The *New York Times* bestselling author **Sherrilyn Kenyon** has over ten million copies of her books in print in twenty-six countries. Her groundbreaking Dark-Hunter vampire novels were an overnight sensation that have given her an international following, with devout fans in more than forty countries, and have landed her on multiple bestseller lists in publications like *The New York Times*, *Publishers Weekly* and *USA Today*. A versatile, award-winning writer, Sherrilyn has carved out multiple bestselling series in numerous genres and subgenres. Writing as Sherrilyn Kenyon and Kinley MacGregor, her series include the Dark-Hunters, the Dream-Hunters, Nevermore, the League and the Lords of Avalon. She lives in Nashville, Tennessee.

Alethea Kontis's short fiction has appeared in *Realms of Fantasy* and *Orson Scott Card's Intergalactic Medicine Show*. In 2005, she co-edited the critically acclaimed SF all-star *Elemental: The Tsunami Relief Anthology* (featuring a story by Kinley MacGregor) and launched her exclusive dark fantasy and horror small press, Nyx Books. Alethea lives in Tennessee and is currently working on a young-adult fairy-tale fantasy novel.

The Dark-Hunter Companion

Sherrilyn Kenyon
with
Alethea Kontis

PIATKUS

PIATKUS

First published in Great Britain in 2007 by Piatkus Books
First published in the US in 2007 by St. Martin's Press, New York

Copyright © 2007 by Sherrilyn Kenyon
Text on pp. 379–84 © 2007 by Kate Johnson
Illustrations © 2007 by Dabel Brothers

The moral rights of the authors have been asserted

Design by Nicola Fergunn
Illustrations by Claudia M. Campos

A CIP catalogue record for this book
is available from the British Library

ISBN 978-0-7499-3867-3

Data manipulation by Phoenix Photosetting, Chatham, Kent
www.phoenixphotosetting.co.uk

Piatkus Books
An imprint of
Little, Brown Book Group
100 Victoria Embankment
London EC4Y 0DY

An Hachette Livre UK Company

www.piatkus.co.uk

The Dark-Hunter Companion

Contents

Introduction

Look what the cow dragged in.
—Artemis

Congratulations!

If you're reading this, you've activated your Dark-Hunter decoder ring or recited whatever ridiculous nursery rhyme Ash thought up this week to decipher this amazingly complicated, intriguing, and mysterious text.

You've also found yourself neck-deep in the biggest pit of divine quicksand this side of the hereafter.

Right now I'm guessing you're a bit confused, and your mind is full of whos, whats, whens, whys, and hows that haven't exactly been answered by a certain representative of upper management who is as arrogant as he is tall and in severe need of a haircut. (Trust me, you're not alone. Get used to it. P.S. Don't tell Ash about the hair comment as I'd like to continue breathing for a bit longer and if I'm dead, you're screwed.)

'Cause I'm here to sort you out.

Lucky you!

Here's the situation in a nutshell: You've bought the farm on a dead-end street. You've bitten both the bullet and the apple, my friend. Your soul cried out for vengeance and I certainly hope you took advantage of it. You should have listened to your mama when she told you to be careful what you wish for. You got more than you bargained for, and there's no going back. We don't do things that way 'round these parts.

I'm here to tell you what you've won.

Consider this handbook your education. Hunter 101. And don't go thinking you got off easy just because there's not a pop quiz at the end.

This is the good stuff. The real deal. In here you'll find out all there is to know about being a Dark-Hunter. How to live. How to kill. Where to go to buy weapons. Where to socialize. Who to talk to ... and who *not* to talk to. Your physical attributes—what you've lost and what you've gained. There's also a history lesson or seven inside that it would behoove you to sit through—one of the first things you'll need to learn is that ancient gods have a habit of popping up in the strangest places. Knowledge is power.

Always has been; always will be.

And stupidity kills. Trust me.

Now for the disclaimer: This book is mutable. It goes with the wind. It changes more often than the mind of a sixteen-year-old Libra with a closet full of clothes and a date in an hour. It's been around for-almost-ever and it's still a continual work-in-progress, kind of like Earth herself. Don't be surprised if you open it up for the thirty-five-thousandth time and find something old, something new, something borrowed, or ... well, you get the point.

This book also won't get *too* deep into the nitty-gritty. You understand there's only so much we can put in print that we wouldn't mind Daimons and pesky Squires (Hey Squire, you think you're the first one to stumble across this book?

Hah!) getting their grubby mitts on. The real down and dirty stuff you'll have to ask the tight-lipped Goth Royal Tallness himself.

Yeah. I wish you a lot of luck with that. I'm sorry but I have to pause so that I can laugh . . .

12:01

12:07

12:16

Back and sober. (Clearing throat) There are other ways to find out certain little secrets, of course ... but those are not for me to divulge. If you are resourceful enough, if you're in the right place at the right time and you have the right passwords and proper identification, it won't be much of a challenge.

At this point, while I'm sure you're appreciating all the knowledgey goodness I'm about to fork over, you might be feeling a little sorry for me—the poor sucker who's been conned into compiling all this nonsense for you then, now, always, and forever until the end of time. Let me set your lovely, selfless mind at ease. Please remember, there are very few people to whom Acheron Parthenopaeus owes a favor.

I am one of them.

So I'll leave you to it then. Curl up in a comfy chair with some millennium-old scotch and feast upon the informative banquet I have prepared for your enjoyment.

Welcome to your new life.

Go kick some ass.

—*Alethea*

THE DARK-HUNTER
COMPANION

So Now You're
a Dark-Hunter . . .

*What to Do, What Not to Do, and
How to Royally Screw It All Up*

*We're not the damned, folks, we're the
categorically fucked.*
—Urian

Take a deep breath.

Turn out the lights.

The reason you're having a hard time reading this is because the eyesight of a Dark-Hunter is the first, and possibly the most difficult, thing to adjust to. Birth is hard, especially the second time around. We'll go in baby steps, all right? Take your time. Are the lights out? Pull the shades, twist the blinds, and put blankets over the curtains.

Sounds insane, I know, but you're going to have to trust somebody sometime. That guy you met on the way in? That's Acheron. When the world inevitably goes to hell, he's one of the only people you will always be able to trust.

I'm one of the other ones.

Now, light a candle. But don't look straight at it since it'll only hurt more.

Here, I'll do the same thing so you don't feel like you're the only weirdo in the universe.

Go on, trust me. You may as well. I'll keep reminding you, so you won't forget. What else have you got to lose?

See, I know you that well and we've barely even met.

So.

You with me?

First lesson: Candlelight and firelight are second only to moonlight when it comes to enhancing a Dark-Hunter's vision. It makes sense if you think about it—these natural sources of illumination are instruments of the gods. Our Dear Lady Artemis is the goddess of the Moon. You are a product of Artemis's handiwork, therefore you are able to see better by the light of her totem.

Honestly, come on. Have you ever heard of the god of Neon or the goddess of Fluorescence?

I rest my case.

But what if it's nighttime? you say. *If I can see better by moonlight, why did I just block up all the windows?*

Three reasons.

Three is a significant number among the gods, didn't you know? Well, you do now.

One: You have to think outside the box for a minute. You can do it. . . . I'll give you a couple of seconds just in case you need them.

Humans are creatures of habit and, despite their amazing innate evolutionary ability to adapt to their environment, they are exceptionally averse to change. People notice change, but they aren't bothered by sameness. Constancy flies under the radar. If you shut up your windows every day and open them wide every night, someone will notice and wonder why. If you just leave them closed—or go so far as to block or board them up—it will be speculated upon and then shrugged off once the guy down the street brings a strange woman home, or the woman next door forgets to wheel her garbage to the curb.

Two: In a perfect world, Dark-Hunters sleep all day and hunt Daimons all night. Of course, if this world were perfect there wouldn't *be* any Daimons or Dark-Hunters. Curses wouldn't exist, the gods would never get angry, we would all love one another, and everything would be rainbows and puppies.

If you're anything like any of your predecessors, you're going to work your ass off all hours of the day and night. You will never be able to predict when you're coming or going—where your next nap or your next meal will be coming from. (Unless you have latent psychic abilities, but for the purposes of this discussion let's assume you don't.) I hear from the ancient Greeks that it's a bit like the army.

Even on cloudy days, daylight is still daylight. There will come a night when you inevitably sleep well past sunrise. That moment, you'll be thanking me for not having to wake up on fire.

Which brings us to three: about that fire.

I'm assuming you've got that candle lit by now. In many ways, that tiny dynamic flicker of energy is the perfect representation of your existence. It can be small, simple, and easy to manipulate. It can be wild, passionate, and unstoppable. It can feed; it can consume. It can save lives just as effortlessly as it can kill.

Above all, its very existence is among the first substantial evidence of the true wrath of the gods.

You know Prometheus, right? (No, I don't mean personally, you nitwit. Though if you do, tell him I said "Hi" next time you see him. And remind him that he owes me five bucks.)

Consider the candle.

Exhibit A.

Prometheus was a Titan, one of the giants who inhabited the

earth before humans. In fact, Prometheus is sometimes credited with making the human race from the earth, in the image of the gods. Perhaps he felt like a father to humans, complete with a sense of protection and obligation. He taught humans the basics of civilization by bringing them fire down from the hearth of Mount Olympus, magic firsthand like none of them had ever witnessed before.

He introduced the world as we know it to . . . well . . . the world as it used to be. In his humility, Prometheus took something that only the gods had complete power over, and he did it for the good and the survival and the progression of mankind. Humans stayed warm. They cooked their food. They thrived. They lived. They evolved.

The gods, however, did not see it that way. They didn't exactly warm to the thought of a more level playing field. They never do. The gods are gods because they are worshipped. A god who is not worshipped loses power. Humans with power begin to question their gods. What Prometheus did for the world not only shook Mount Olympus to its core, it fractured its foundation.

It also doomed Prometheus—who held the secret to how the gods could remain the ultimate power in the universe . . . but would not tell them.

Zeus, in his rage, chained Prometheus to a rock and left him to the carrion birds. Every day, his liver is eaten out by a vulture; and every night, it grows back again. Over and over and over, until the end of time. Pretty much forever-and-ever. Amen.

Now.

Consider the candle.

It is a testament to what you are—a player in the game set into motion by the wrath of the gods. An immortal being charged with a secret, and the protection of the human race. You are a champion who bears a burden of tremendous responsibility . . . and tremendous suffering. But don't lose faith. Just remember:

You wouldn't have been chosen if you weren't strong enough to handle what you're about to face.

After all, what doesn't kill you ... just really pisses you off.

How It All Went Down

When you've spent a lifetime being betrayed by everyone around you, it's really hard to let that go.
—Acheron

I'm guessing you forgot both the white stones and the bread-crumbs, so you're probably a bit hazy on the details of what brought you to the gingerdamned house. Let me recap.

You were wronged. Big-time. Happens to everybody ... but what happened to you was beyond forgiveness. Beyond redemption. Someone deserved to pay, King Solomon style, and karma would have had no problem with it.

The part you didn't know about—behind the scenes, under the skin, in the ether—was that when a soul is wronged so unjustly, it cries out. And it's not just a baby's cry, or that noise you make when you hit your thumb with a hammer. It's the sound of ultimate betrayal: the sound a heart makes when it's breaking, the sound of the sky falling. It is the voice of the Phoenix when she rises up from the ashes.

That sound echoes in the ears of the gods, and most of them wave it away like an errant fly.

Except for Artemis.

To Artemis that's the sound of another job applicant filling out the paperwork and requesting an interview.

She came to you in that moment. You'll remember her: tall, red hair, body to die for, and the aura of a snake? (If you are a snake enthusiast, I apologize.) She offered you your last request: She offered you an Act of Vengeance. In return you swore your allegiance to her and her cause, to become a soldier in her nine-thousand-year-old army against the Daimon parasites who prey upon the earth.

To seal the deal, you gave her your soul. (That's usually how bargains with immortals go down, so don't go feeling particularly unique.) She laid her hand upon you and extracted it—you have her double bow-and-arrow symbol marking the spot, but you won't remember the pain. It's a bit like childbirth that way. Some memories you just don't need to keep.

After Artemis took your soul, she brought you back to life. Immortal life. Yup, you could quietly live forever now, with no fear of disease or death. (Only your life from this point will now be loud and messy, so you may want to be careful. See "How to Die".) You were born again as a Dark-Hunter, and you had twenty-four hours in which to exact your revenge.

If you ultimately decided not to take advantage of that window of time, I am obligated to tell you that you can't go back. The road only goes forward, and there are no second chances. For better or worse, Artemis has your soul until Shadedom or Rebirth.

The part that no one is forcing me to tell you is that I admire you. It takes a person of extreme moral character to walk away when faced with the opportunity to lower themselves to the depths of their greatest enemy. That act takes a person with a seemingly endless capacity for love, and there are few enough of us in the world. I value that. And I commend you; no fine print, no strings attached.

What You Got Out of the Deal

*I can hear your heart beating faster, your blood
flowing through your veins as you sit there wondering
whether or not I would really hurt you.*
—Kyrian Hunter

You may think you're a vampire. You are not. You cannot fly and you cannot turn into a bat (one particular Dark-Hunter sorcerer notwithstanding). Unless you were formerly a Were-Hunter, you cannot shapeshift. Do not try either of these things at home or anywhere else. You'll just look stupid. And trust me, with cameras being what and where they are in this century we will all laugh at you for decades to come.

There are thousands of Dark-Hunters. No two Dark-Hunters are alike, and no two Dark-Hunters have the exact same combination of superpowers. Like snowflakes. A few things are pretty constant, though—such as the traits Dark-Hunters were given to mirror the Daimons, so that they may better track their enemy.

Almost all Dark-Hunters' eyes are jet-black and, like an eagle's, densely packed with light-sensitive sensory cells. You will rarely see a fellow Dark-Hunter without a decent pair of sunglasses. It's one of the first things I recommend you pick up for yourself. If you have a Squire (you lucky dog), this may have already been taken care of for you.

Speaking of dogs: You now have pointed canine teeth, ones that you will eventually learn to stop cutting your lips on. In time you will also train yourself to know instinctively the exact degree of a smile that will conceal this feature . . . and the degree in which to show it to its best advantage. You will become a master of the difference between a laugh and a threat, but you have to give yourself time.

And if you're lisping, don't worry. That doesn't last long. Just don't try to intimidate anyone verbally while it remains, otherwise you might damage your ego. And our reputations.

Just because you have these teeth does *not* mean you have to drink blood. (Dark-Hunters who do so are called Feeders, and to say that Acheron frowns upon the subject would be a gross understatement.) You started out as a human, so you do not need blood or human souls to survive. The basic physical human needs still apply, however. Dark-Hunters, when they're not busy working, normally eat three meals a night. And yes, they still have to go to the bathroom.

You will be unable to cast a reflection; this is a power Artemis bestowed on her Hunters as the perfect camouflage. Some Dark-Hunters report that they can cast one if concentrating... but again, that takes time. For now, don't worry about what your hair looks like. The Daimons you dust can report you to the fashion police in hell.

As you have probably discovered already, your vision is not your only heightened sense perception. (And yes, that smell *is* you ... you should probably go take a shower.) You can smell and hear and think and see and feel more than any human, more than any animal ... possibly more than anyone save a Were-Hunter, or a god. It's a bit overwhelming at first, but the *more* of the world that's currently jamming itself into your brain right now will quiet down as you learn control. Trust your biological clock: You will know now when the sun is setting and, similarly, when it's about to rise again.

Each Dark-Hunter possesses a certain degree of mind control—use it wisely. Each also has the ability to heal quickly, often within twenty-four hours. Quicker, if a Dream-Hunter is involved. Which is a good thing, because while you—as an immortal—are immune to addictive substances, you are also immune to anesthetic. When you are injured, you will feel a natural urge to sleep. Go with it. Just make sure you're in a safe place where the rising sun won't turn you into a fried crispy Hunter. Remember, you will sleep for quite a few hours so take precaution before you succumb to it.

Now that you have none of your own, you are particularly sensitive to the presence of a soul, which is how you will be able to instantly discern the difference between an Apollite and a Daimon, and how you can feel a baby's soul inside its mother's womb.

Other powers you might develop include psychic abilities like telekinesis, mind reading, and precognition. (Once you have the ability to see the future, you will never lose it. So if you've had it before, no worries—if you just now got it, good luck.) You could also have healing powers, or control over certain elements. There's no way to tell until you use them, so keep an eye out. Pay attention. And be careful.

Powers That Be

With my background and genetic makeup, buddy,
you're lucky I'm as normal as I am.
—Katra Agrotera

You can't be sure which of these you will develop with your new birthright, if any. But definitely be on the lookout for signs. Better safe than sorry.

Keep in mind, too, that gods have one, many, or all of these powers. When you're thinking about giving one a piece of your mind, consider what the consequences might be.

Aerokinesis   The ability to mentally manipulate wind and air flow.

Animation   The ability to bring inanimate objects to life or to free a person from petrification.

Astral Projection   The ability to separate and control one's astral body. The out-of-body experience can be achieved by dreaming or deep meditation. Astral projection is sometimes considered a form of telepathy or clairvoyance. Remote viewing is a specifically directed form of astral projection. Depending on the strength of the projector's ability, the astral body may even be able to interact (speak or move objects) with its surroundings.

Atmokinesis   The ability to mentally manipulate changes in the weather, up to and including the bringing or banishing of pressure systems, clouds, rain, storms, hurricanes, and tornadoes.

Aura Perception   An aura is the spiritual energy field that emanates from a person or object. Most often, auras convey the feelings and emotions of the person or object involved in a range of colors. An aural perceiver has the equivalent of a permanent mood ring decoder for everyone and everything in his path.

Biokinesis   The ability to heal, or perform other biological manipulation. A biokinetic can knit tissue together just as easily as he or she can stop a breath, or a heart.

Chlorokinesis   The ability to mentally manipulate plants. A chlorokinetic also sometimes has a bit of clairvoyant ability, but only in regards to plants. The plant can "speak" to a chlorokinetic, conveying sounds, images, and sometimes even the entire passing of a sequence of events.

Chronokinesis   The ability to mentally manipulate time. Weres can surf the Rytis to travel through time, but the rest of us seem to be slaves to this relative.

Clairaudience   The ability to aurally perceive words or sounds originating on the spiritual plane. Clairaudients are also able to hear sounds at low and high frequencies not audible to the human ear.

Clairsentience   The ability to perceive the atmosphere or origin of a person, place, or thing by way of feeling; often associated with psychometry. Clairsentients are also called empaths. Always trust the "gut feeling" of a clairsentient.

Clairvoyance   The ability to visually perceive events that are taking place elsewhere or sense places that are not in view. Some clairvoyants can also see certain types of spirit or foreign energy. The term *clairvoyant* often includes both clairaudients and clairsentients. Clairvoyants are usually also able to see auras.

Cryokinesis   The ability to mentally manipulate ice, or cold in general. The antithesis to pyrokinesis. Cryokinetics are especially helpful around avalanches and icebergs. They are also immune to frostbite.

Divination   The art of predicting the future. (See Precognition.)

Electrokinesis   The ability to mentally manipulate electricity and electric fields. Trained electrokinetics are able to produce force fields as shields for protection. As a rule, Were-Hunters seriously hate these people as they tend to make them change forms. So if you have this, give our furry friends a break and stay away from them.

Energy Blasts (Godbolts)   If someone blasts you with energy, that someone is a god, or has somehow acquired god-powers. A Dark-Hunter has never been known to develop this power naturally.

Ferrokinesis   The ability to mentally manipulate metal. This power was especially valued during the Middle Ages, with all those innocent, tasty knights in armor running around.

Geokinesis   The ability to mentally manipulate the earth. Especially powerful geokinetics can cause or stop earthquakes and active volcanoes.

Gravitakinesis　The ability to mentally manipulate gravity. Usually considered generic telekinesis, unless the gravitakinetic has the ability to manipulate his *own* gravity. Which would just be way cool.

Hydrokinesis　The ability to mentally manipulate water. Hydrokinesis is useful for purifying water when trapped on a deserted island, and summoning or finding it when lost in the desert. Especially powerful hydrokinetics can calm tsunamis, hurricanes, or storms, but generally it is not in the hydrokinetics' power to actually cause these things to happen. A hydrokinetic can, however, control waterspouts and the direction a river can travel. And considering that the human body is about 75 percent water . . . it's not as wimpy a power as you might think.

Magnetokinesis　The ability to mentally manipulate the magnetic field; usually associated with ferrokinesis. And the X-Men. But please note, we have much cooler wardrobes.

Mediumship/Necromancy　The ability to see and communicate with the dead. Some mediums need an object through which the spirit can communicate, like a Ouija board. Some mediums are possessed by the spirit, and it communicates through them by speaking or automatic writing. Some simply see them, and talk to them or feel their emotions and intentions. Since you're a Dark-Hunter, you never want a spirit inside you. You have no soul and it will take possession of you, which is not a good thing. Remember what happened to Alexion. You guys don't have the same regenerative abilities he did. You will be terminated.

Omnilingual　The ability to quickly memorize and/or decipher any foreign language.

Omnipotence　The ability to do anything you want to. Again, reserved for the gods, so try not to make any of them angry. And stay out of Ash's way.

Omniscience   The true know-it-all, an omniscient literally does see and know everything. Again, this power is pretty much limited to the more powerful gods, like Zeus. Or Acheron, who will never share his knowledge with you, so don't ask.

Photokinesis   The ability to mentally manipulate light. Unfortunately, photokinetically created light doesn't have the exact properties of natural sunlight and cannot kill Daimons, but it's awfully handy in a dark cave, or if your opponent has a migraine.

Power Absorption   The ability to absorb another person's powers, leaving that person powerless. Usually that other person is not another Dark-Hunter, seeing as the proximity alert will weaken both this and the other Dark-Hunter's powers. Daimons technically have this ability; when they drain the souls of a powerful person, they inherit those powers for a period of time until the soul wanes. Gods have this power, as they are able to absorb the powers of their defeated foes (if the foe is another god) indefinitely.

Power Bestowal (Conduit)   The ability to bestow powers upon another person or evoke the latent powers of others. Again, this doesn't usually happen Dark-Hunter to Dark-Hunter. But if you somehow discover you've been "blessed" with this particular gift, be careful whom you approach, especially humans with gypsy or god blood. You never know what latent power might be sleeping inside them. Daimons shouldn't be a problem for someone with this power, as they can only possess the powers of the last soul they stole.

Depending on the type of power and the strength, the bestower can give a person temporary powers (usually based on the bestower's proximity), or permanent ones.

Power Mimicry   Like power absorption, mimicry is the ability to absorb another's powers. In this case, however, the mimic is able to leave the other person's powers intact. Which could be a good thing or a bad thing depending on who the other person is, and whether or not they're on your side.

Power Negation   The ability to cancel out or diminish the powers of others. This ability is kind of inherent in all Dark-Hunters, thanks to Artemis, since close proximity to any of your brethren results in a mutual power drain.

Power Sensing   The ability to sense or recognize the powers of another person. Depending on the strength and ability of the senser, it could be a generic idea of the presence of powers, or the knowledge of the other person's exact abilities. Apollites have the ability to sense other Apollites as well as Daimons, based on their blood connection to the god Apollo. Similarly, Dark-Hunters can normally sense the presence of another Dark-Hunter (if the draining of their powers isn't a dead giveaway) and you will be able to sense a Daimon from a mile away (a slight exaggeration, but you get the idea).

Precognition   The ability to perceive events before they happen. Sometimes it is only expressed in vague dreams while asleep, other times it is clear and occurs at will and when awake. The events seen may take place in the near future, or the far future. They are also only one of many possible outcomes—some events can be avoided if the right measures are taken.

Presentience   Presentience is precognition in the form of more abstract senses, emotions, or feelings … kind of like a mood ring of prediction. This power is also associated with clairsentience.

Psychokinesis   The ability to mentally will events to happen, or will objects to move. (See Tactile Telekinesis.)

Psychometry   The more beloved an object is by its owner, the more of the owner's energy is retained inside that object.

Similarly, the stones of old houses and castles may retain some memory or recording of especially passionate events that have taken place in their midst. Psychometry is the ability to sense this energy and relate details about the past or future condition of an object, person, or location, usually by being in close contact with it.

Pyrokinesis   The ability to mentally manipulate fire, or heat in general. The antithesis to cryokinesis. Pyrokinetics are especially helpful around erupting volcanoes and forest fires. Pyrokinetics are usually fire-retardant . . . but the sun will still kill you.

Remote Viewing   The ability of a directed clairvoyant who can travel to a specific person, time, or place to be able to see what someone is doing, or what events are taking place. Often used by spies to overhear secret plans, or to discover the hiding place of documents or treasure.

Shapeshifting   This power is usually limited to Were-Hunters, but not always. If a Were-Hunter becomes a Dark-Hunter, like Ravyn Kontis, he retains this power—the two are not mutually exclusive.

Sonokinesis   The ability to mentally manipulate sound waves. A sonokinetic is a great friend to have at a concert, a crowded bar, or a political cocktail party. They are particularly useful when in need of a distraction, as trained sonokinetics are exceptionally good ventriloquists. Sonokinetics rarely ever go deaf, but if one decides not to listen to you, he or she can literally tune you out.

Spiritual Possession   The ability to take complete and total control of another person's body via astral projection or mind transfer. Spathi Daimons, such as Desiderius, have the ability to do this if their original body is killed and they are allowed to float about disembodied in the ether. Ghosts and other departed spirits are especially eager to possess the body of a Dark-Hunter, since it is a souless vessel in prime condition, so always be on your guard.

Tactile Telekinesis   The ability to manipulate objects by touching them. People who are tactile telekinetics can carry massive objects with very little effort. They also have to be very careful that no one witnesses them picking up cars and cement trucks and whatnot.

Technopathy   The ability to manipulate electrical fields and/or devices. Associated with electrokinesis and magnetokinesis, technokinetics stand apart for their particularly useful ability to fix broken electronics and corrupted computers. There are a few technopathic Squires who work on maintaining the Dark-Hunter Web site.

Telekinesis   A matter of mind over matter. Telekinesis is the ability to manipulate and control objects with the mind, often in ways not visible to the naked eye. A telekinetic can lift and move inanimate objects; some more powerful telekinetics can also manipulate people into doing things against their will. Poltergeist activity has often been attributed to telekinetics.

Telepathy   The ability to read the thoughts of others. Some telepaths can make themselves be heard by others, and particularly powerful ones can mentally communicate with a person or persons with no telepathic ability. All gods are telepaths, and those Apollites most closely descended from Apollo, like Cassandra Peters, have some latent telepathic ability.

Teleportation   Just like in *Star Trek*, teleportation is the ability to disappear from one place and reappear in another almost instantaneously. Were-Hunters have this ability, and Daimons can teleport through laminas. One cautionary note: If a bolt-hole or lamina appears, don't follow the Daimon into it. You will get eaten. FYI: Corbin has this power.

Dark-Hunter Creed

Let me give you the job description. Me, Dark-Hunter.
You, Daimon. I hit. You bleed. I kill. You die.
—Zarek

We are Darkness. We are Shadow. We are the Rulers of the Night. We, alone, stand between mankind and those who would see mankind destroyed. We are the Guardians. The Soulless Keepers. Our souls were cast out so that we would not forewarn the Daimons we pursue. By the time they see us coming, it's too late.

The Daimons and Apollites know us. They fear us. We are death to all those who prey upon the humans. Neither Human, nor Apollite, we exist beyond the realm of the Living, beyond the realm of the Dead. We are the Dark-Hunters. And we are eternal.

Just Say No

Even the devil may cry when he looks around
hell and realizes that he's there alone.
—Acheron

There are certain things a Dark-Hunter must do (kill Daimons, stay alive), and there are certain things that will get you in so much trouble with Acheron even the Shades will remember your name. There is a code of honor that's a bit like the Ten Commandments, but less written-in-stonish.

The Fourteen Cardinal Rules

1. Never expose your powers to uninitiated humans.
2. Be a part of the world, but never in it.
3. Never be in the presence of a god.
4. Never let sunshine touch you.
5. An unconscious Dark-Hunter is a dead Dark-Hunter.
6. No significant others.
7. Never touch your Squire.
8. No family, no friends who knew you before you died.
9. Let no Daimon escape alive.
10. Never speak of what you are.
11. You cannot be in the presence of another Dark-Hunter.
12. Whatever you do to another Dark-Hunter, you will feel tenfold.
13. You walk alone.
14. Keep your bow mark hidden.

Sounds easy, right?

Well, if it's so easy, why do we have to keep reminding Dark-Hunters about it?

1. Never expose your powers to uninitiated humans. Exposing your powers exposes all of us to public scrutiny—you, me, the Apollites and Daimons, the gods and goddesses, even the existence of Atlantis itself (and you really don't want to go there). For obvious reasons—like the fate of the world as you know it—it's best if the world thinks we are all products of stories and legends, Hollywood and folktales. Never ever prove to them that you are real. More important, just weigh how badly the gods would punish you against that fifteen minutes of fame.

2. Be a part of the world, but never in it. You *will* be forced to interact with the human world. You can't exactly save them if you don't interact with them, right? Just remember, you are an observer, not a participant. Leave no witnesses. Stay in the background. Be discreet with your prey. Daimons turn to dust, so there's never a body to worry about. See? Half the work's already done. Make sure you take care of the other half.

3. **Never be in the presence of a god.** Since you are soulless, you are an anathema to the gods. You certainly don't want to be on one's bad side, and you don't exactly want to be on one's good side. Gods fight a lot. And you know, the friend of my enemy and all that. You shouldn't come up against this too much, since all but Artemis are forbidden to lend you aid of any kind. More on that in "Great Gods All Mighty".

4. **Never let sunshine touch you.** This one's sort of self-explanatory, really. Thanks to Apollo, daylight equals death. If you're feeling particularly masochistic, skip straight on down to the section on "How to Die". Go on. I'll wait right here.

5. **An unconscious Dark-Hunter is a dead Dark-Hunter.** When you are injured, you will want to sleep. It's a natural instinct. Your body will heal in its sleep. With the aid of a Dream-

What to Do If You're Close to Exposure

1. Ignore all Daimons. Saving yourself just became more important than saving the world. Besides, you can catch them later.
2. Run. (There is no playing this off.)
3. Hide. (Garages, woodsheds, public toilets, and so on. *Avoid occupied tombs.*)
4. Call a Squire. (Always keep a body bag in your trunk.)
5. Stay calm. What's the worst thing that could happen? Oh, yeah, you burst into flames. Never mind. Panic all you want.

Remember, a Light-Hunter is a *Dead*-Hunter.

Hunter, it will heal even faster. *Don't* fall asleep outside of your safety zone. Never leave yourself vulnerable.

6. No significant others. Your *only* priority is mankind. Dereliction of duty is grounds to be classified as a Rogue (a one-way ticket to total extinction). Keep your priorities straight. Significant others will distract you and detract from your oath. You're on a nondisclosure agreement as it is with the whole Dark-Hunter powers thing, so any sort of long-term relationship is doomed from the start.

I'm not telling you to repress your urges, I'm just saying limit it to a one-night stand (with a *human*, you moron, not an Apollite for heaven's sake and, whatever you do, *never* a Daimon), and move on. It's safer that way for everyone involved. And don't worry about having a child, or begetting one on someone else—Dark-Hunters are sterile.

The first thing a new Dark-Hunter is quick to point out is the existence of copious modern-day exceptions to this rule. Kyrian and Amanda Hunter, Tabitha Devereaux and Valerius Magnus,

Talon and Sunshine Runningwolf...yes, it does happen. (Life wouldn't be much fun if it didn't.) Just don't ever count on it happening to *you*. For the truly masochistic, there is more information later on, in "The Out Clause".

7. Never touch your Squire. Squires. They may be hard to live with, but it's pretty damn hard to live without them. You rely on them to protect you while you rest and to pull your butt out of harm's way in a pinch (and in the daylight). Do yourself a huge favor and don't go falling in love with yours. Your Squire will do anything for you. If you care about yours, do this for them.

The Squire Council tries to avoid pairing up Squires and Dark-Hunters of the opposite sex (or the opposite desired partner, in case that happens to be the same sex), but it happens from time to time. People in the workplace and all that. Just *don't*. Affairs of the heart inevitably lead to the death of either the Hunter or the Squire. No entanglements.

8. No family, no friends who knew you before you died. You are *dead*. Never forget it. It's cruel to both the Hunter and the family to know what you have become. You have loved, and now you must let go. It puts your family in jeopardy, making them prime targets for Daimon attacks. For everyone's sake, never return to your origins, your descendents, or contact any family or friends who may still live to recognize you.

9. Let no Daimon escape alive. You were created to kill them. (If for some reason you don't, when Ash comes around you gonna have some 'splainin' to do, Lucy.) Never toy with your prey. The longer they live, the greater the chance the souls they carry will die. Kill the Daimons; save the humans. Let me repeat that: Kill the Daimons; save the humans. Humans and Apollites, while they have their failings, are what you were sent here to protect. Once an Apollite turns Daimon, though, it's fair game.

Daimons by nature are cowards. They talk big, and their bark is worse than their bite, literally. The courageous ones are Spathi Daimons. These are their warrior class who do hunt and pursue Dark-Hunters. Don't get cocky. Learn the difference. The Spathi have sun tattoos. They swear allegiance to Apollymi. They will face you and fight to the death and they are very good at what they do—expect it.

10. Never speak of what you are. Sometimes it is best for legends to stay legends. All Dark-Hunters are forbidden to have their likeness captured, in any medium. The last thing you need is a bunch of renegade teenage paparazzi hunting you down like Doctor Who. The only time you can break this rule is in the event of dire circumstances. Humans *must not know* you exist. Film provides lasting proof that you don't age and it makes it easy for humans to recognize you. Those two things are bad. *Very* bad.

11. You cannot be in the presence of another Dark-Hunter. Just in case one of you was harboring any ill will, to prevent Dark-Hunters from combining their powers they are forbidden from ever being in each other's company. To do so is to feel an instant drain on your powers. A few minutes' company with your comrades-in-arms is fine, but any lengthy stay and you will deplete each other.

This also prevents the Dark-Hunters from banding together and going up against the gods . . . a nice touch on Artemis's part. Acheron is the only Dark-Hunter you will be able to walk beside for an extended period of time without passing out, but Acheron was the first. He's . . . different.

12. Whatever you do to another Dark-Hunter, you will feel tenfold. To help maintain the above rule, Artemis added a bonus. If you do attempt to physically harm another Dark-Hunter, the pain you inflict upon your victim you will feel tenfold. (And here you thought paganism with its threefold rule was tough.) Don't worry, you will stop long before he's even close to dead; it will be physically impossible for you to continue. That much pain is just not worth it. Think twice before striking.

13. You walk alone. You are the boogeyman. You are the scary thing that goes bump in the night. The main directive of the

What to Do if Your Picture Is Snapped

- Try to get it back. (You catch more flies with honey . . .)
- Break the camera. (Last resort, please. Respect other people's property.)
- Destroy the pictures *and* negatives. (Don't forget the negatives.)
- Carry a big magnet. (Digital cameras *love* magnets.)
- If an old photo appears out of the blue, try to convince everyone that you look just like your great-great-great-great-grandparent.

Always be aware of:
Tiny digital cameras
Camera phones
ATMs
PDAs
Police cameras
CCTV
Web cams

(Send your Squire into Best Buy.)

Dark-Hunter code is to be alone. You cannot team up, even to help each other. It sucks, but that's the way it is. The only friend you're allowed is your Squire. Take care of them. (But don't—you know—take *care* of them.)

14. **Keep your bow mark hidden.** Never let anyone see your double bow-and-arrow mark. You are known for that, and by letting it be seen you can be exposed to humans . . . or Daimons. The bow mark should be guarded and protected at all times.

What to Do If Your Tattoo Is Not in a Place That's Easy to Hide

Women
Makeup
Arm-length gloves
Thigh-high corset boots
Catsuits
Plate necklaces and chokers

Men
Makeup (if you're brave enough)
Leather bands
Vambraces
Spiked collars
Bandannas
Face masks (Although I wouldn't suggest entering a convenience store if you opt for this one.)

Wages

I'm not paid to be fair. I'm paid to kick Daimon ass.
—Acheron

Yes, this is a job, and yes, you do get paid. There are no raises, no benefits—other than, you know, massive strength and immortality—and no 401(k) plan. If you want to set it aside for retirement or spend it as soon as it lands on your dining-room table, it's up to you. More than likely, you will have sufficient funds to do both, with a bit left over after to buy a small country.

Speaking of which . . . Artemis does have a tendency to drop your pay packet in on you when—and where—you least expect it. She hasn't quite gotten the whole "direct deposit" idea down just yet. She's more of a "trunk full of jewels and precious stones on the hood of your Maserati" kind of gal. If you do have some precious furniture in your house, you might want to make some sort of arrangement with her beforehand. But always be prepared to kiss it goodbye.

Choosing Your Home

I'm the one, as I recall, who kept telling you to embrace the ridiculous.
—Leo Kirby

I know, it's an odd subject to put before weapons, but consider: A Dark-Hunter's home is his castle. It is your safe haven, your base of operations, your first line of defense, your port in a storm . . . you with me?

Before purchasing property with all that loot Artemis dumps on you every so often, you (or your Squire) need to do some thorough research. There are two main reasons:

Soul-searching In case you haven't figured it out already, Dark-Hunters don't fare well around holy places. Back in the old days of Dark-Hunters living in crypts, those were usually built on unconsecrated ground, and were each a significant distance from any other grave.

Think about it this way: Disembodied souls and spirits are always eager to take up residence in a nice, healthy, immortal body with no soul, such as yourself. So while you can enter a church—even bless yourself with holy water if you're into that kind of thing—don't spend a whole lot of time there. You are beachfront property for the dearly departed, baby, and there's no such thing as time-share.

If you do become possessed by a soul, one of two things will happen. If the soul is a strong one, it will take over your body. That's it. End of story. End of you. You may have heard stories of the Dark-Hunter Ulric? Maybe not. In a nutshell, his body was taken over by the disembodied soul of the Spathi Daimon Desiderius. That one killed a lot of people, a lot of Dark-Hunters. We don't talk about it much. It's still too painful.

If the soul is a weak one, may the god of your choice have mercy on you. You will hear this weak soul within you—tortured and screaming, begging and whimpering like a whipped dog. It is enough to drive you mad, and it will. The only choice you have

at that point is to kill yourself and set the soul free—if you condemn the soul to wither and die within you, you break the Code,
and are no better than a Daimon. So make sure when you buy a
house that you are the only preternatural critter calling it
home.

Open invitation If the home you decide to occupy has ever
in its existence been a bed-and-breakfast, hospital, restaurant,
community center—any gathering place of some sort—any Daimon can enter without an invite.

So, what have we learned, boys and girls? Always do a thorough property search. Buy a new house, or have one declared
ghost-free by a licensed psychic.

One more side note if you're stationed in the United States:
Always be on the lookout for undisclosed Native American burial
grounds. You don't want those puppies sneaking up on you, no
sirree. Think *Poltergeist* without the happy ending.

Weapons

If something as pathetic as a Greek Fury can take me down
in a fight, I deserve to die.
—Sin

Here we come to the obligatory weapons section. I know, I
know . . . most of this stuff you probably already know. You've
got a favorite; we've all got favorites. But indulge me on this one.

There are certain things you might not think about, certain
cultures you haven't explored yet. Well, now's the time. Experiment. Have some fun. Learn something new. Who knows, you
might like it.

At the end of the day, use whatever you want as long as it gets the job done. But you're not allowed to say you don't like something until you've tried it at least once.

And if you do find something, can I tell you I told you so?

Feel free to use this list as the first errand you have your Squire run for you. Yes, you're immortal and in peak condition, but a well-honed blade always cuts quicker and deeper. Don't waste your time by being sloppy.

A lazy Dark-Hunter is a dead Dark-Hunter.

No, it's not a saying, but it probably should be.

Most of these things can be procured, modified, or customized by Kell or Liza. They'd be happy to take your order ... just don't be impatient. Remember that you're not the only Dark-Hunter in need of a weapon. Have a care and use some tact. You catch more flies with honey. And chocolate.

Also, don't forget handy-dandy old eBay. Sure, you may have buckets of cash lying around, but a bargain is still a bargain. And you never know what you're going to come across. Be inventive!

Athame   Ritual ceremonial dagger, usually with a short handle and double-edged iron blade.

Atlantean Dagger   Dagger with a wavy, etching-covered blade from hilt to point. Only known weapon able to kill a Charonte demon. The last known Atlantean dagger was destroyed by Ash, so if you find one, you might not want to tell him.

Bo   Japanese staff weapon that originated as a means for carrying sacks of grain or buckets of water from the shoulders. Normally about six feet in length, a bo can be fashioned from a variety of materials.

Body Bag   Useful in case you're ever stuck in sunlight with no place to go. Made of nonporous black or white plastic, they are available in a variety of densities. Get the thickest possible, and make sure it's new or you get the whole spirit-possessing-you mess.

Boot-Sheath Stiletto   Pretty much a necessity. A thin blade designed for stabbing rather than cutting, a stiletto can be made as short as three inches. This weapon became popular during the Middle Ages and Renaissance for its ability to pass through chain mail.

Boot-Toe Knife   One of the most popular weapons among Dark-Hunters. Portable, lightweight, easily concealed, and easily missed by anyone searching you for weapons. And hey, you never leave home without your shoes. . . .

Butterfly Knife   Quick to open; easy to conceal. A fad in the 1980s among teenagers and martial artists, this type of knife is now banned by many states in America. It was nicknamed the butterfly knife by soldiers stationed in the Philippines in World War II.

Claws   Articulated silver finger sheaths that usually culminate into a sharp point. They can be used as talons to scratch and slay enemies. This is the weapon of choice for Zarek of Moesia or any Hunter who likes to get down and dirty with their kills.

Crossbow   Favored by the Greek armies of Dionysus and made popular in Europe during the Middle Ages, this weapon is now mostly used for target shooting and sport hunting. Bows are typically made of ash or yew . . . but Kell can always hook you up with modifications if this happens to be your weapon of choice. And he can make a groovy one that hides up your sleeves.

Dirk   Celtic straight-bladed dagger used as a backup to a broadsword, or to swear a ceremonial oath. Dirks have the benefit of being small, lightweight, and easy to conceal.

Double Ax   Also known as a labrys, this two-headed ax was widely used in Ancient Minoan, Thracian, and Greek symbology to represent Zeus. In Scandinavian mythology, this ax was used to represent their thunder god, Thor.

Dummies   The most widely available for weapons training are wooden dummies, which come in a variety of woods and sizes. Then there are punching bags (I'm told Valerius used to dress his in a Hawaiian shirt) in the shape of people. Some Hunters have been known to put fangs on them just for effect.

Glaive   A long-reaching shaft weapon, like a spear, only a glaive has a much longer blade (anywhere from one to two feet in length).

Grenade/Grenade Launcher   The grenade gets its name from the word *pomegranate,* a popular fruit if you know your mythology. (And if you do, tell Hades "Hi".) This small bomb can be filled with a variety of things such as shrapnel (for destruction) or smoke (for distraction) or gas (for incapacitation of your enemy). The grenade launchers do tend to be a little hard to hide though. The last one I remember hearing about was being used by Spathi Daimons to attack Wulf in Minnesota.

Halberd   This fancy ax with a long spike at the top is mounted on a pole shaft. It was used in battle against cavalry and other mounted foes. The halberd was once the primary weapon of the Swiss Army. Wielders were known as "pikemen".

Handclaws   Used by the ninja to cross ice, climb trees, and scratch messages in stone, glass, wood, or the bodies of their opponents.

Hurlbat   An all-metal throwing ax with either a point or a blade (or both) sharpened onto all conceivable (and some contrived) ends. Whatever—or whomever—you hurl this one at is going to be hurting . . . and hopefully, dust.

Kama   This small, handheld scythe originated as a farming implement in Japan and China. (Favored by Cassandra Peters Tryggvason.) The handle can be made of wood or metal, and is usually the length of the user's forearm. The short, curved blade can be used for slashing, stabbing, or deflecting an opponent's weapon.

Katana   Japanese single-edged longsword. Japanese swords are differentiated by length—the shorter form of this sword is called a *wakizashi*. The katana is traditionally worn sharp-side up.

Kevlar   Kevlar is DuPont's light but strong fiber, with a strength-to-weight ratio five times that of steel. It comes in various grades: Kevlar 29 is the grade used for body armor. Even though they can't kill you, bullets can still slow you down. A Kevlar jacket is a handy item to have around. Do note, however, that Kevlar decomposes when exposed to chlorine, so don't go using it as a flotation device in your neighbor's pool. It also has adverse effects in UV light . . . but since I'm pretty sure you're not going to be sunbathing in it, I'm not going to worry. There are other fabrics on the market as well, like Dyneema, which can be purchased from retailers selling tournament-quality fencing equipment.

Kunai   Ancient Japanese trowel with a sharpened tip. It looks a bit like a chisel with a loop at the end, where it could be attached to a cord, to be worn around the neck or affixed to another weapon. Like many other weapons, the kunai was originally used as a gardening tool. But, like many other gardening tools, it was discovered that the sharp-tipped kunai was especially effective against Daimons.

Mace   Like a club only heavier, deadlier, much cooler, and much older—the first wooden maces date back to 12,000 B.C. Not popular with the Romans, the mace came back into fashion during the Middle Ages when metal flanges were added that could dent or pierce armored knights.

Mat   This plastic-covered foam can be procured in a variety of colors, shapes, sizes, widths, and foam densities. The question to ask yourself is: How hard do you want to hit the ground?

Panic Alarm   Most often kept on a key chain to page your Squire in emergencies. But remember that since you have heightened hearing, it will hurt when used.

Punching Bag   A fairly modern invention in the world of athletic training, this water- or grain-filled sack comes as a "heavy bag" (hanging) or "standing bag" (freestanding with a wide, round base). Heavier bags will sway less; water-filled bags weigh more. Be careful, though—too heavy and you may as well be punching the wall.

Retractable Knives   Kell makes these handy-dandy carbon steel puppies with Velcro wrist-fasteners.

Sai   Another weapon whose origin lies in ancient Japanese agriculture, this unsharpened dagger can be used lethally (stabbing) or nonlethally (disarming your opponent). Traditionally, sais are carried in threes (one at either side and one in back)— unless you're a Ninja Turtle.

Scramasax   This is a Viking blade—a cross between a curved machete and a crude sword that tapers to a point at its end. The shorter scramasax (as short as six inches) was commonly used as an eating utensil, while the longer ones (up to three feet) were used in farming.

Shobo   A shobo consists of a small piece of wood connected to a ring worn around the finger. Adopted by the Japanese ninja for its simplicity and concealment factor, it was used for striking an opponent's pressure points. Of course, there's only one "pressure point" you need to worry about on a Daimon. Go for it.

Shuriken   Commonly known as "ninja throwing stars", these supplemental Japanese blades can be made of anything and only some are shaped like flat stars (*hira-shuriken*). The *bo-shuriken* (a metal spike sharpened at one or both ends), may be of greater use to Dark-Hunters.

Srad   A circular dagger; an ancient Celtic weapon that can be thrown or used hand to hand.

Stake   An oldie but a goodie. Not fancy, but it does the job. Both wood and steel are acceptable.

Sword   Long, bladed weapon. Kind of easy to use. The pointy part goes into your victim's body.

War Fan   Used in Japanese feudal warfare. Can come in a variety of shapes, sizes, and materials. The Dansen uchiwa fighting fan is made of iron, and was used more like a shield. (Kell specializes in a smaller one, roughly eleven inches long, with a razor-sharp edge.) An iron-spoked Tessen fan can also be used as a club, for throwing, or for aid in swimming.

Watch   Seems silly, but it is a good idea to have a watch, with the alarm set to go off twenty minutes before sunrise. You never know when you'll get distracted right before sunup.

How to Die

Dying's easy. It's living that's hard.
—Zarek

No Dark-Hunter likes to hear about the death of another.

Like Daimons, Dark-Hunters turn to dust upon death. I pray you never have to witness it . . . but you will. You can't die from a gunshot wound or a blow to the head or a drink spiked with Drano. Crosses and garlic are as useless on you as they are on Daimons.

But you're not invincible. Your body is gifted with regenerative powers, but some things even the gods themselves can't fix.

Remember rule number five: An unconscious Dark-Hunter is

a dead Dark-Hunter, and a dead Dark-Hunter only takes about five minutes to decompose.

There are four ways a Dark-Hunter can die:

1. **Total dismemberment** (Though I can't imagine partial is too easy to come back from. Avoid wood chippers.)
2. **Sunlight**
3. **Beheading**
4. **Stabbing the bow-and-arrow tattoo** (You're not supposed to know about this one, Hunter, so as soon as you turn the page you won't remember that you've ever read it.)

Those of you from the Middle Ages will remember the punishment of being hanged, drawn, and quartered. Contrary to popular opinion, the quartering part comes from Dark-Hunters. If quartered and buried separately, you are dead.

The reason sunlight can kill you is because Artemis is the goddess of the Moon. The reason it kills Daimons is because they were cursed by Artemis's twin brother Apollo, god of the Sun. Isn't it pretty how it all fits together like that?

Apollo hates you with a passion just because of what you are. He won't hesitate to rid the world of your hide if he catches you in his domain. Never let a ray of sunlight come into contact with your body. Umbrellas and coats will not shield you from daylight—any part of you that is exposed to daylight will burn. There is no SPF high enough.

Make sure to know where your safety zones are. Have more than one safe place to run to should you be trapped after sunup. Squires are handy, but remember there's only so much they can do.

If you die as a Dark-Hunter, you die without a soul. You cannot cross over into a happy hereafter. You become a Shade, trapped forever in a painful, horrific place that makes hell look like paradise. In Shadedom, you exist insubstantially on the mortal plane. You have no body, but full cognition. No one can see you, or hear you, or touch you. When a human walks through your "body", their soul rips through you like broken glass. You are always hungry, always thirsty, and always lonely. Nothing can sate your hunger or thirst or mind. Ever.

Forever.

The Out Clause

Everyone wants someone they can hold and love. Someone who will be there to help pick up the pieces when everything falls apart.

—Acheron

Before I go into this one, consider the benefits of being a Dark-Hunter. You have a well-paying job, literally all the time in the world, and pretty much nothing can touch you. Now consider mortality. Death. Disease. Stubbed toes and paper cuts. Reading glasses and gray hair.

If you fall in love, it better be someone you're willing to die for . . . because that's exactly what you're going to do. Only slowly this time. And you don't come back.

Each out clause varies by Dark-Hunter, and is a secret even to them. Beware of when you find it—you will be drained of your Dark-Hunter powers for a period of time. But *if* you find it, you know that regaining your soul is within your grasp.

Well, technically, it will lie in the grasp of your beloved. Artemis keeps your soul inside a medallion that swirls any and every color of the rainbow. A pure, loving heart must hold this medallion in the palm of her (or his, if that's your thing) hand and hold it, while you are drained of your powers.

It's not as easy as it sounds. The medallion is not meant to be held by mortals, and so it burns the flesh irreparably. It is a torturous, unyielding pain . . . but your true love must *not let go*. If they do, your soul will be lost forever and you will be doomed to live as a Shade for all eternity.

So: medallion in hand, drained of your powers. With me so far? Good.

Because then you have to die.

Worse than forcing your lover to bear the pain of the soul medallion is asking them to kill you. And no halfways. Your heart *must* stop beating. Staking is best.

Once your heart stops beating, your lover must place the medallion over the mark where your soul was captured; this area is conveniently marked somewhere on your body by a clever double bow-and-arrow mark. It is where Artemis touched you when she took your soul, and that exact place is where the soul needs to reenter the body.

If you're very lucky and your love is pure, you are reintroduced to the mortal coil.

Every few hundred years there's a rash of Dark-Hunters who find true love and make a break for it. To them I say, *Vaya con Dios.*

Or . . . you know . . . not.

There is one nifty part—if and when your soul is returned to you, you will have the option of remaining in the service of Artemis. Ex-Dark-Hunters have found it difficult to give up their day . . . er . . . night jobs and intimate circle of friends.

But hey—there's one easy way around all of this.

Just don't fall in love.

Pyramid of Protection

Honey, there's always hope.
—Selena Laurens

There are three branches of Hunters: Dark-Hunters; Were-Hunters; and Dream-Hunters. Together they form the Pyramid of Protection. These warriors keep mankind safe from all the different kinds of predators who could easily kill or enslave them.

Most often the branches work alone, but they do team up together for not only human protection, but also the protections of other Hunters, Apollites, gods, and ultimately the world itself.

They're the good guys. You want them on your side. And they're all hugely powerful, so you *really* don't want them as your enemies.

Dark-Hunter.com

Be part of the world, but never in it.
—Acheron

At first glance, this Web site might look like a book series and a role-playing game. Don't be fooled. We did that on purpose. Aren't we clever?

Dark-Hunter.com is the place to go to keep in touch with other Dark-Hunters around the world, around the clock. It is a lonely life you will lead, but that doesn't mean you're completely alone. Since proximity to another Dark-Hunter will drain your powers, the Internet is the perfect solution for a bit of healthy social activity with like-minded folks. (And you thought it was invented by the government.) Brag about your kills, imagine new and inventive ways to kill the enemy, vent about the one that got away. It's all right here.

The labyrinthine Web site was originally set up by several Squires. Tad Gardner, Carl Samuel, Daphne Addams, and—until recently—Nick Gautier maintain the information and keep the safeguards up-to-date. There are so many twists and turns . . . it's a bit like a library housed in some forgotten catacombs.

All of the records are kept here. If something should happen to this book—and Acheron doesn't take your head off—you can always find what you're looking for on the site. You just may be looking for a very, very long time.

Dream-Hunter.com   This is to give you an idea of the important gods for ye non-Greek people. It will also explain to you the different Dream-Hunters and what their functions are.

dailyinquisitor.com/bbs/index.php   This is the message board where our members gather from all over the world. You'll definitely want to check that out.

Katoteros.com   Don't think we're alone with having our own Web site. In this day and age, the Daimons have their own, too. Keep an eye on it. It'll give you all kinds of nifty info.

SherrilynKenyon.com   This is the author we keep hearing about who knows way too much about our world. We're not sure how she got her info, but she's scarily tuned into us.

Were-Hunter.com   These are our friends, the Were-Hunters. The site explains key elements about them and introduces you to their world.

Quick Reference Slang

I'd rather be vindictive than smart.
—Solin

Most of these terms you'll pick up along the way . . . heck, you might even invent a few over the years. But just so you're not completely in the dark, here are a few words and phrases that are common in Dark-Hunter circles.

Act of Vengeance The night a Dark-Hunter is given to extract his or her revenge on whoever wronged them and caused their death. It ends with the dawn.

Apollite The cursed descendents of Apollo, who either die on their twenty-seventh birthday or choose to become Daimon. More on them in chapter 6, "How to Roast a Daimon".

Arcadians Humans who can take animal form. They are descendents of a human father and an Apollite mother. More on them in chapter 3, "Were-Hunters".

Blood Hunt The search for a Rogue Dark-Hunter. A successful blood hunt ends in the death of the hunted.

Bolt-Hole Astral opening between dimensions that can be used by Were-Hunters or Daimons. Also called a lamina.

Buffites Human vampire slayers. It was inevitable, wasn't it? Just be glad you're not called Angels.

Carmillas Women looking for Daimons to turn them into immortal vampires. Also referred to as Complete Morons.

Daimon An Apollite who has chosen to steal human souls to fool their bodies into maintaining their life. More on them in chapter 6, "How to Roast a Daimon".

Dark-Hunter   Someone who has sold their soul to Artemis for one single Act of Vengeance, and will now spend eternity hunting Daimons. You ready?

Day-Slayer   Daimon myth about one of their kind who can move in daylight and who will one day come to lead them back into Apollo's favor.

Day-Surfer   A Dark-Hunter who dies by sunlight. If you want to be a surfer, give Savitar a call and get your jollies out in the ocean.

Deadmen Walking   Humans who serve Daimons (usually because they have been promised immortality). Daimons will promise their food anything if it will make it stick around and stay fresh for that much longer.

Diktyon   Magical net Artemis uses when hunting. Pretty cool. Pray it's never used on you.

Expire   To kill a Daimon.

Fabio/Kato   Derogatory term for a Daimon stemming from the fact that they are all blond and good-looking.

Feeder   A Dark-Hunter who drinks blood. If you must, do so cautiously. Ultimately, though, feeding can only lead to trouble. Best to avoid it altogether.

Four Realms   Time, Space, Earth, Dreams. These are what the Pyramid of Protection guard. There is only a small group of individuals who can walk all four. Yeah, the tall Atlantean is one of them.

Full Alert   When all hell is breaking loose, literally, and Daimons are emerging from their bolt-holes en masse. Most likely to happen in New Orleans during Mardi Gras. Only Acheron can call a Full Alert.

Inkblot   Slang for Daimon. Named after the black mark that appears on a Daimon's chest after turning from Apollite. It is this spot that must be pierced to free the souls and to kill the Daimon.

Kalosis   The mysterious nether region where Apollymi the Destroyer is imprisoned. It is the Atlantean hell realm.

Katagaria   Plural term for the animal branch of the Were-Hunters. They are animals who can take human form. Katagari is the single term.

Katoteros   The mysterious nether region where Acheron lives. It is the Atlantean heaven realm and was once the home of the gods.

Kori   A servant of Artemis. They are found in her temple on Olympus.

Kynigostaia   Homer's history of the Dark-Hunters that was lost.

Laminas   Bolt-holes the Spathis use to travel. The rabbit hole leads straight to Kalosis. Don't follow.

Oneroi   Dream-Hunter champions who protect those who are asleep. They also help Dark-Hunters to heal psychologically and physically. It is sometimes used as the generic term for any sleep god.

Ords   Slang for "ordinaries"—normal humans who have no idea about the world around them.

Patria   A Were-Hunter clan.

Rogue   A Dark-Hunter who has spurned the ways of Artemis and turned against Acheron and his Dark-Hunter brethren. No longer protecting humans, they are a threat to humanity. Pretty much an instant death sentence. You're always welcome to question authority . . . but don't.

Rytis   The ripple that allows Were-Hunters to travel forward and back through time.

Scooby   Derogatory term Lykos Were-Hunters use to insult one another, meaning a stupid or cowardly pup.

Scuds   Young Daimons out to prove themselves worthy.

Sentinels   Chosen by the Fates, they are members of the Arcadian Were-Hunters who protect the humans and Arcadians from the Katagaria.

Shade   Dark-Hunter who dies before his or her soul can be returned. Shades have translucent, ashen skin and dark eyes. They are doomed to an eternal unlife without powers, where they cannot touch anything and cannot be heard by anyone but the Oracles. They crave food and water but cannot eat or drink.

Shadedom   The existence of being a Shade. If you can go so far as to call it an "existence".

Skoti   Dream predators hooked on excess emotions. They infiltrate sleep so they can tamper with and seduce dreamers in order to get their emotional fix. Skotos is the singular term.

Slayers   Katagaria or Arcadians who are driven to madness by their hormones. They kill indiscriminately.

Spathi   Warrior class of Daimons who will pursue and kill Dark-Hunters.

Squire   Servant to the Dark-Hunters. (Just don't go using the word *servant* around one of them.)

Strati   Katagaria soldiers. Often confused with Slayers, Strati only kill to defend themselves, their pack, or their territory.

Telikos   Armageddon. End of the world. Death to all. You get the picture.

Temple of Artemis   Artemis's home on Olympus.

UHF   Universal Hunter Food: pizza. Quick, easy, and fast.

Van Helsings   Another term for human vampire slayers.

Whelps   Young Were-Hunters who have reached puberty, mastered their hormones, but have yet to harness all their powers. Again, it's a derogatory term.

Dark-Hunter Directory

Your Fellow Soldiers

He's a vampire, isn't he? I knew it!
—Selena Laurens

There are thousands of Dark-Hunters all over the world. Trying to keep track of them all on paper would be like trying to print a global phone book. (Plus, we don't exactly want to give away the locations of some of our operatives, if you know what I mean.) With that in mind, here is a list of just a few Hunters you may have already encountered, or ones that you'll be hearing stories about soon enough.

Hopefully this list will give you some small bit of insight into who might be guarding your back, what harsh world they came from, and what made them who they are today. It will tell you more about those who have taken advantage of the out clause, but still fight the Daimons on the side of Artemis.

It is also meant to serve as a memorial to those Dark-Hunters who have come before and passed away in the line of duty. We honor them by always being conscious of just how mortal we immortals can be.

If you need to get in touch with any of these Hunters, view their pictures and profiles, or run a background check, you should find all you need and more on www.Dark-Hunter.com.

Alexion   Alexion is not a name, it's an Atlantean title. The Alexion we know and love today is technically neither human nor Dark-Hunter nor Shade . . . he's one of those Acheron classifies as "other". His original incarnation was Ias of Groesia.

Ias was the third Dark-Hunter created after Acheron, and he's the whole reason there's an out clause to begin with. Ias, as a human, was killed by his wife's lover. Trusting that Ias's wife's love for him was pure (their first mistake), Acheron entrusted her with Ias's soul medallion.

However, even Ash can be wrong sometimes. The unfaithful wife, unwilling to bear the pain and bring Ias back to humanity, dropped the medallion and instantly doomed Ias to Shadedom. (And don't think she just got away with that. Happily, Ash turned Ias's wife into stone.)

Ash took pity on Ias. He gave him form (of sorts) and took him to live beside him in Katoteros. He bestowed upon Ias the title of Alexion and branded him with Acheron's mark: a gold sun with three lightning bolts.

Unfortunately, Acheron at the time was still coming into his role and was not aware of the full extent of his powers, so—unlike many Acheron has revived since—Alexion can never be truly human again. As a Shade his senses are muted; his lot is to observe life, not live it.

His duties include watching over Simi and keeping her out of trouble. Alexion can also pass judgment on Dark-Hunter groups that are trying to overthrow Acheron's authority, but he can't be outside Acheron's domain for any longer than ten days. No Dark-Hunter retains a memory of the white-coated Alexion once he has passed judgment and returned to Katoteros.

Alexion, like Simi, can only be killed by an Atlantean dagger from the Destroyer herself. He can explode Daimons with a thought. He can hear the Shades as they wail in their living hell. He does not eat; he drinks Ash's blood to survive. (Though he does like popcorn . . . it has something to do with the consistency.)

He currently lives in Katoteros with Ash, Simi, and Dangereuse St. Richard, Alexion's Dark-Hunter true love who was brought to Katoteros by Acheron after her death.

HAIR/EYES: blond/hazel-green
POWERS: godlike
FEATURED NOVEL: *Sins of the Night*

Alousius   (deceased) A Scottish Dark-Hunter, Alousius was killed by Daimons. Prior to his death, he had lived in Seattle since 1875.

BORN: March 14, 1516
BIRTHPLACE: Aberdeen, Scotland
HEIGHT: six foot three
HAIR: blond
POWERS: telekinesis
CURRENT LOCATION: deceased

ap-Owain, Ryn   Ryn was a Welsh prince whose family was betrayed and wiped out by an ambitious neighbor. In a vengeful rage, he led a suicide charge against his enemy and was left for dead.

BORN: April 25, 1400
BIRTHPLACE: Gwynedd, Wales
HEIGHT: six foot five
HAIR/EYES: black
POWERS: pyrokinesis
AGE AT DEATH: twenty-four
CURRENT LOCATION: Santa Cruz, California

Arien   Arien began her life as the kindhearted daughter of a thief. She dedicated her life to helping others, until a clansman accused her of sorcery and blamed her for the death of his wife. Arien and her father escaped into the hills, where they were then betrayed by her lover. Her father was hanged, and Arien was burned as a heretic.

BORN: A.D. 1052
BIRTHPLACE: Gwynedd, Wales
HEIGHT: five foot ten
HAIR/EYES: dark brown
POWERS: precognition
CURRENT LOCATION: New York, N.Y.

Baughy, Christopher (aka Rogue)   Nickname: Kit. A known Dark-Hunter.

BORN: July 4, 1702
BIRTHPLACE: London, England
HEIGHT: six foot four
HAIR/EYES: black
POWERS: cryokinesis
CURRENT LOCATION: Chicago, Illinois

Belle   (deceased) Belle was a tall, blonde, gum-chewin', tequila-drinkin' Dark-Hunter with a Texan drawl as deep as the Mariana Trench. In her heyday, Belle traveled with a Wild West show. Legend has it that she shot the reporter who failed to mention she was a better shot than Annie Oakley, and that she reputedly threw the party that started the Great Fire of Chicago.

Belle was killed by Daimons during an ambush in Seattle.

BORN: November 9, 1869
BIRTHPLACE: Austin, Texas
HEIGHT: six feet
HAIR: blonde
POWERS: atmokinesis

Blade   A Saxon peasant who rose to knighthood on merit alone, Blade eventually became a mercenary for William the Conqueror. He was assassinated by his lover during the 1066 Norman Invasion after he snuck her through enemy troops to safety.

BORN: A.D. 1032
BIRTHPLACE: Northumberland, England
HEIGHT: six foot four
HAIR/EYES: dark brown
POWERS: telekinesis
CURRENT LOCATION: Atlanta, Georgia

Brady, "Jess" William Jessup (aka Sundown)   Orphaned at age five, Jess was a gunslinger, train robber, and cardsharp by age sixteen. He obtained the nickname "Sundown" because they claimed he always did his best work after dark. The bounty on his head was enough to persuade the best man at Jess's wedding to shoot him in the back. The best man collected . . . and, thanks to Artemis, so did Jess.

Jess is the only Dark-Hunter that Zarek has ever confided in (they met while playing Myst online). Not surprisingly, he wears a black Stetson.

BORN: August 14, 1869
BIRTHPLACE: Possum Town, Mississippi
HEIGHT: six foot five
HAIR/EYES: dark brown
POWERS: precognition, telekinesis
AGE AT DEATH: twenty-four
CURRENT LOCATION: Reno, Nevada

Cael   A Celtic Dark-Hunter whose wife (Morag), brother, washerwoman mother, and sister (Corynna) were all slain by Vikings in 904. Cael's nobleborn father had sold them all into slavery to save his own wretched life. He probably knew that the Vikings didn't want slaves—they wanted people on whom to practice their fighting skills. Cael was forced to watch as his entire family and his beloved wife were killed before his eyes.

And then came vengeance.

An artist of sorts, Cael makes recycled trash sculptures that he keeps at his home in the basement underneath the Happy

Hunting Ground (an Apollite bar) in Seattle. His only friend through the centuries has been the Dark-Hunter/Were-Hunter Ravyn Kontis.

In 2006, Cael's Apollite-turned-Daimon (by accident) wife, Amaranda, fed him the blood of a Daimon to save him from dying—an act that caused his black eyes to be streaked with amber.

BORN: September 2, 879
BIRTHPLACE: Cornwall, England
HEIGHT: six foot six
HAIR/EYES: black/black and amber
POWERS: psychometry, telekinesis
CURRENT LOCATION: Seattle, Washington

Callabrax of Likonos   Nickname: Brax. A Dorian warrior (Dorians are the forerunners of the Spartans), Callabrax was one of the original Dark-Hunters. He, like many other of his Dark-Hunter brethren, enjoys keeping track of his Daimon kills.

BORN: ?
BIRTHPLACE: ?
HEIGHT: six foot five
HAIR/EYES: black
POWERS: ferrokinesis
CURRENT LOCATION: Dallas, Texas

Campbell, Maxx   A Dark-Hunter Highlander currently located in Glasgow. Maxx's Squire is Keller Mallory's father.

BORN: June 12, 1419
BIRTHPLACE: Northern Scotland
HEIGHT: six foot four
HAIR: blond
POWERS: teleportation, telekinesis
CURRENT LOCATION: Glasgow, Scotland

Corbin   Nickname: Binny (to a chosen few). A Dark-Huntress, Corbin is a former beloved Greek queen who married and was widowed young. Her reign was uncontested until her brother-in-law made a pact with a barbarian tribe to sack the city and burn it to the ground. She died trying to save her servants and their children.

Corbin gets her kicks out of sneaking up on people. Her Squire is Sara Addams.

BORN: January 17, 190 B.C.
BIRTHPLACE: Athens, Greece
HEIGHT: five foot ten
HAIR: auburn
POWERS: chronokinesis, teleportation
AGE AT DEATH: twenty-six
CURRENT LOCATION: St. Paul, Minnesota

Cromley   (deceased) Dark-Hunter killed by Desiderius.

BORN: August 19, 1610
BIRTHPLACE: Liverpool, England
HEIGHT: six foot six
HAIR/EYES: black
POWERS: pyrokinesis

Danesti, Esperetta   Nickname: Retta. The daughter of Vlad Tepeş (aka Dracula or Vlad the Impaler), Esperetta grew up isolated in a nunnery in the Caucasus. From the moment of her birth, it was decided that she would be a gift to the Church to atone for her father's sins. Retta had no desire for anything else ... until the day Velkan saved her from a fate worse than death (see Velkan Danesti). Retta fell instantly in love with the handsome warrior prince. They were married in secret and— because he was a sorcerer—Velkan bound her soul to his so that they might remain together for all eternity.

Killed by Retta's father, Velkan took up Artemis's deal to become a Dark-Hunter. He swore vengeance upon Vlad, and killed him. But because they had been bound by sorcery, when Velkan was reborn as a Dark-Hunter ... so was his soul mate.

BORN: December 25, 1452
BIRTHPLACE: Wallachia, Romania
HEIGHT: six feet
HAIR/EYES: auburn/blue
POWERS: longevity
CURRENT LOCATION: Transylvania
FEATURED STORY: "Until Death We Do Part" in the *Love at First Bite Anthology*

Danesti, Velkan   Velkan was the illegitimate son of a Hungarian sorceress-princess and a Moldavian prince who—like the infamous Vlad Dracul—was a member of the Order of the Dragon. Velkan grew up at his father's side, fighting invaders. His brothers were captured and enslaved by their enemies.

Rather than be turned into a slave, Velkan sold his soul to the devil for freedom. He vowed that no one would ever enslave or tame him. At age fifteen, he fought and freed his one brother who still lived.

At twenty-six, Velkan captured a band of invaders who had attacked and robbed a group of nuns on their way to Trigoviste There in their midst, he found a novice who they had captured with the intent to rape and kill her.

This novice from Wallachia was none other than Esperetta, the daughter of Vlad Dracul, one of his father's most hated enemies. Despite her ancestry, Velkan took her to his home and cared for her . . . and fell in love with her. (See Esperetta Danesti.)

Velkan has a scar that runs from the corner of his left eye to his chin. During his days as a Moldavian warlord, he wore black armor bearing the golden emblem of a coiled serpent, and a dragon-shaped helm.

He owns two huge Tibetan mastiffs: Bram and Stoker.

BORN: September 8, 1450
BIRTHPLACE: Moldavia, Romania

HEIGHT: six foot four
HAIR/EYES: black
POWERS: telekinesis, shapeshifting, pyrokinesis
CURRENT LOCATION: Transylvania
FEATURED STORY: "Until Death We Do Part" in the *Love at First Bite Anthology*

Diego   Born the spoiled son of a rich aristocrat, when Diego wanted to be a sailor, his father gave him a boat and the best captain to train him. With the influx of gold from the New World and the stories of riches to be had, Diego turned his attention to the Aztec nation. He was reportedly on his way to El Dorado when his second-in-command decided to hand him over to a group of headhunters. Vengeance ensued, and Artemis got herself a new Dark-Hunter.

BORN: A.D. 1532
BIRTHPLACE: Toledo, Spain
HEIGHT: six foot four
HAIR/EYES: black
POWERS: aerokinesis, electrokinesis, telekinesis
CURRENT LOCATION: East Los Angeles, California

Dragon   Dragon is the illegitimate son of a Western merchant and a Japanese woman. Trained as a ninja by his uncle, he was betrayed by his samurai overlord and handed over to his archrival. Dragon still walks the path of the ninja, making time to take on students—often inner-city kids and women from shelters—and train them in the martial arts. He believes that no one should ever be defenseless. Dragon was the sensei of Susan Michaels.

His real name is unknown. The nickname, Dragon, was given to him because of the red dragon tattoo that marks his left arm. He has a strange fascination for Zoe, and he often talks to Ravyn and Cael.

BORN: January 3, 1332
BIRTHPLACE: Okinawa, Japan
HEIGHT: six feet
HAIR/EYES: black
POWERS: hydrokinesis, power mimicry, power sensing
AGE AT DEATH: twenty-six
CURRENT LOCATION: San Francisco, California

Eamon　(deceased) A Scottish Dark-Hunter, formerly Squired by Celena.

BORN: A.D. 1518
BIRTHPLACE: Scotland
HEIGHT: six foot five
HAIR: blond
POWERS: divination, clairvoyance

Ephani　An ancient Amazon Dark-Huntress stationed in Mississippi. Ephani became a Dark-Hunter sometime around 1000 B.C. She was formerly Squired by Celena.

BORN: circa 1000 B.C.
BIRTHPLACE: Greece
HEIGHT: six foot two
HAIR: red
POWERS: cryokinesis
CURRENT LOCATION: deceased

Erius　(deceased) Erius was a Dark-Hunter who thought he could be a god. He tried to lead the Dark-Hunters to revolt against Acheron. He has been a Shade now for more than two thousand years.

BORN: 2349 B.C.
BIRTHPLACE: Sparta
HEIGHT: six foot six

HAIR/EYES: black
POWERS: geokinesis

Euphemia   (deceased) Nickname: Effie. Formerly a Greek slave woman, Effie was a Dark-Huntress stationed with Viper in Memphis. She was vivaciously funny, and smart to boot. Effie was decapitated by Stryker's Daimons.

BORN: ?
BIRTHPLACE: Athens
HEIGHT: six feet
HAIR: blonde
POWERS: gravitakinesis

Fitzgilbert, Badon   A known Dark-Hunter.

BORN: A.D. 1151
BIRTHPLACE: Hexham, England
HEIGHT: six foot six
HAIR: blond
POWERS: hydrokinesis
CURRENT LOCATION: Columbia, South Carolina

Gallagher, Jamie   James Cameron Patrick Gallagher was born in the back of a sweatshop in the Irish slums of New York. Jamie later became a gangster during the American Prohibition era. At the age of twenty he was working for the infamous Ally Malone. His mother disowned him because of it.

Quick to anger, he took nothing from anyone and refused to be tamed until the day a Portuguese immigrant's daughter crossed his path. Instantly in love, Gallagher defied everyone to claim Rosalie for his own. He adored his wife and was trying to go straight when fate intervened.

Jamie was shot down in the street by police officers when he was on the way to the hospital to see his wife and their newborn son.

He is one of the youngest of the Dark-Hunters and is still getting used to his powers and responsibilities. He is wild, untamed, and extremely unpredictable.

BORN: December 24, 1900
BIRTHPLACE: New York, N.Y.
HEIGHT: six foot four
HAIR/EYES: black
POWERS: telekinesis, atmokinesis, chronokinesis
Featured Story: "A Dark-Hunter Christmas"

Hawke, Jonathan   Jonathan Hawke was the son of an English gambler and a Powhatan mother, so he has both a deep respect for nature and incredibly good luck. Hawke took to the sea at age eleven and won his own ship at age nineteen in a game of chance. When the Revolutionary War broke out, he became a blockade runner to aid his fellow Americans. He died during the fighting when the woman he loved turned out to be a British spy.

BORN: July 4, 1753
BIRTHPLACE: Blue Ridge Mountains
HEIGHT: six foot six
HAIR/EYES: black
POWERS: geokinesis, gravitakinesis
CURRENT LOCATION: Yorktown, Virginia

Hunter, Kyrian (aka Kyrian of Thrace)   An ancient Greek ex-Dark-Hunter. Born prince and sole heir to the throne of Thrace circa 180 B.C., Kyrian was disinherited when he married an ex-prostitute against his father's wishes.

As a legendary Macedonian general, he cut a trail of slaughter through the Mediterranean during the Fourth Macedonian War. Chroniclers wrote that Kyrian would break the Roman stranglehold on the known world and claim Rome for his own. The motto on his shield read: "Spoils to the Victor".

Kyrian would probably have succeeded in conquering the world, had he not been betrayed by his wife (Theone) and delivered into the hands of his enemies. He was tortured for weeks and then executed in 147 B.C. by Valerius (not to be confused with the Dark-Hunter Valerius, who is Valerius's grandson . . . but I can see you're confused anyway. There, there. It will pass in a minute).

A Lynyrd Skynyrd fan and car enthusiast, Kyrian is married to Amanda Hunter and is the father of Marissa Hunter. Kyrian was killed by Desiderius/Ulric in 2005. He was revived soon after and made immortal by Acheron.

BORN: 179 B.C.
BIRTHPLACE: Thrace
HEIGHT: six foot five
HAIR/EYES: blond/green
POWERS: telekinesis, clairvoyance
AGE AT DEATH: thirty-one
CURRENT LOCATION: New Orleans, Louisiana
FEATURED NOVEL: *Night Pleasures*

Ias of Groesia   This ancient Greek Dark-Hunter was one of the first three created along with Callabrax and Kyros. He had only been a Dark-Hunter for two days when Acheron met him. (See Alexion.)

Jean-Luc   A pirate Dark-Hunter, noticeable by the gold loop earring in his left ear. He was stabbed once by Tabitha Devereaux. (It was dark, she said.)

BORN: A.D. 1692
BIRTHPLACE: Nice, France
HEIGHT: six foot six
HAIR/EYES: black
POWERS: telepathy, telekinesis, ferrokinesis
CURRENT LOCATION: New Orleans, Louisiana

Kassim   (deceased) A Saracen prince in the Middle Ages who fought against the European Crusaders, Kassim was betrayed by one of his own and given over to an enemy who took Kassim's life in revenge for the death of his son. So Kassim took it back, with interest . . . vengeance is a vicious cycle.

Kassim was stationed in Jackson, Mississippi, until Ash moved him to Alexandria. He was with Kyrian and Amanda Hunter in New Orleans when Desiderius returned to wreak havoc upon the city. He was killed while protecting Marissa Hunter from the Dark-Hunter Ulric, who was possessed by Desiderius at the time.

BORN: A.D. 1103
BIRTHPLACE: Syria
HEIGHT: six foot six
HAIR/EYES: black
POWERS: photokinesis, omnilingual

Kell   A former Visigoth warrior whose tribe was destroyed by a Roman army, Kell and his brother were sold into slavery and trained as gladiators. He was executed when he attempted to murder Emperor Valens. Not surprisingly, Kell doesn't really deal well with anyone from Rome. He hates Valerius, big-time.

The son of a metalsmith, Kell also makes weapons for the Dark-Hunters. Combining ancient techniques with modern technology, his weapons are virtually indestructible. Because of his age, he is also able to provide the Dark-Hunters with the weapons they had in their ancient worlds.

He has a girlfriend, which is a constant source of irritation for Acheron. He plays drums in a band called Never Never, and he makes his own guitars. His Squire is Jamie Blackstone, a runaway he rescued off the streets, fostered, and then offered the position to when his own Squire retired.

He is exceptionally fond of peanut butter and jelly sandwiches.

BORN: November 22, 345
BIRTHPLACE: Dacia (Romania)
HEIGHT: six foot five
HAIR/EYES: brown
AGE AT DEATH: twenty-five
CURRENT LOCATION: Dallas, Texas

Kontis, Ravyn   An Arcadian Dark-Hunter/Were-Hunter leopard, Ravyn is the son of Gareth Kontis. Ravyn was mated to Isabeau (a human), who betrayed Ravyn's Were pack to the humans while the male Weres were out hunting.

The hunting party realized that the women and children were being slaughtered when the bonded males began to die instantly. The remaining males in the pack turned on Ravyn and killed him (Wales, 1673). Ravyn then called on Artemis to seek revenge on Isabeau and her people.

When he made the bargain to become immortal, Ravyn lost the ability to teleport, travel through time, and day-walk as a man. He can walk in daylight only in the form of a very small Arabian leopard. In this form, he is often mistaken for a cat. Ravyn is stationed in Seattle, where his family owns a sanctuary (the Serengeti Club), but because of the laws of both Hunter-kind, they are never to associate. He is classified as an *exoristos,* which forbids any member of his clan from even speaking his name.

After recently mating with Susan Michaels, Ravyn asked Susan not to petition Artemis for his soul so that he might remain a Dark-Hunter.

BORN: 304 B.C.
BIRTHPLACE: Athens, Greece
HEIGHT: six foot six
HAIR/EYES: black
WERE-FORM: leopard, often very small Arabian
AGE AT DEATH: six hundred and thirty-five

Kyros of Seklos   (deceased) An ancient Greek Dark-Hunter, Kyros was one of the first three created, along with Callabrax and Ias. Kyros fought beside Alexion/Ias as a soldier, but he never told Ias about his unfaithful wife because he knew the knowledge would kill him. Oh, how right he was.

Kyros was stationed in Aberdeen, Mississippi, when he went Rogue with the Dark-Hunter Marco. He tried to turn other Dark-Hunters against Acheron by spreading vicious rumors. He later redeemed himself, by dying to save Alexion's life.

BORN: ?
BIRTHPLACE: Greece
HEIGHT: six foot five
HAIR: blond
POWERS: telekinesis

Magnus, Valerius   A former ancient Roman general who led conquests throughout Greece, Gaul, and Britannia. His undefeated army made even the Roman Consul tremble in fear. This Valerius is not to be confused with his grandfather—also Valerius—who tortured Kyrian of Thrace to death (though Valerius the younger was present at Kyrian's crucifixion). Valerius the younger also witnessed Kyrian come back and take his revenge on Valerius the older.

Val's father, Gaius Magnus, was a well-respected senator and completely evil bastard who forced his son to physically punish his half-brother Zarek. Val later came back as a Dark-Hunter himself to kill his own brothers after they turned on him and crucified him.

Despite this, Zarek still harbored little love for Val, and enjoyed shooting lightning bolts at him once he married Astrid and obtained his god-powers.

Val was sent to work in New Orleans after Kyrian's return to mortality. And in a move that shocked everyone, he went and fell in love with (and married!) the deliciously insane Tabitha Devereaux.

Valerius is an avid reader of science fiction. He always wears a designer suit, no matter what the occasion. He doesn't play well with most Dark-Hunters and it is imperative we keep him far away from Kell and Zoe, as well as other ancient Greeks and a large number of Celts, Vandals, Huns, and other groups who weren't friendly with Rome.

Valerius was given nectar of the gods (and therefore immortality) by Zarek and Astrid as a wedding gift. Astrid's bonus wedding gift was ambrosia—to bestow upon Val his own god-powers, so he could give Zarek as good as he got.

BORN: 152 B.C.
BIRTHPLACE: Rome
HEIGHT: six foot six
HAIR/EYES: black/blue
POWERS: godlike
AGE AT DEATH: thirty-four
CURRENT LOCATION: New Orleans, Louisiana
FEATURED NOVEL: *Seize the Night*

Marco   (deceased) From the Basque region of France, Marco was a renegade Dark-Hunter who, along with Kyros, aided Daimons and tried to turn other Dark-Hunters against Acheron. He was stabbed and decapitated by a group of Spathi Daimons.

BORN: A.D. 1701
BIRTHPLACE: Spain
HEIGHT: six foot six
HAIR/EYES: black
POWERS: telepathy

Menkaura   A Nubian priest Dark-Hunter, Menkaura has a tattoo of the Eye of Horus on his right bicep.

BORN: 3452 B.C.
BIRTHPLACE: Egypt
HEIGHT: six foot seven
HAIR/EYES: black
POWERS: animation, atmokinesis
CURRENT LOCATION: Seattle, Washington

Miles   (deceased) A renegade Dark-Hunter that the justice nymph Astrid fancied herself in love with . . . until he tried to kill her.

BORN: A.D. 1384
BIRTHPLACE: Sussex, England
HEIGHT: six foot two
HAIR: blond
POWERS: sonokinesis

Morginne   A Dark-Huntress who tricked Wulf Tryggvason into trading souls with her, cursing him so that no human or animal would be capable of remembering him five minutes after they left his presence. (Acheron used a drop of Wulf's nephew's blood to soften the blow of this curse, so that Wulf's blood relatives would be able to remember him.) Morginne escaped the clutches of Artemis so that she could spend eternity with the Norse god Loki.

BORN: April 14, 432
BIRTHPLACE: Wales
HEIGHT: five foot ten
HAIR/EYES: black
POWERS: astral projection, sorcery
CURRENT LOCATION: Valhalla

Olavsson, Treig   A Dark-Hunter whose Squire is Brynna's father.

BORN: A.D. 767
BIRTHPLACE: Oslo, Norway
HEIGHT: six foot four
HAIR/EYES: black
POWERS: sonokinesis
CURRENT LOCATION: Portland, Oregon

Parthenopaeus, Acheron (Ash)   An ancient immortal Atlantean, the leader and trainer and first of the Dark-Hunters. Son of King Icarion and Queen Aara, Acheron is the elder twin brother of Styxx. He makes his home in Katoteros. Talon Runningwolf refers to him as "T-Rex".

Ash has a handprint scar on his neck. It comes and goes about as often as he changes the color of his hair. His presence will not drain your powers. He's one of the few Dark-Hunters who gets carded at bars. He's also the last face you'll ever see if you piss off the gods.

Much more than that you want to know, and I'm not at liberty to tell you. Let's just leave it at that and move along.

BORN: 9548 B.C.
BIRTHPLACE: Didymos
HEIGHT: six foot eight
HAIR/EYES: varies/silver
POWERS: omniscience, omnipotence, omnilingual
CURRENT LOCATION: Wherever he wants to be

Phobos   His name means "fear" in Greek. This Dark-Hunter is the son of Neoptolemus and grandson of Achilles, both of whom fought in the Trojan War. His mother was Andromache, a concubine and war prize. (She was Hector's wife.)

Phobos was betrayed and killed by a vengeful woman who used him to gain access to his brother's palace and then enslaved his whole family.

BORN: 1999 B.C.
BIRTHPLACE: Sparta, Greece

HEIGHT: six foot five
HAIR: blond
POWERS: telekinesis, ferrokinesis
CURRENT LOCATION: Nashville, Tennessee

Porter, Diana The Porter family, along with their entire wagon train, were led out into the Mojave Desert by a corrupt guide and left there to die. Diana is one of the few Dark-Hunters who is also a peacekeeper ... and yet she has a strange fascination with guns.

BORN: A.D. 1865
BIRTHPLACE: Boston, Massachusetts
HEIGHT: six feet
HAIR: blonde
POWERS: sonokinesis
CURRENT LOCATION: New Mexico

Renegade Born an Anasazi warrior or shaman (only his hairdresser knows for sure), Renegade is an ancestor of Shadow, a Zuni warrior.

BORN: A.D. 961
BIRTHPLACE: unknown
HEIGHT: six foot seven
HAIR/EYES: black
POWERS: telekinesis, atmokinesis
CURRENT LOCATION: El Paso, Texas

Romanov, Dimitri A Russian prince and cousin to Tsar Nicholas II, Dimitri grew up as a close member of the royal family and was a general in the Russian White Army. When the Revolution came, he did everything he could to get his cousins to safety. Unfortunately for him, his second-in-command learned of his activities. In order to curry favor with the new regime, he had Dimitri arrested. Dimitri was executed the day before Nicholas.

Dimitri's attempt to rescue the royal family is what led to their executions.

BORN: September 8, 1884
BIRTHPLACE: Tsarskoe Selo, Russia
HEIGHT: six foot five
HAIR/EYES: light brown
POWERS: telepathy
AGE AT DEATH: thirty-three
CURRENT LOCATION: New York, N.Y.

Runningwolf, Talon   Also known as Speirr of the Morrigantes, Talon's father was a Druid high priest. His mother was a Celtic queen who abandoned her tribe in order to be with the man she loved.

When Speirr and his sister Ceara were orphaned at a very young age, Speirr returned to the clan and was forced to survive the punishment that his mother ran away from so that his sister might be given the food and protection he—but a child himself—could not provide for her. Speirr grew up and married his true love, Nynia, who later died in childbirth.

Speirr/Talon became a Dark-Hunter through a very sticky set of circumstances. In A.D. 558, when his beloved uncle, Idiag, died, Speirr swore vengeance on the northern clan who had murdered him, a Gaulish clan under the protection of the god Camulus. Speirr then went and killed Camulus's son, bringing the wrath of the war god down upon himself.

Unbeknownst to everyone involved, it was Camulus's other, illegitimate son who had murdered Idiag and framed Speirr, thus prompting his retaliation—but the damage had been done.

To appease the god, Speirr offered himself up as a sacrifice. This offer the clan accepted . . . but not until they had first sacrificed Ceara in front of her brother. She was only sixteen years old.

As a Dark-Hunter, Talon walked between this realm and the next with the help of Spirit Guides. He lost power whenever he felt negative emotions. After his marriage to Sunshine Running-wolf, he was made immortal by his patron goddess, the Morrígan.

Despite being officially off the hook and out of Artemis's employment, Talon keeps up with his Dark-Hunter duties. He still bears the body tattoos designed as a tribute to the Morrígan. He is also the only Dark-Hunter to bear the permanent soul medallion scar on his own palm. He used his powers to absorb the deformity from his wife so that she might continue to pursue her living as an artist.

Talon rides a Harley-Davidson motorcycle. He owns at least four more, a Viper, and four alligators. Okay, well, maybe he doesn't exactly *own* the alligators. But if you ever do stop by his house, be sure to say "Hi" to Beth for me.

BORN: A.D. 532
BIRTHPLACE: Northern England
HEIGHT: six foot five
HAIR/EYES: blond/amber
POWERS: telekinesis, astral projection, atmokinesis, biokinesis, limited mediumship, power absorption
PREFERRED WEAPON: srad
AGE AT DEATH: twenty-seven
CURRENT LOCATION: New Orleans, Louisiana
FEATURED NOVEL: *Night Embrace*

Russenko, Viktor   (deceased) A Dark-Hunter who was killed in Little Rock, Arkansas.

BORN: A.D. 1792
BIRTHPLACE: St. Petersburg, Russia
HEIGHT: six foot four
HAIR/EYES: black
POWERS: telepathy

Safrax   An ancient Greek Dark-Hunter.

BORN: 5108 B.C.
BIRTHPLACE: Greece
HAIR: blond
POWERS: He doesn't let others know them.
CURRENT LOCATION: Los Angeles, California

Samia   The last of her Amazon tribe, Samia is as lethal as she is beautiful. She is fond of her Dark-Hunter brethren, but not exactly men in general.

BORN: 52 B.C.
BIRTHPLACE: Southern Greece
HEIGHT: six feet
HAIR/EYES: brown
POWERS: telekinesis
CURRENT LOCATION: Detroit, Michigan

Santiago, Rafael   A pirate ex-Dark-Hunter with a shaved head and scrollwork tattoos, Rafael was born the son of a Brazilian "merchant" and a freed Ethiopian slave. He grew up on board his father's ship and learned piracy at the knee of some of the most famous pirates in history. He was the youngest member of the Brethren of the Coast.

Rafael followed in his father's footsteps until the day his father was murdered. He vowed vengeance and went after the pirates who were responsible. One by one, he made them pay. Or at least he thought.

Once his vendetta was settled, Rafael decided he would retire with the love of his life so that they could enjoy his riches and raise the children he wanted to have. It was on their wedding night that one of the pirates he'd thought was dead returned to exact his own revenge. Rafael's newly wedded wife died in his arms, their vows unconsummated.

Stationed in Columbus, Mississippi, Rafael refused to believe Kyros's Rogue stories about Acheron, thus saving himself from Alexion's judgment. Rafael owns a boat, a possession he values more than the life of his Squire (Jeff Brinks). Rafael's soul—and humanity—was restored to him by Celena, former Squire of Ephani.

Oh—and Rafael resents being compared to Taye Diggs, no matter how much they may look alike.

BORN: A.D. 1636
BIRTHPLACE: Tortuga, Haiti
HEIGHT: six foot six
HAIR/EYES: bald/black
POWERS: telekinesis
CURRENT LOCATION: Columbus, Mississippi
FEATURED STORY: "A Hard Day's Night Searcher"

Sara   (deceased) A Dark-Huntress who was killed when cornered by Daimons after sunup. Sara was formerly Squired by Celena.

BORN: A.D. 1614
BIRTHPLACE: England
HEIGHT: six foot one
HAIR: blonde
POWERS: atmokinesis

Sebastian (aka Viper)   One of the original Thirteen of Glory who accompanied Pizarro to the Inca city of Tumbrez more than five hundred years ago, this Spaniard Dark-Hunter is now assigned to Memphis, Tennessee. His mother was a Moor. So that he is not confused with his car, Viper drives an Aston Martin Vanquish, of which I am very jealous.

BORN: ?
BIRTHPLACE: Toledo, Spain
HEIGHT: six foot four

HAIR/EYES: black
POWERS: telekinesis
CURRENT LOCATION: Memphis, Tennessee

Sin   Once a powerful Sumerian god of the Moon, Fertility, and the Calendar Year, Sin's godhood was stolen by Artemis. It was his twin brother, Zakar (Sin was actually born one of triplets, but his father killed the eldest over a prophecy), who found him barely alive, wrapped in a diktyon in the desert. Zakar saved his brother's life; a favor that Sin later returned in spades.

Sin's major grudge is not so much against Daimons as it is the gallu demons. He possesses a cane weapon, last of the thin blades created by his pantheon, that will kill the gallu. He, Zakar, and his daughter, Ishtar, were the ones who originally trapped the Dimme and banished them from this world.

Sin is blood-bonded to his beloved Katra, thanks to Acheron's intervention. Katra later bestowed upon Sin her own Greek-Atlantean powers in order to save him from death by a Sumerian dagger. He returned them with a kiss. (Sigh.)

He can most often be found in the penthouse above his casino in Las Vegas, accompanied by his non-Squire, Kish, his Daimon casino manager, Damien, and Katra, of course.

BORN: the dawn of time
BIRTHPLACE: Ur
HEIGHT: six foot seven
HAIR/EYES: jet-black/topaz
POWERS: godlike
CURRENT LOCATION: Kyshtym, Las Vegas, Nevada
FEATURED NOVEL: *Devil May Cry*

Smith, Janice   An African-American Dark-Hunter with a Caribbean accent, Janice was transferred to New Orleans from the Florida Keys during the return of Desiderius.

BORN: A.D. 1760

BIRTHPLACE: Trinidad
HAIR/EYES: black
POWERS: necromancy
CURRENT LOCATION: New Orleans, Louisiana

Spawn   An Apollite Dark-Hunter, Spawn lives in Alaska. He can read thoughts, even through the phone.

BORN: A.D. 702
BIRTHPLACE: Ukraine
HEIGHT: six foot seven
HAIR: blond
POWERS: telepathy
CURRENT LOCATION: Alaska

Squid   A known pirate Dark-Hunter.

BORN: A.D. 1594
BIRTHPLACE: Portugal
HEIGHT: six foot three
HAIR/EYES: black
POWERS: He won't say.
CURRENT LOCATION: varies

St. James, Xander   The illegitimate son of a Gypsy fortune-teller and an English lord, Xander carries a partial soul. He was a sorcerer in his past life, and his powers are still rooted in darkness. He is also very, very protective of his Squire, Brynna. Nobody's quite sure how he became a Dark-Hunter ... but I can tell you that of all of us, he does know who—or what—Ash really is.

BORN: A.D. 1781
BIRTHPLACE: London, England
HEIGHT: six foot five
HAIR/EYES: black
POWERS: He never reveals them to anyone but his victims
CURRENT LOCATION: Richmond, Virginia

Streigar   (deceased) A Dark-Hunter who was trapped by vampire-hunting humans, Streigar died from exposure to daylight.

BORN: A.D. 898
BIRTHPLACE: Denmark
HEIGHT: seven feet
HAIR: blond
POWERS: ferrokinesis
CURRENT LOCATION: deceased

St. Richard, Dangereuse   Nickname: Danger. (She was named for the grandmother of Eleanor of Aquitaine.) Born the daughter of a French actress and a French nobleman, Danger grew up on the stage. She loved her family and her life, right up until the French Revolution tore her world apart. Caught between the two warring factions, Danger refused to see the noble half of her family killed.

Using her connections in the theater, she tried to smuggle her father and noble half-siblings into Germany. Her husband, Michel, was the one who betrayed her into the hands of the Committee. Danger was killed, shot by her husband, while trying to protect her small brother and sister from the guillotine. She was stationed in Tupelo, Mississippi, when Alexion was sent back to stop Kyros and the other renegade Dark-Hunters from banding against Acheron.

Danger was killed and became a Shade … which would be an awful fate if it (and the benevolent Acheron) hadn't afforded her the ability to live alongside her true love Alexion in Katoteros.

BORN: A.D. 1752
BIRTHPLACE: Paris, France
HEIGHT: five foot two
HAIR/EYES: chestnut/brown
POWERS: telepathy

CURRENT LOCATION: Katoteros
FEATURED NOVEL: *Sins of the Night*

Syra of Antikabe (aka Yukon Jane)   An Amazon warrior Dark-Hunter from the fourth century B.C., Syra was originally stationed in the Yukon as a punishment, after maiming a king who had annoyed her.

BORN: ?
BIRTHPLACE: Greece
HEIGHT: six feet
HAIR/EYES: black
POWERS: telekinesis
CURRENT LOCATION: Yukon

Thorssen, Bjorn   (deceased) A Viking warrior Dark-Hunter, Bjorn was killed by Thanatos in Alaska.

BORN: January 5, 801
BIRTHPLACE: Denmark
HEIGHT: six foot eight
HAIR/EYES: black
POWERS: telepathy

Trieg   A Dark-Hunter stationed in Greece. The Dream-Hunter Arikos was summoned by Acheron to help Trieg deal with the death of his family. Arikos remained Trieg's Dream-Hunter until he turned Skotos.

BORN: ?
BIRTHPLACE: Scotland
HEIGHT: six foot six
HAIR/EYES: black
POWERS: telekinesis
CURRENT LOCATION: Greece

Troy   (deceased) A Dark-Hunter who was burned to death in a holding cell.

BORN: A.D. 1801
BIRTHPLACE: Indianapolis, Indiana
HEIGHT: six foot three
HAIR/EYES: black
POWERS: atmokinesis

Tryggvason, Wulf   Wulf is the only Dark-Hunter who was never granted an Act of Vengeance. He was a Viking warrior born to a Christian mother and Norse father—to honor them he wears a necklace bearing both a crucifix and Thor's hammer. His mother was captured and given to his father as a prize after a raid. She bore him two more children after Wulf—Erik and Brynhild—and then disowned Wulf and Erik when she discovered they had become raiders like their father.

Wulf was tricked by the Dark-Huntress Morginne into giving up his soul and trading it with the Norse god Loki. Since he was wrongfully brought over by another Dark-Hunter, his powers are very different from the rest of his brethren. The most curious power of all is that of amnesia, the result of a curse laid on him by Morginne. No human or animal is capable of remembering him five minutes after they leave his presence. Acheron used a drop of Wulf's nephew's blood to soften the blow of this curse, so that Wulf's blood relatives would be able to remember him.

He is married to ex-Apollite (and direct descendent of Apollo) Cassandra Peters. They have a son, Erik.

BORN: A.D. 750
BIRTHPLACE: Hammerfest, Norway
HEIGHT: six foot six
HAIR/EYES: black
CURRENT LOCATION: Twin Cities, Minnesota
FEATURED NOVEL: *Kiss of the Night*

Ulric   (deceased) A Dark-Hunter from Biloxi. The spirit of Desiderius took over Ulric's body and went on a killing spree. His victims included: Tia Devereaux; Cherise Gautier; Kyrian and

Amanda Hunter; and the Dark-Hunter Kassim. Ulric/Desiderius was finally defeated (stabbed and beheaded) by Valerius Magnus and Tabitha Devereaux.

BORN: A.D. 1498
BIRTHPLACE: Brussels, Belgium
HEIGHT: six foot four
HAIR: blond
POWERS: sonokinesis

Zarek of Moesia   Zarek of Moesia is not kind. To be fair, he comes by it honestly—after several lifetimes full of getting the short end of the stick.

Zarek was born the unwanted son of a Greek slave and the Roman Senator Gaius Magnus. Instead of being killed as his mother had instructed, he was brought to his father. The unforgiving Gaius reintroduced Zarek to slavery, and made him a whipping boy for his half-brothers. As a slave, Zarek last worked for Carlia, a beautiful Roman woman who wanted Zarek to warn her and her lover when her husband was coming. She later told her husband that Zarek raped her.

To add insult to injury, Zarek was so filthy that when he appealed to Artemis for his vengeance she did not touch him to transform him into a Dark-Hunter—she only poked him with a stick and injected him with ichor to give him immortality and physical Dark-Hunter traits. So in all those nine hundred years full of twenty-four-hour days of summer, Zarek never was susceptible to death by sunlight.

Yeah, I'd be bitter, too.

In the Dark Ages, Zarek lived in a village (Taberleigh) that was attacked by the first incarnation of Thanatos. When Zarek hunted Thanatos back to the Apollite village where he sought asylum, Thanatos threw an Apollite in front of him as a human shield (Dirce), and Zarek accidentally killed her.

Thanatos could not be killed by Zarek, only Acheron could

manage that. But when Ash used his god-powers in front of Zarek to kill Thanatos, he messed with Zarek's mind to make him forget what had happened. Because of that, the massacre of the Apollite village was blamed on Zarek, and Artemis banished him to Alaska for nine hundred years. He was even banned from both the online Dark-Hunter bulletin boards and the chatrooms on the Dark-Hunter Web site.

Rumors began to pop up about Zarek. He was a known Feeder who preyed on human blood, so he did not deny the accusations that he was psychotic, or that he had cut up and eaten the last Squire Ash sent him. His hostility even scared the Dream-Hunters, who would not come to heal him while he slept.

Zarek was sent to New Orleans for Mardi Gras, where he sided with the mischievous god Dionysus and then betrayed him by not letting Dion kill Sunshine Runningwolf. Months later, Zarek fell in love with Astrid, the justice nymph who was sent by Themis to pass judgment on him. Astrid determined Zarek's innocence (despite his arrogance), and they were married. After their wedding, Astrid fed Zarek ambrosia so that he could return with her to Mount Olympus. He abused his power for a while, choosing to constantly hurl lightning bolts at the Dark-Hunter Valerius.

Valerius was given nectar of the gods (and therefore immortality) by Zarek and Astrid as a wedding gift. Astrid's bonus wedding gift was ambrosia—to bestow upon Val his own god-powers, so he could give Zarek as good as he got.

BORN: 155 B.C.
BIRTHPLACE: Viminacium, Moesia
HEIGHT: six foot six
HAIR/EYES: black
POWERS: godlike
PREFERRED WEAPONS: silver finger-claws
FEATURED NOVEL: *Dance with the Devil*

Zoe   A Dark-Huntress from New York City who now lives in Seattle, Zoe was the daughter of an Amazon queen. She was originally killed by Valerius's brother Marius Magnus before coming back as a Dark-Hunter. In the tradition of many Amazons, Zoe *reeeeally* can't stand men . . . to the point of preferring women as her intimate companions.

BORN: 150 B.C.
BIRTHPLACE: ?
HEIGHT: six foot five
HAIR: auburn
PREFERRED WEAPONS: whip, bow
CURRENT LOCATION: Seattle, Washington

Were-Hunters

Their Bark Has Nothing on Their Bite

The Were-Hunters may be fuzzy,
but they're seldom warm.
—Kyl

The Allagi

The mythic birth of the Were-Hunters is called the *Allagi*. But instead of forcing you through some dusty archaic translation, I'm just gonna sum it up for you. (You're welcome.)

You already know that Apollo cursed the Apollites and everything went to hell with that. (There's more in chapter 6, "How to Roast a Daimon", if you need to jump ahead for details, but I'm guessing you've got the basics.)

Many years later, the sorcerer king Lycaon of Arcadia unknowingly fell in love with and married an Apollite woman. He knew she had a few strange habits—what nobleborn lady didn't need to preserve her beauty by staying out of the sun?—but he loved her so much that he was willing to overlook them. She bore him two sons and then—you guessed it—she went and died at the unnaturally youthful age of twenty-seven. Lycaon, distraught and all too powerful for his own good, declared that Apollo's curse would not plague his bloodline. He would see to it that his sons would outlive him.

Genius, scientific intelligence, and good intentions. We have the atomic bomb for the same reason we have the Were-Hunters.

And so, Lycaon began his terrible experiments on the Apollite people. He gathered up as many of them as he could and used his magic to . . . change them, to alter their makeup on a level so basic that it might fool the curse of a god. He tortured them and killed them so that he might find a way for them to go on living, so that his sons might go on living. He experimented on them as if they were animals.

And then he experimented on them *with* animals.

Using arcane magicks, he took a page out of Apollo's book. The Apollites were cursed with the traits of beasts, so that's where Lycaon decided to start. He spliced the essence of the Apollites with predators renowned for their strength and superior survival skills. Bears, for their teeth and deadly claws. Panthers, for their agility and hunting skills. Leopards, for their almost supernatural ability to go undetected. Lions, for their speed and ability to work together. Tigers, for their size and lack of natural predators. Jackals, for their long legs and cunning ways. Wolves, for their heartiness and stamina. Hawks, for their swift and deadly beaks and their keen eyesight. The mad king even captured the legendary dragon, with all its might, magic, and majesty.

Lycaon hoped that if he could combine an Apollite's life force with those of these animals it would make them powerful enough to somehow break the curse.

For better or worse, Lycaon's experiments worked. Instead of living only twenty-seven years, these new Apollites now had life expectancies of close to a thousand. As he expected, they were strong, quick, powerful, and deadly. Their life spans were suddenly elongated to twelve times that of any human. And because they were born of magic and descended from the psychic pure-blood Apollites, they ended up with a lot of innate bonus powers such as telepathy, telekinesis, and shapeshifting.

After choosing from among their new monstrous cousins, the king blended his sons with a dragon and a wolf—he decided that those were the most powerful of the animals he had experimented upon. He had thwarted Apollo's curse; he had defied the will of a god with his own human hand.

The Fates were not happy when they found out.

Clotho, Lachesis, and Atropos all came to Lycaon and demanded that he kill his sons, unnatural abominations that they were. It was not for man to change a fate handed down by the gods, and this should be Lycaon's punishment.

Yeah. That went over like a lead balloon.

When he would not comply, Clotho cursed this new race—"They will spend eternity hating and fighting until the day when the last of them breathes no more"—and then sent Eris to plant mistrust among them.

Chalk one up for the Fates.

The second you have to chalk up to science. Due to the dual nature of Lycaon's research, he was responsible for not one but two sets of laws: those of both heaven and earth. He was not going to get away with breaking either of them.

The first Law of Thermodynamics states that energy is neither created nor destroyed. Whatever you put in, you will get out. Because each member of this new Were race consisted of essentially half an Apollite and half an animal, whenever Lycaon blended the two beings together he created two new, separate beings: one with an animal's heart and one with a human's.

Plato's theory about humans being two halves of the same person was based on the Were race.

The animal-hearted Weres were called *Katagaria*—a term meaning "miscreant" or "rogue". Born in the body of their predator skin, they could only become human at puberty, when their magical powers were genetically "unlocked". Conversely, the *Arcadians*—named after Lycaon's own people—were born as humans, a fact that was used as the argument for Arcadians being a cut above their animal cousins. The Arcadians thought—and still do—the Katagaria needed close supervision and monitoring. They believed the Katagaria should be controlled, and contained.

Likewise, the Katagaria were mistrustful of their human counterparts. Humans are so often deceptive. They constantly deal in lies and subterfuge. If a wolf dislikes you, he attacks you openly, without question or hesitation. If a human dislikes you, he can smile to your face, and then stab you in the back. As Clotho predicted, it wasn't long before war broke out between these two groups. That war continues on to this day. There are villains and heroes on both sides.

The direct descendents of the sons of King Lycaon took the surname Kattalakis. The name belongs to the Lykos and Drakos branches on both the Arcadian and Katagaria sides.

Through experience some of us have learned certain characteristics specific to each patria. For instance, that Were-panthers and -tigers cannot stand to be blinded, and that—like with most animals—chocolate is lethal to some Weres. Were-Hunters also mimic their animal brethren by preferring to move quickly to avoid or capture their enemies. Because of this, many Were-Hunters prefer racing bikes to standard automobiles. (Hah! Like an Aston Martin is *standard*. Most Dark-Hunters have garages packed with Bond cars. Don't worry, you will too, in time.)

Slayers and Sentinels

Everyone has scars from their life.
—Wren Tigarian

The Arcadians and Katagaria each have designated soldiers who fight and protectors who watch over the women and children of the group. Their societies and existence are extremely complex, though they will most often segregate themselves to be with their own kind. For example, an Ursulan (bear) Katagari will live in a clan (patria) of other Ursulan Katagaria, while an Ursulan Arcadian will live with other Ursulan Arcadians. You won't generally see a bunch of random Were-Hunters bedding down comfortably in a mismatched pack.

I suppose one could consider it a bit racist . . . but while the human side of a Were has no problem mating with another human Were, their animal sides still have big mental hurdles to jump when it comes to intimate relations with a different species. The psychology is just a lot easier when a Were runs with his own pack. Especially the Katagaria.

Katagaria follow the basic law of nature: Kill or be killed. The Katagaria have their own form of soldiers, the *Strati,* who seek out Rogue Arcadians. (You've no doubt figured it out by now—if it's Rogue, it's got a death warrant.) Much like their predatory ancestors, Strati will not engage an enemy unprovoked. They will only kill to defend themselves, their pack, or their territory.

Speaking of animal instinct, it is a common Katagaria tradition to mount (as in, on the wall) your first kill. Say it with me: "Ewwww". I bet most Katagaria wives hope their husband's first kill is a Daimon. It's kind of hard to mount a pile of dust.

It is also polite to refer to Katagaria by their animal selves. For example, you may address Vane Kattalakis as "Wolf". It's a bit like the equivalent of a "Doctor" or "General" honorific. The term *Were,* however, is a major insult to the Katagaria since the term is taken from Old English and means "man"—they pride themselves on being animals. They don't mind the term *Were-Hunter* because it implies they are hunting men, which they are. It is normally fine to use the term *Were* when discussing them casually, like here, but it's definitely not something you want to call them to their face. Katagaria do not like to be reminded of, or referred to by, their human half, and Arcadians in the main prefer to never think of themselves as anything but.

In times of desperation, a Were-Hunter's body will resort to the form of its truest nature. It is almost impossible for Katagaria to maintain human form when injured, and the reverse is true for Arcadians. Consider this if you've got an injured Katagari on hand—you're going to need a vet and an explanation for why you're suddenly in a crowded place with an exotic animal. If an Arcadian is hurt while in his human form you've not got much to worry about. If the Arcadian was in animal form when injured, be prepared to give them your shirt and/or coat, especially in inclement weather, and do your best to keep them from getting ticketed for public indecency.

It is also difficult for either species to maintain constant form when zapped by an electrical impulse . . . but more on that in a bit.

There are those Katagaria who are not able to rein in the natural, hedonistic impulses of their animal souls, and they eventually succumb to the madness of their blood. These Katagaria are true, unredeemable animals, and are called *Slayers*.

Below are the Most Wanted Katagaria who have dubbed themselves the Sons of Vengeance. Remember, each one is lethal, fast, and deadly. They possess an animalistic charisma that enchants human women to the point that such women will often protect them at any cost and are willing to die for the Katagaria. They have no known weakness and are loyal only unto themselves. Most are loners who will attack with little to no provocation. Their animal forms rule them and they are as dangerous in human form as they are in animal state.

Do not try to apprehend. They are to be destroyed on sight. Their bounties carry a triple bonus for anyone who can provide a hide as proof of the kill.

Watch for them—they could be in your neighborhood any day.

Some Arcadians refer to all Strati as Slayers, but that's somewhat of a sweeping generalization laced with a heap of latent hostility.

Arcadian soldiers are called *Sentinels* and they usually patrol

MOST WANTED KATAGARIA
aka
The Sons of Vengeance

Paris Sebastienne
Patria: Litarian (lion)
Last Seen/Fought: Oklahoma City, Oklahoma, 1989

Ilarion Konstantinus
Patria: Drakos (dragon)
Last Seen/Fought: Toronto, 2002

Icarus Kallikedes
Patria: Gerakian (falcon/hawk)
Last Seen/Fought: Paris, 1860

Jasyn Kallinos
Patria: Gerakian (falcon/hawk)
Last Seen/Fought: Richmond, Virginia, 2000

Lysander Stephanos
Patria: Tigarian (tiger)
Last Seen/Fought: The wilds of the Orient, 1817

Fang Kattalakis
Patria: Lykos (wolf)
Last Seen/Fought: New Orleans, Louisiana, 2002

Vane Kattalakis
Patria: Lykos (wolf)
Last Seen/Fought: New Orleans, Louisiana, 2002

Trey Xanatos aka Ax, Trion
Patria: Tigarian (tiger)
Last Seen/Fought: Scotland, 1742

in groups of four. A Sentinel's main duty is to track and kill Slayers. (You can see now where the Strati-Slayer confusion, conscious or not, would cause a bit of trouble.)

Only a select few Sentinels are born to each patria, and they are chosen by the Fates. They are stronger and faster than the rest of their species. They are immune to everything but the common cold and a couple of odd diseases, like the one that takes away their ability to do magic.

Arcadian Sentinels can be recognized by the geometric designs covering one side of their face—a birthmark that appears at maturity. Most use their powers to hide these markings.

The Strati do not share the facial markings that brand Sentinels. However, it should be noted that the legendary Kathoros Daimons—a sect more evil than their Spathi brethren—have similar facial markings. Encountering a Kathoros is exceptionally rare . . . but that doesn't make it impossible.

Were-Hunters can kill Daimons but usually don't, as they are cousins to the Apollites, and therefore cousins to their foul brethren as well. Were-Hunters also tolerate the existence of Dark-Hunters, but not generally well. Most powerful beings don't like to share that power, and when it comes to the Weres, it's all about being the one in control—the leader of the pack.

Mating

If you ever threaten Vane or his brothers again,
I'm going to show you just how human I am.
I will don my camouflage, hunt you down,
and skin you while you scream.
—Bride McTierney

Mating is a serious affair in the Were-world. Mating is not just sex; it is the discovery of a soul mate. That soul mate is one chosen by the Fates. As many of the animals that Lycaon crossed the Apollites with were ones who mated for life, the prospect of finding a soul mate for most Weres is as natural as breathing.

I did say *natural*, not *easy*. For some species, mating involves a hunt or a chase. For some, the female must have reached maturity and be ready to receive the male. For some, it is just the divining of the proper pheromones. Then all of this animal instinct has to be weighed against the two Weres as humans, with all the pain and emotional baggage that goes along with that.

Like I said, not easy. But even the most basic animal heart cannot argue with Fate. They all succumb eventually. And if they resist . . . well, you'll see.

Once the soul mates have discovered each other, beautiful Greek scroll-markings burn themselves into the palms of the male and female after they have sex. The markings mirror each other exactly, showing parental lineage, and the ancient cipher can only be read by another Were. It looks a bit like a delicately detailed henna tattoo. Unfortunately, it isn't quite as harmless.

While they bear the mark the couple must be careful, as each will carry the scent of his or her mate. This complication has put a Were in mortal danger more than once. Once an enemy has pegged a Were, that Were will be tracked by his scent. A Were's scent is the one thing he cannot change or hide with magic.

Once the mating marks appear, the happily doomed couple has three weeks in which to consummate the mating—an act over which the female has total control. She is the one who must decide whether to take her partner into her body and accept him as a mate.

This is a tribute to the first law of Weres: "Nothing a woman gives is worth having unless she gives it of her own free will". (I have a feeling this has a great deal to do with the Fates being women . . . but for gods' sakes don't quote me on that.)

If for any reason she does not, and the couple does not

consummate their relationship within the allotted weeks, the Fates have declared that they must live out the rest of their very long lives without another mate.

And there's more.

Such solitary damnation has less of a biological impact on the female of the species. She is still able to copulate with whomever she pleases—she just won't ever be able to have any children.

Those are only the Fates' laws, however. The clan laws are not so benevolent. They are strict about who and what they will allow into their patria, Fates be damned. In certain Arcadian groups, punishment for a female mating with a despised Katagaria male is that she be "given" to the unmated men of the clan.

Few women survive such a punishment.

What the male of the species must face if he decides to reject his chosen soul mate is just as cruel. He is rendered not only sterile, but also unable to perform the sexual act with any other woman, ever again, so long as his rejected mate lives.

To make it worse, it's not something the couple can just change their minds about later. The couple must make the decision within the allotted time, and they must make the right one. It's *forever*. Their future depends on it.

You don't really ever want to cross the path of a Were that has turned against his soul mate. Talk about bitter; you haven't seen a person with serious issues until you've met one of these folks. (See Markus Kattalakis.)

Now, once mated, there are two classifications of how strong the bond between each couple could possibly be: *claimed mates* and *bonded mates*.

Each couple is given the chance to decide whether or not to claim each other. Like almost every other decision in a Were's life, the decision to bond or not to bond is once again eternal and irreversible.

In order to bond, during the consummation of their love the

couple must clasp their mating-marked hands together. Then, each must recite the words of the Bonding Spell:

> I accept you as you are, and I will always hold you close in my heart. I will walk beside you forever.

Directly after the Bonding Spell, the Weres succumb to the *thirio*—their passionate animal instinct. They give in to their wild side, and their canine teeth elongate.

At this time, the couple can officially bond with each other by mutually sinking their teeth into each other, drinking their partner's blood, and combining their life forces. It may sound scary and more than a bit stomach-turning, but in the world of the Were-Hunters, the bonding is a sacrament. It is beautiful and natural, and it is a testament to true love.

Just as it is the female's choice to claim her mate, bonding is also totally within the female partner's control. However, resisting the thirio is apparently much easier than resisting a soul mate.

The act of choosing to not claim her mate is more common practice among the indecisive female Arcadian Weres. Very few Katagaria females refuse their mates. To them, claiming your mate is simply accepted as the way things should be.

Once formally bonded, if one of the Were couple should die, the other will die as well. The only exception to this is if the female Were is with child. If a Were is pregnant when her mate dies (or is killed), she will outlive her partner only long enough to give birth to her litter. (See Anya.) If the couple is not bonded, then when one mate dies, the other is free to mate again.

So you can see why the Arcadians tend to be a bit hesitant about committing. Forever in Were-Hunter years is a pretty long time.

Also, while Arcadians and humans can mate due to their similar human base-form, it is not possible for Katagaria and humans to do so. Okay, okay, I know we're never supposed to say never. It *is* possible, but there would never be any children from such a union.

However, all human males (and Dark-Hunters, where applicable) should heed this warning: Keep an eye on your woman. It is said that the Weres can seduce any woman alive just by saying her name.

Believe it or not, but know this: Vane Kattalakis said my name once. Sometimes, in the moments before I fall asleep, or just before I awake, I hear him repeat it in that low, predatory voice, calling to my soul.

Don't get me wrong; I don't envy his mate Bride in the least. That much power is simply too frightening for most of us folks to handle.

Just like Dark-Hunters, each Were and his powers are unique, but there are some traits common to each patria. These traits are discovered through eyewitness account . . . and generally whenever the Were-Hunters slip and flat-out tell us. For example, thanks to Dante Pontis, we can now include certain specific information about Were-panthers.

Forget what you know about humans and their social habits; women rule the roost in the world of the Panthiras Katagaria. Typical female Were-panther behavior is to mate, get pregnant, and then leave the cubs for the men to raise. Daughters remain in the pack until puberty. After that time they form a pack with other females from their own group and leave to search for mates. (Contact with any male outside her clan is forbidden until the female's first menstrual cycle.)

This is one of the more defining differences between Katagaria and Arcadians; Arcadian pantheresses do not abandon their children until adulthood, as befits their human nature. (At which point, of course, it's hard to say who exactly is abandoning whom.)

We know that pregnant Katagaria are Daimon magnets due to

their soul strength and power. An unborn child is a Daimon delicacy as it is, with its unlimited soul-sustaining power. Were-mothers have *litters* of children—anywhere from two to six and possibly more—and though the birthrate is higher than that of their animal cousins, there is still an unfortunate chance for infant mortality.

Were-mothers are also inherently extremely powerful beings, oftentimes more so than their male counterparts. This may have to do with the inherent power of the mother, the combined untapped powers of her unborn children, or both. Put that all together and you have a Daimon smorgasbord fit for a king ... or a queen and her army.

Magic and Time Travel

Nothing is ever truly set by fate.
In one blink, everything changes.
—Acheron

While mating is heavily influenced by the animal instinct of the Weres, there are some characteristics that can only be attributed to their human and Apollite natures. One of the traits the Were-Hunters inherited from their sorcerous forefather was ... well ... sorcery. And, like any other hereditary attribute, some Weres are simply better at it than others.

Most Katagaria have trouble maintaining their human form until nightfall. In turn, it is easier for Arcadians to turn animal at night. Part of this is due to the mostly nocturnal nature of the beasts they descended from, and part of it has to do with the cosmic forces of the moon—the leftover curse from their Apollite ancestry. On any given day, it is easiest for a Katagari or Arcadian to remain in their birth form, but the moon—and the forces that surround it—can amplify a Were's powers, for better or worse.

Sometimes during the full moon (a force powerful enough to wreak havoc on any untrained Were's powers), an Arcadian can't help but turn animal . . . thus giving birth to the popular were-wolf legends of today.

Then there are Aristi, a rare breed of Arcadian who can wield magic almost effortlessly. In the Arcadian realm, the Aristi are considered gods. (See Vane Kattalakis.) And why not, right? If they've got the powers, other Weres just call 'em like they see 'em. Not that I think any Aristos would last three rounds in a cage match with one of the twelve Olympians . . . and neither do the Aristi, who are too smart to provoke such a duel.

At the other end of the spectrum, those without innate magical abilities can still perform basic Were acts, but they cannot do things as complicated as, for instance, shapeshifting with their clothes on.

There are more forces at work between the moon and the earth besides the tides, and it is these and other natural forces which govern both the scope and limitations of Were-powers—natural forces, such as storms, and the electricity born within them. (It is said that Benjamin Franklin's "key on a kite string" experiment originally had something to do with the discovery of Were-Hunters in his midst . . . but that has yet to be proven, thank the gods.)

Because of their reliance on natural gravitational, magnetic, and electrical forces, you may notice that a faint electric crackle heralds a Were's change in form. It is a natural side effect, as they are relying on natural electrical impulses to make this change. That reliance on these forces of nature is what makes Weres so susceptible to electricity-based weapons and torture devices such as metriazo collars, fazers, Tasers, and cattle prods.

In the case of a metriazo collar, tiny ionic pulses are sent from the collar into the body of a Were-Hunter. This prevents the trapped Were-Hunter from using his or her magic powers. (It can only be removed by magic or a whole lot of strength, making it an effective neutralizer for a Were-Hunter.) The collar will also stop a shapeshifter from changing shape.

A fazer is a customized Arcadian Sentinel weapon developed specifically to target Katagaria Slayers. It sends a jolt of electricity through the victim, making their magic go berserk and rendering them unable to hold on to either animal or human form. If the jolt is strong enough, there is the possibility that the Were-victim might "fall out" of his body altogether.

Tasers and other stun-type weapons are slightly less powerful than fazers. These are weapons that use electrodes to relay a brief, high-voltage charge to incapacitate victims without killing them. That charge, of course, is what will incapacitate your not-so-average Were-Hunter. These devices are a lot easier for humans to get their hands on, especially with regards to self-defense, and so are more common.

Along with the ability to harness the powers of nature, the Weres can also time travel. With the exception of the Aristi, most Weres only wield enough power to time-jump by the light of the full moon. They use the *Rytis*—invisible energy waves that run through everything in the natural world—to move through space and time.

Certain social rules exist regarding time-jumping—for instance, no Were-Hunter is allowed to remove a human from their time period without the human's permission. (Demons and gods are exempt from this rule. Come to think of it, demons and gods are exempt from *most* rules.) It is also worth noting that magnetic and electrical changes of the aurora borealis make it impossible for Were-Hunters to travel too far north, so Alaska and some parts of Scandinavia and the Ukraine are basically Were-Hunter-free zones.

The Weres share the psychic abilities of their Apollite cousins in varying degrees, but only the Katagaria can willingly give up their powers to another Were or bestow them upon a human. It's not a much-talked-of practice and it is rarely ever done, since most Katagaria Were-Hunters are understandably reluctant to completely surrender their magic to another unless it is a case of extreme circumstances.

Never, ever let a Daimon kill a Were-Hunter if it is at all within your power to stop it. When a Daimon claims a Were-Hunter soul, the Daimon absorbs their powers until that very strong, very virile soul dwindles inside them. You do not want any Daimon to have that sort of leverage. He'll take that upper hand, and he'll smash you flat with it . . . right before he kills you.

Patria

You want to fuck with Artemis, fuck with Artemis.
You want to fuck with me . . . make out your will.
—Savitar

Like each animal is broken down into a distinct scientific genus and species, so the Were-Hunters are broken into *patria*, familial descriptions of each race that Lycaon mixed with Apollite blood. These are:

Balios *(jaguars)*	Niphetos Pardalia *(snow leopards)*
Drakos *(dragons)*	Panthiras *(panthers)*
Gerakian *(hawks, falcons, and eagles)*	Pardalia *(leopards)*
Helikias *(cheetahs)*	Tigarian *(tigers)*
Litarian *(lions)*	Tsakalis *(jackals)*
Lykos *(wolves)*	Ursulan *(bears)*

As mentioned before, most Weres in their lifetime will only ever be born into, run with, find their mate in, and die amongst the patria of their birth. In the last few hundred years the

widespread presence of known sanctuaries (thanks to the Inter-
-net) has afforded Weres more opportunities to intermingle, but
even that is only normally done on a social basis. Jackals especially have been known to stay far away from other Were branches,
but they will always have a representative member to speak for
them at the Omegrion.

The *Omegrion* is the ruling council of the Were-Hunters. Similar to a senate, one representative from each of the Arcadians
and Katagaria is sent to voice the concerns of that patria to the
Omegrion. That representative is known as the *Regis*. The
Omegrion makes laws that govern all Were-Hunters. It is responsible for setting up sanctuaries and safe houses. The members of
the Omegrion can also call out a blood hunt for anyone who is
determined a threat.

Savitar oversees the Omegrion, though nobody's exactly sure
how he got the job. Based on how most of the Weres work, one
can only assume Savitar—with all his Zen and mighty power—is
the essential alpha male. He plays the role of impartial mediator
between the Arcadians and the Katagaria. The Omegrion meets
on Neratiti—Savitar's island home off the coast of . . . wherever he
decides to put it. Despite having the Omegrion over for the occasional powwow, Savitar himself still remains a mystery to even
the Weres. No one is allowed past the council doors of the
Omegrion meeting room.

The human saying "curiosity killed the cat" apparently came
from an Arcadian panther who once tried to take a look around
Savitar's palace. And no, satisfaction did *not* bring it back.

Another interesting tidbit I learned when I heard the "curiosity"
story is that there are no Arcadian jaguars anywhere in the world.
Savitar destroyed them all when they "pissed him off big-time".

Were-Hunter or not, I suggest you don't piss off Savitar . . .
even little-time.

The same goes for Artemis (are you surprised?), with regards
to the current state of the jackal patrias. In the ancient world,

the Tsakalis' numbers were legion. And then, centuries ago in Egypt, they fought for Bast against Artemis. War was openly declared by the goddess on their species (both Katagaria and Arcadian). They have since been hunted to near extinction. While some of their Arcadian clans have tried to make peace with Artemis, those of the Katagaria refuse.

MEMBERS OF THE OMEGRION

A = Arcadian   *K = Katagaria*

BALIOS
(A) extinct
(K) Myles Stefanopoulos

NIPHETOS PARDALIA
(A) Anelise Romano
(K) Wren Tigarian

DRAKOS
(A) Damos Kattalakis
(K) Darion Kattalakis

PANTHIRAS
(A) Alexander James
(K) Dante Pontis

GERAKIAN
(A) Arion Petrakis
(K) Draven Hawke

PARDALIA
(A) Dorian Kontis
(K) Stefan Kouris

HELIKIAS
(A) Jace Wilder
(K) Michael Giovanni

TIGARIAN
(A) Adrian Gavril
(K) Lysander Stephanos

LITARIAN
(A) Patrice Leonides
(K) Paris Sebastienne

TSAKALIS
(A) Constantine
(K) Vincenzo Moretti

LYKOS
(A) Vane Kattalakis
(K) Fury Kattalakis

URSULAN
(A) Leo Apollonian
(K) Nicolette Peltier

Safe Houses

You just have to learn to hum a lot so you don't hear
their bullshit echoing in your head.
—Damien Gatopoulos

There exist throughout the known world *limani*—sanctuaries where humans and animals can gather without fear of being hunted. Each sanctuary has its own laws, but by rights, all limani must abide by human law first and foremost. More information on these and other safe houses can be found online at www.Dark-Hunter.com.

PELTIER HOUSE
688 Ursulines Avenue
New Orleans, Louisiana 70116
(504) 555-1635
Hours of Operation: 24/7
Motto: Don't bite me, and I won't bite you.

This premier New Orleans biker bar in the heart of Vieux Carré is owned by the Peltiers, a Katagaria bear clan. The owners, Nicolette and Aubert Peltier (known affectionately to all as Mama and Papa Bear), decided to found Sanctuary as a safe zone after two of their cubs (Bastian and Gilbert) were brutally killed by Arcadian Sentinels. Mama and Papa Bear currently run Sanctuary with the help of their twelve children.

Sanctuary is also home to the Howlers, the popular house band for the club. Their specialty is heavy metal with lots of attitude. They play covers as well as original songs, and are always ready to play requests from the ladies. For other entertainment, Sanctuary has pool tables, video machines, and pinball, and

Sanctuary

Our menu changes daily—depends on how Mama's feeling.
Please ask your server for the specials!

All entrées include the salad bar.
(You must eat your vegetables, cher.)

Sanctuary Staples

Papa Peltier's Seafood Boil Cajun-seasoned fresh shrimp, crab, crawfish, sausage, potatoes, and corn-on-the-cob, boiled to perfection. Served with crackers and Papa's Bayou Sauce. $12.95   *(for two)* $21.95

Cherise's Gumbo Bes' you ever et, cher. Chicken, andouille sausage, shrimp, crab, and okra. Served on a bed of Louisiana long-grain rice. *Cup* $5.95   *Bowl* $9.95

Jumpin' Jambalaya Andouille sausage with chicken and/or shrimp, spiced enough to make your mama blush. Served on a bed of Louisiana long-grain rice.
Chicken $11.95   *Shrimp* $12.95
Combo $14.95

Mama's Barbecue Lovingly rubbed and slow-roasted pork, pulled off the bone and presented on a toasted bun with your choice of sauces: Wimpy, A-Cha-Cha, and Simi-style. Sandwich served with fries; platter served with two vegetables of the day.   *Sandwich* $9.95   *Platter* $12.95

Prime Rib 8, 16, or 22 oz. of melt-in-your-mouth USDA Grade A Prime. The only sexier pieces of meat are our staff, but you'll have to get those numbers on your own. Served with two vegetables of the day.   *8 oz.* $12.95   *16 oz.* $18.95
22 oz. $24.95

Those with special dietary needs, please call one hour ahead so we have adequate time to procure and prepare your order.

poker tournaments three nights a week. There's also an ongoing tattoo contest ... be sure not to go up against an Arcadian Sentinel, or you're sure to lose.

When visiting Sanctuary, you will often hear requests for the bartender to "Hold the human hair". As Were metabolism is very high thanks to their animal ancestry, Sanctuary always has on hand a full complement of liquor strong enough to make any human completely drunk with one shot. The experienced staff at Sanctuary has been instructed not to dispense this alcohol to humans. The menu is varied, but specializes in Cajun and carnivorous delights (exotic entrées available upon request). All meats are served fresh from the kill that morning with a loving smile.

Like any other limani, Sanctuary has its rules. Number one: Spill No Blood. Your attitude is welcome, but check any and all weapons at the door. This is the place to come and hang out, be seen, and just drink and eat in peace. If two warring parties are present and both want to leave, the hunted gets a head start, and the hunter is not allowed to follow. As a last resort, there is also a room full of cages in case some animal decides to get nasty. Sanctuary also boasts a resident vet, medical doctor, and Were himself, Carson Whitethunder (accredited).

Another rule of note: Lynyrd Skynyrd's "Sweet Home Alabama" is a song played on the jukebox only to warn Sanctuary's clientele of the presence of Acheron. As much as you might like to hear it, please think twice before making your musical selection.

Adjacent to the bar, Peltier House is the living quarters for Sanctuary's hidden animal population (including the dragon in the attic). This historic mansion was constructed in 1801. It has more alarms than Fort Knox and is always guarded by at least two Peltier family members.

Top Five Requested Songs at Sanctuary

1. "Splendid Suicide" by Warchild
2. "Winterborn" by Crüxshadows
3. "(Don't Fear) the Reaper" by Blue Oyster Cult
4. "Bad Magick" by Godsmack
5. "Get Stoned" by Hinder

DANTE'S INFERNO
Twin Cities, Minnesota

This happening Goth nightclub gets its name from its owner, Katagaria Were-panther Dante Pontis. Be warned, this isn't Sanctuary and Dante will kill anyone who threatens his people. In fact, Dante will kill just about anyone who makes him angry. At last count that was estimated to be about one out of every five people. You could be next.

Technically, because of his hotheadedness, Dante's Inferno is not an officially registered limani with the full amenities granted such. But you can be pretty sure that if you're under Dante's roof—provided you're on his good side and you're not a Daimon—you're just fine.

Of course, while you're there, you should also have fun. Indulge in the mixes of Dante's house DJs—if you're lucky, Romeo Pontis will grace your groove with his charmed Pied Piperesque beat—when on the dance floor, you are required to let yourself go. If you have trouble relaxing, be sure to stop by the bar and have a Blood-tini, or order up a round of Fabio Bombs. You'll be jiving in no time.

If you've got the munchies, don't hesitate to order up some of the Inferno's fabulous appetizers. If you feel the need to enjoy your meal in solitude, take a break down in the soundproof pit, equipped with its own bar and subtle ambiance. If dancing's not

Dante's Inferno

"Abandon all hope, ye who enter here."

SHOT LIST

SWEET	HARD	EVIL
Hair of the Were	Inkspot	Sacred Heart
Witch's Tit	Rising Sun	Woodshed
Igor	Soul Sucker	General's Tears
Oracle	Redhead	Destroyer
Paradiso	Ferryman	Damnation
Convivio	Purple Purgatory	Faust's Fire
Divine Comedy	Vita Nuova	La Guerra
Canto	Gravedigger	Mephistophelean Hot Shot

THE ORPHEUS WALL

Want your name to go down in infamy? Be part of Dante's Orpheus Wall. Nine shots of your choice—one for each circle of Hell. You're thinking: "No sweat," right? Wrong. After all, Orpheus went to Hell *and then came back,* didn't he? Just remember, there is no shame in turning around before you reach the top . . .

SPECIALTY BEVERAGES

THE DESCENT   Our nine-layer house favorite, served in a unique slatted mug for you to mix your own demise.

BLOODY MARIE   In honor of the legendary voodoo priestess—she'll kick your ass.

RESURRECTION SHUFFLE   Jalapeño-infused liquor guaranteed to wake the most stubborn dead.

FABIO BOMB   We'd tell you what's in it, but you won't remember in the morning anyway. . . .

BLOODTINI   Served Shaken, Stirred, Dirty, or Spartan.

SWEET HOME ALABAMA ICED TEA   Long Island's got nothing on the South.

No Daimons Allowed
Please don't forget to tip our sexy and talented waitstaff. If you're too drunk to remember, you are too drunk to drive home . . . or come back.

your thing, you can spend your cash at the superstocked arcade, sporting all the latest and hottest new games.

Of course, if dancing's not your thing and you happen to be young and blond, you'll have to forgive the staff if they're ... more than a little suspicious.

Top Five Requested Songs at Dante's Inferno

1. "Ashes to Ashes" by Warchild
2. "Boulevard of Broken Dreams" by Green Day
3. "Taking Me Alive" by Dark New Day
4. "My Immortal" by Evanescence
5. "Charlotte Sometimes" by The Cure

THE SERENGETI CLUB
Seattle, Washington

This popular singles club is the domain of the Were-leopard Kontis patria. The building is recognizable from the outside by its black, mirror-tinted windows.

Show off your best down one of the many blacklight hallways leading to the state-of-the-art fiber-optic-lit dance floor. If the earth moves beneath your feet as you shimmy and shake you're not imagining it ... eighteen subwoofers are strategically and subtly planted beneath you. You will feel the rhythm, that's a guarantee. Check out your local listings to see which fabulous live bands or guest DJs will be rocking Serengeti's dance floor Friday and Saturday nights.

Every weekday night is karaoke night, so warm up your vocal cords and come on down. Bring some friends—the more the merrier—and they'll have to say yes to Tuesday's two-dollar draft

The Serengeti Club

Monday is Student Night
Every Tuesday is $2.00 Draft Night!
Wednesday is '80s Night!

FRIDAY AND SATURDAY DANCE UNTIL DAWN

▓ DAILY SPECIALS ▓

MONDAY
25¢ Oysters on the Half Shell
Happy Hour 5–7 P.M.
Student Night!

TUESDAY
Ninth Street Nachos
Happy Hour 5–7 P.M.
$2.00 Draft Night!

WEDNESDAY
Voodoo Chicken Salad
Happy Hour 5–7 P.M.
'80s Night!

THURSDAY
25¢ Wings—Spicy as you like 'em!
Happy Hour 5–7 P.M.

FRIDAY
Blackened Chicken Sandwich Basket
Dance Until Dawn

SATURDAY
Habañero Poppers
(Can you handle it?)
Dance Until Dawn

SUNDAY
All-You-Can-Eat Shrimp

Happy Hour Every Monday–Thursday 5–7 P.M. | 2-for-1 Margaritas
Check out our never-ending selection of imported and microbrewed beers

night. If putting on the hits is not your bag, join one of Serengeti's darts, poker, or pool tournament leagues.

You'll never have to sing for your supper, though—the Serengeti Club offers a full-service restaurant to satisfy your every craving. (And if you haven't tasted Terra Kontis's homemade French fries, you have not experienced heaven.) Serengeti also does banquets and private party packages—call ahead to make an appointment.

The Kontis clan will take care of you from the time the party starts until the wee hours of the morning. If you've partied a little too hard, one of Gareth Kontis's sons will be happy to escort you home in the Serengeti courtesy van (just don't embarrass yourself and try to take the Kontis boy with you). Get home safely, sleep soundly, and live to party another night away at the Serengeti Club.

The Serengeti also houses a small emergency clinic complete with hospital beds and basic supplies, should any extenuating circumstances arise. Alberta, the Serengeti's staff doctor, will happily nurse you back to health . . . or put you down, whichever's necessary.

Top Five Requested Songs at the Serengeti Club

1. "Fergalicious" by Fergie
2. "Between Me & You" by Eight O'Clock Vendetta
3. "Without Me" by Eminem
4. "Beautiful Liar" by Beyoncé and Shakira
5. "Stupid Girls" by Pink

Were-Hunter Directory

Here are a bunch of folks you might run into, hear stories about, ask to watch your back when you're in trouble, or run the other direction from if you happen to see them coming. (Those Were-Hunters really get around.) Scattered throughout are also some common terms used by and about the Were-Hunters.

Acmenes   A Katagari dragon, one of Bracis's clan.

Aloysius   (deceased) One of the tessera sent after Vane. Aloysius was killed by Bryani Kattalakis.

Anya   (deceased) Lykos Were-sister of Vane and Fang who mated with the fallen Strati warrior Orian. Since their souls were bonded Anya should by all rights have died when Orian died, only she was pregnant at the time. Unfortunately, the den was attacked by Daimons and Anya was killed before she could give birth.

BORN: A.D. 1463
BIRTHPLACE: Essex, England

Apollonian, Leo   Contrary to his given name, Leo is an Arcadian Were-bear. He represents the Arcadian Ursulan patria at the Omegrion as Regis of his clan.

Archigos   The leader of a patria.

Aristos/Aristi   A rare breed of Arcadian with the ability to wield magic effortlessly. The most powerful of their kind, the Aristi are considered gods in the Arcadian realm and are guarded zealously by patria who would gladly die for them.

Aristotle   Regis of the Rogue panther clan who kidnapped Pandora Pontis from the future. (Not to be confused with Aristotle Tigarian.)

Arnulf   Known Arcadian Were-Hunter.

Book of Dragons   The Book of Dragons explains the origin of the Arcadian Draki. It was taken from the Library at Alexandria by Sebastian Kattalakis the day before the great fire and given to Channon MacRae as a birthday present.

Bracis   A Katagari Were-dragon who killed Sebastian Kattalakis's sister, Antiphone.

Constantine   This antisocial Arcadian Were-jackal is Regis of his Tsakalis patria.

Cresting   Term used to describe Were females at the height of their sexual peak.

Diki   Trial by combat in Were culture.

Dragon Tapestry   Woven by Antiphone Kattalakis in seventh-century Britain, the tapestry tells the story of Lycaon and his brother. In essence, it embodies the origin of the Arcadian Draki and the eternal struggle between good and evil. The tapestry currently resides in the Richmond Museum in Virginia.

Exoristos   Term for an exiled Were. No member of the exiled Were's former patria is allowed to even speak his name. (See Ravyn Kontis)

Fazer   A dangerous Sentinel weapon developed specifically for the Katagaria. The fazer sends a jolt of electricity through its victim, making their magic go berserk and rendering them unable to hold on to either animal or human form. If the jolt is strong enough, there is a possibility that the victim might "fall out" of his body altogether.

Filos   The Katagaria term for a male pack member (affectionate). Can also mean "pack" or "brotherhood".

Gavril, Adrian   This Arcadian Were-tiger represents his patria at the Omegrion as the Arcadian Tigarian Regis.

Giovanni, Michael   A Katagari Were-cheetah, Michael is Regis of his Helikias patria.

Griffen, Taran   Bartender and waitress at Sanctuary, Taran is a major night owl who loves her job and lives to tease the regulars.

Hawke, Draven   Regis of the Katagaria Gerakian patria.

Isabeau   (deceased) Ravyn's human mate. Isabeau betrayed Ravyn's Were pack to her human family. They slaughtered all the patria's women and children while the men were out hunting. She was later killed by Ravyn as his Act of Vengeance when he opted to become a Dark-Hunter.

James, Alexander   This Arcadian Were-panther represents his patria at the Omegrion as the Arcadian Panthiras Regis.

Kallikedes, Icarus   Were-Hunter of the Gerakian patria. Icarus was last seen in Paris in 1860.

Kallinos, Jasyn   A legendary Were-hawk with a price on his head. A hero to the Katagaria and the devil to the Arcadians, Jasyn once lived to kill and stalk and maim. Don't cross him on a bad day. In fact, it's probably safest not to cross him at all. The only person he ever trusted tried once to hand him over to the Arcadians. It is rumored he ate that friend.

Only the bravest of the Sentinels have faced Jasyn, and Arion Petrakis, the Gerakian Arcadian Regis, has vowed to see him dead. The two of them play a deadly game of hopscotch and one-upmanship. Sooner or later, one of them is bound to kill the other.

BORN: 4685 B.C.
BIRTHPLACE: Thracia, Greece
HAIR: blond

Kattalakis, Antiphone   (deceased) Sister of Sebastian and Damos. Antiphone was killed by Bracis and his Katagaria in seventh-century Britain. She was responsible for weaving the legendary Dragon Tapestry.

Kattalakis, Bride   (née McTierney) The bonded mate of Vane Kattalakis, Bride owns the Lilac and Lace Boutique in New Orleans. She graduated from Tulane University. Before Vane, Bride had a horrible streak of boyfriends that ended with Taylor, a bastard who couldn't accept Bride as she was and broke up with her in a FedEx letter he charged to her account. (Did I say bastard already?) Her mother and father are both veterinarians who met in grad school and married upon graduation. Bride is the youngest of three siblings—her sister lives in Atlanta, and her brother works for a firm in the New Orleans business district. She has no love for her mother-in-law, Bryani.

HAIR/EYES: auburn/amber
FEATURED NOVEL: *Night Play*

Kattalakis, Bryani An Arcadian Sentinel Lykos Were-Huntress, Bryani is mother to Vane, Fang, Anya, Fury, Dare, and Star. She chose to live in Dark Age Britain, and dress kind of like something out of a *Xena* episode. Her father was Regis of the wolf clan before Vane.

Bryani was captured and raped by a pack of Katagaria . . . at which point it was discovered that by some bizarre twist of fate she had been mated to one of them (Markus). Disgusted at the prospect, Bryani refused to complete the mating ritual. Unfortunately, she was already pregnant. After giving birth to a litter of six children of both human and animal base forms, Bryani took the three human children away with her and left the animals for Markus to raise.

Bride McTierney kicked her butt once. She hasn't forgotten. Happily (for us), Bryani was banished to a fifth-century arena on an island to battle her husband for eternity.

Kattalakis, Damos Arcadian Were-dragon, and Drakos Regis in the Omegrion, Damos is the eldest of the direct Kattalakis Drakos descendents. He is the brother of Sebastian Kattalakis, and cousin of Darion. His parents, along with 90 percent of his patria, died after a brutal Slayer attack (thought to be led by Darion). His powers are legendary and his skills as a leader are beyond question.

Damos is haunted by his dark past, and he has sworn to seek out every Slayer in his time period. He will keep his people safe at any cost—even when it means banishing his own brother. The survival of his patria rests upon his shoulders. It is a responsibility he doesn't take lightly.

BORN: A.D. 530
BIRTHPLACE: Wessex, England

Kattalakis, Dare   The Arcadian brother of Vane, Star, Fang, Anya, and Fury. Dare was raised by Bryani, along with his Arcadian sister Star.

BORN: A.D. 1463
BIRTHPLACE: Essex, England

Kattalakis, Darion   A Katagari Were-dragon and warlord of great powers, Darion is a cousin of Damos Kattalakis. He is also Damos's greatest enemy. They have a blood feud that stems from the very beginning of their creation. Darion is the leader of his patria and is rumored to be the Slayer behind the attack that killed Damos's parents. Should they ever cross paths, there is little doubt that neither one of them will survive.

Damos represents all Katagaria Drakos as Regis in the Omegrion.

BORN: 5925 B.C.
BIRTHPLACE: Arcadia, Greece

Kattalakis, Dimitri   Dimitri is cousin to Damos, Sebastian, and Makis, and brother to Perseus. He is the anchor for his tessera and provides the stability they need. He functions as a peacemaker when necessary, but due to his volatile temper Dimitri is sometimes distracted from that calling. You don't want to be that distraction. You might want to say a prayer for whoever is.

BORN: A.D. 812
BIRTHPLACE: Hexham, England

Kattalakis, Fang   Katagari Were-Hunter and brother of Vane, Dare, Star, Anya, and Fury, Fang loves to crack bad jokes. The undisputed black sheep of the family, Fang asks for nothing and expects to get it. ("If you keep low expectations," Fang says, "you'll always be happily surprised.")

Alienated from all of his family and filos except Vane and Anya (before she died), he walks the world alone. He is the true lone wolf. Fang is a drifter, and the worst sort of scoundrel.

Fang was harmed badly when attacked by Daimons alongside Vane. Vane rescued himself and his brother and took Fang to Sanctuary to recuperate. What Vane didn't count on was Fang becoming completely (and dangerously) smitten with Aimée Peltier.

BORN: A.D. 1463
BIRTHPLACE: Essex, England
HAIR/EYES: black/hazel
WERE-FORM: brown timber wolf

Kattalakis, Fury   Brother of Vane, Fang, Anya, Dare, and Star. He was born in human form and lived with his brother Dare and sister Star under the care of their Arcadian mother Bryani until puberty, when his Katagari-half took over (the opposite of what happened to Vane). Bryani tried to kill Fury when she discovered his true animal nature.

Vane saved Fury's life when he first joined the pack by swearing brotherhood to him if he helped protect Bride McTierney. Fury is unreliable and selfish, but because of his mixed birth (and the fact that no one trained him to use his magic powers), he relies on his animal strength. When it comes to fighting, there are few better. Now he is the leader of the pack that used to shelter Vane and Fang. He claims the role of Katagari Lykos Regis at the Omegrion but he is pretty much just a figurehead, as he will always side with his brother Vane.

Not a great conversationalist. Fury's favorite saying is, "No good deed goes unpunished."

BORN: A.D. 1463
BIRTHPLACE: Essex, England
HAIR/EYES: blond/turquoise
WERE-FORM: white timber wolf (distinguishing brown spot)

Kattalakis, Makis An Arcadian Drakos born between Damos and Sebastian, Makis is the identical twin of Theren, who died protecting their sister from Slayers. Though he travels with Damos, Makis still longs for the return of Sebastian and the reunification of their scattered patria.

Makis takes great pleasure in the hunting and execution of the Slayers, and has vowed to track down everyone who was responsible for the slaughter of their village. He is relentless and cold to the Katagaria. To them, his name is synonymous with death. He will not rest until he lays waste to all bearing the blood of those who attacked his people.

BORN: A.D. 535
BIRTHPLACE: Wessex, England

Kattalakis, Markus A Katagari Were-Hunter and father of Vane, Fang, Fury, Dare, Star, and Anya. Markus tried to force the unwilling Bryani to accept him as a mate and failed, thus dooming him to a bitter life of powerless sterility. He later turned on his own sons, wanting to kill Vane and Fang for "allowing" their sister Anya's death to happen. Markus made deals with Daimons for magic since he could no longer wield any. He was eventually banished to a fifth-century arena on an island to battle his wife for eternity.

WERE-FORM: brown timber wolf

Kattalakis, Matarina Markus's youngest adopted daughter. Matarina was always very fond of Vane and Fang.

Kattalakis, Sebastian Arcadian Sentinel Drakos Were-Hunter and youngest of the direct Drakos Kattalakis descendents. Sebastian is the grandson of King Lycaon, and a prince of Arcadia. Always at odds with his older brother Damos, Sebastian was excommunicated from his patria after the death of his sister Antiphone. He wears a gold medallion around his neck that belonged to his mother.

Sebastian is mated to a twenty-first-century human, Dr. Channon MacRae.

BORN: October 3, 545
BIRTHPLACE: Hexham, England
HEIGHT: six foot five
HAIR/EYES: black/greenish-gold
WERE-FORM: dragon with blood-red and black scales
CURRENT LOCATION: Richmond, Virginia
FEATURED STORY: "Dragonswan"

Kattalakis, Star Arcadian sister of Vane, Dare, Fang, Anya, and Fury. Star was raised by Bryani, along with her Arcadian brother Dare.

BORN: A.D. 1463
BIRTHPLACE: Essex, England

Kattalakis, Taron Taron is the leader of his patria and the great-grandson of the first Lykos Katagaria. Proclaimed a Slayer when he turned twenty-eight, he has spent his adulthood thwarting the Sentinels after him.

Taron is still searching for his sister and two brothers who were lost to the patria during an attack. It is believed they were taken by the Arcadians and made into slaves. Taron won't rest until he finds them and restores them to the lands where they were born. Until that day comes, he has vowed to lay waste to every Arcadian he can find.

BORN: A.D. 10
BIRTHPLACE: Gaul

Kattalakis, Theren   (deceased) This Arcadian Drakos was the identical twin of Makis. He died protecting their sister from Slayers.

BORN: A.D. 535
BIRTHPLACE: Wessex, England

Kattalakis, Vane   Arcadian Sentinel, Lykos Were-Hunter, and Aristo. Firstborn of the Kattalakis litter, Vane was born Katagaria but changed to Arcadian at puberty (opposite from his brother Fury). The Arcadians proclaimed him a Slayer on his twenty-fifth birthday, and they have pursued him ever since. The bounty on his head is staggering. As an Aristo his powers are legendary; few Sentinels have dared challenge him. Those who have, paid with their lives.

Vane was doing a favor for the Dark-Hunters (protecting Sunshine Runningwolf) when Daimons attacked his pack and slaughtered his pregnant sister, Anya. Their father turned against him because of this. As a result, he and his brother Fang were subjected to the timoria. They were imprisoned in metriazo collars and left to the elements, the alligators, or the Daimons, whichever came first.

As Murphy's luck would have it, it ended up being the latter. Vane managed to save both himself and his brother, but during their escape, Fang was almost fatally wounded by Daimons. Vane took Fang to Sanctuary to recover from his wounds.

Vane worked as a bartender at Sanctuary while Fang was ill, and was later banished from the safe house for attacking Stefan, who had come to kill Fang.

Vane was mated to Bride McTierney in 2004. He represents the Arcadian Lykos patria at the Omegrion and, through his brother Fury, pretty much represents the Katagaria branch as well.

BORN: A.D. 1463
BIRTHPLACE: Essex, England
HAIR/EYES: mottled dark brown/green
WERE-FORM: solid white timber wolf
FEATURED NOVEL: *Night Play*

Konstantinus, Ilarion   The last surviving member of his Drakos filos, Ilarion was captured by humans when he was barely eight years old. He lived in captivity for four years where he was brutally tortured and cruelly displayed. He finally escaped, but not before his throat was damaged so badly by the humans that he could no longer speak.

Ilarion learned to hide where no one could find or track him. He trusts no one and refuses to let anyone near him. Antisocial to the extreme, he only interacts with women when his passionate appetite requires it. His powers are equal to, if not greater than, any Kattalakis.

BORN: A.D. 435
BIRTHPLACE: Norway

Kontis, Dorian   Nickname: Dori. An Arcadian Were-leopard and brother of Ravyn Kontis. Dorian is the bonded mate of Terra and twin of Phoenix. Dorian often says he came into the world with one purpose: to harass his brothers and keep them from hurting each other.

He is a fair man, and he possesses a most wicked sense of humor. Aside from his mate, he prefers to keep to himself. As a young Sentinel, he was charged with the harsh duty of putting down one of his littermates who succumbed to the trelosa. Many say that his heart died that day.

He resides at the Serengeti Club, alongside his family. He also represents his patria at the Omegrion as the Arcadian Pardalia Regis.

Born: March 10, A.D. 675
Birthplace: Athens, Greece
Height: six foot two
Were-Form: leopard
Current Location: Seattle, Washington

Kontis, Gareth   This Were-leopard is the father of Dorian, Phoenix, and Ravyn Kontis. Gareth is the owner of the Serengeti Club in Seattle. He was not formally bonded to his mate, and so survived when the Were pack was slain by the humans.

Kontis, Georgette   (deceased) The unbonded Were-leopard mate of Phoenix Kontis. Georgette was killed alongside her children when Isabeau betrayed the Weres and the humans attacked the clan.

Kontis, Phoenix Nickname: Nix. Arcadian Were-leopard Sentinel, twin to Dorian, and reluctant brother to Ravyn Kontis. He was born five minutes before his twin brother, Dorian, and is fond of saying that he took all of his brother's meanness. In fact, his brother and two sisters are the only creatures he will interact with peacefully.

He was also Ravyn's murderer, back when his brother's human mate betrayed the Were pack. Phoenix was not formally bonded to his mate at the time (Georgette), and so he was doomed to survive when the humans slew his wife and children.

Cold and calculating, he is one of the few Sentinels who works alone and as such, he keeps the tattoo on his face hidden. As he says, he's never been a team player and he's too old now to change his ways.

He resides at the Serengeti Club with his family.

Born: March 10, A.D. 675
Birthplace: Athens, Greece

HEIGHT: six foot two
WERE-FORM: leopard
CURRENT LOCATION: Seattle, Washington

Kontis, Ravyn　　An Arcadian Dark-Hunter/Were-Hunter leopard, Ravyn is the son of Gareth Kontis and brother to the twins Phoenix and Dorian. Ravyn was mated to Isabeau (a human) who betrayed Ravyn's Were pack to her human family while the male Weres were out hunting.

The hunting party realized that the women and children were being slaughtered when the bonded males began to die instantly. The remaining males in the pack, led by Phoenix, turned on Ravyn and killed him (Wales, 1673). Ravyn then called on Artemis to seek revenge on Isabeau and her people.

When he made the bargain to become an immortal Dark-Hunter, Ravyn lost the ability to teleport, travel through time, and day-walk as a man. He can walk in daylight only in the form of a very small Arabian leopard. In this form, he is often mistaken for a cat.

Ravyn is stationed in Seattle, where his family owns a sanctuary (the Serengeti Club), but because of the laws of both Hunterkind, they are never to associate. He is classified as an *exoristos,* which forbids any member of his clan from even speaking his name.

After recently mating Susan Michaels (a very strange hand dealt by the Fates, since Ravyn is a Dark-Hunter and is not supposed to be able to mate . . . on top of the incredible rarity it is for a Were to be given the chance to mate twice in one lifetime), Ravyn asked Susan not to petition Artemis for his soul so that he might remain a Dark-Hunter.

BORN: 304 B.C.
BIRTHPLACE: Athens, Greece
HEIGHT: six foot six
HAIR/EYES: black

WERE-FORM: very small Arabian leopard
AGE AT DEATH: six hundred thirty-five
CURRENT LOCATION: Seattle, Washington
FEATURED NOVEL: *Dark Side of the Moon*

Kontis, Susan (née Michaels) Susan is the bonded mate of the Were-Hunter/Dark-Hunter Ravyn Kontis. She won the Sterling Award in 2000 for Investigative Reporting. Her career was later ruined when she wrote a story exposing a senator's questionable spending practices, and then found out her source was bogus. She is currently employed by the undercover Squire Leo Kirby at the *Daily Inquisitor* in Seattle.

Susan's father abandoned her and her mother when Susan was three. Years later, her mother died in a car wreck. She learned to sword fight in the SCA, and was once a martial arts student of the Dark-Hunter Dragon.

Susan was almost made a Squire by her boss when trouble started brewing around Ravyn in 2006. This would have forbidden her inevitable relationship with Ravyn, only she missed being officially sworn in and got off on a technicality. Clever Leo.

HAIR/EYES: dark blonde/blue
CURRENT LOCATION: Seattle, Washington
FEATURED NOVEL: *Dark Side of the Moon*

Kontis, Terra A Were-leopard, and Dorian's bonded mate. This lovely, tall brunette works in the kitchen at The Serengeti Club.

HAIR/EYES: brown/blue
WERE-FORM: leopard
CURRENT LOCATION: Seattle, Washington

Kontis, Zatira (deceased) Were-leopard and sister to Ravyn, Phoenix, and Dorian. Zatira died in 1673 alongside their mother, Phoenix's wife and children, and the rest of their village when the humans attacked.

Kouris, Stefan The Katagari Were-leopard who represents his patria at the Omegrion as the Pardalia Regis.

Kouti, Sefia Pandora Pontis's surviving sister. She is mated to a Katagari panther.

Kyriakos, Terecles Terecles was born to one of the now rare Tsakali (jackal) patrias who spurned Artemis. He is the archigos of his patria, and has vowed to see them survive no matter what. He and his patria move constantly and their location is unknown at this time. He could be in the past, present, or future.

He is ruthless and exacting. No one wants to cross him. It is said he can only be tamed for very short periods of time and only by the hand of a tempting woman.

Born: 892 b.c.
Birthplace: Carthage
Height: six foot five

Laminas/Limani The Atlantean term for "haven". This refers to portals between worlds (bolt-holes). The word is also used to describe any Were-Hunter sanctuary or safe house.

Leonides, Patrice An Arcadian Were-lion, Patrice is Regis of the Litarian patria.

MacRae, Channon, Dr. A History professor at the University of Virginia specializing in pre-Norman Britain. Channon's mother died of cancer when she was nine. She is mated to Sebastian Kattalakis.

Hair/Eyes: honey brown/blue
Featured Story: "Dragonswan"

Marvin the Monkey Small brown spider monkey with a fondness for carrots. Marvin is the only real, non-Were animal in Sanctuary, and is its mascot. Watch out: He likes to steal billiard balls off the tables during games. He likes fruit, and is very good friends with Wren Tigarian.

Current Location: New Orleans, Louisiana

Metriazo Collar   This thin silver collar sends tiny ionic pulses into the body of a Were-Hunter, thus preventing its victim from using his magic powers. It will effectively stop a shapeshifter from changing shape, and can only be removed by magic.

Moretti, Vincenzo   Since Were-jackals keep to themselves, not much is known about this Katagari Were-Hunter. He represents the Tsakalis patria at the Omegrion as Regis of his clan.

Nearas   The term used to describe virgin Were females who are cresting.

Omega Wolf   Slang term for the scapegoat of the pack whom everyone picks on.

Orian   (deceased) Strati warrior who was the bonded mate of Anya Kattalakis, sister to Vane and Fang. By all rights Anya should have died when Orian died, only she was pregnant at the time.

Patria   Name for the family grouping of Were-Hunters of the same race and animal genus. The existing Were patria are: Balios (jaguars), Niphetos Pardalia (snow leopards), Drakos (dragons), Panthiras (panthers), Gerakian (hawks, falcons, bald eagles), Pardalia (leopards), Helikias (cheetahs), Tigarian (tigers), Litarian (lions), Tsakalis (jackals), Lykos (wolves), and Ursulan (bears).

Peltier, Aimée   The only daughter of the Peltier clan, Aimée works at Sanctuary as bookkeeper and waitress, as well as taking care of all the necessary permits and bribes. She fell in love with Fang Kattalakis while nursing him back to health after a Daimon attack. (A dangerous proposition for Fang.) Anyone else who looks at Aimée gets a meeting with her brothers and father in the back room.

BORN: Brussels, Belgium
WERE-FORM: bear
CURRENT LOCATION: New Orleans, Louisiana

Peltier, Alain   The eldest Peltier son, Alain manages the bar for his parents. He is also the bouncer no one wants to cross.

WERE-FORM: bear
CURRENT LOCATION: New Orleans, Louisiana

Peltier, Aubert (aka Papa Bear)   Patriarch of the Peltier clan. At seven feet tall, no one messes with Papa Bear. (He does give great hugs, though.) A lot of fun and easygoing, Papa Bear believes in giving everyone a chance—until they prove him wrong. He is fiercely protective of Mama and their children. Especially Aimée.

WERE-FORM: bear
CURRENT LOCATION: New Orleans, Louisiana

Peltier, Bastian   (deceased) A Peltier son, Bastian was killed by Arcadian Sentinels as a cub along with his brother Gilbert.

Peltier, Cherif   One of the Peltier quadruplets, Cherif works as a bartender and waiter at Sanctuary. He also doubles as a bouncer when needs be, as most of the Peltier brothers do.

WERE-FORM: bear
CURRENT LOCATION: New Orleans, Louisiana

Peltier, "Cody" Francois   The fraternal (older) twin of Kyle, Cody tends to let the mischievous Etienne lead him astray. He works as the band's roadie. He keeps their equipment working, and runs the soundboard at night.

WERE-FORM: bear
CURRENT LOCATION: New Orleans, Louisiana

Peltier, Devereaux   Nickname: Dev. One of the Peltier quadruplets, and bouncer at Sanctuary. Dev keeps a close eye on all the females at the bar to make sure no one harasses them—unless they want to be harassed—with the exception of Aimée. No one touches her. Keep an eye out for his bow-and-arrow tattoo, which he has because he thinks it's funny. He is not a Dark-Hunter.

WERE-FORM: bear
CURRENT LOCATION: New Orleans, Louisiana

Peltier, Elizar   Nickname: Zar. He's the Peltiers' next to the oldest, but by far the biggest on brains in the bunch. He loves wordplay, and is always quick with a comeback. A businessman and investment broker, Zar usually deals with Bill Laurens. He also has very little patience for Serre or Etienne.

WERE-FORM: bear
CURRENT LOCATION: New Orleans, Louisiana

Peltier, Etienne   One of the middle sons, Etienne is a bit of a black sheep who continually gets into trouble, gets his brothers into trouble, and drives his family insane. He does, however, respect his mother—he just doesn't listen to her.

WERE-FORM: bear
CURRENT LOCATION: New Orleans, Louisiana

Peltier, Gilbert   (deceased) A Peltier son, Gilbert was killed by Arcadian Sentinels as a cub along with his brother Bastian.

Peltier, Griffe   In the Peltier clan, Griffe is twin to Serre. Sanctuary's resident mechanic and electrician (he likes to live dangerously), he works on the motorcycles and keeps the band and houselights up and running.

WERE-FORM: bear
CURRENT LOCATION: New Orleans, Louisiana

Peltier, Kyle   Youngest of the Peltier brothers and twin of Cody, Kyle works part time at the bar as a waiter while he finishes college. Unwitting patrons have commented on the fact that the wrestle bear shares his name. Yeah . . .

WERE-FORM: bear
CURRENT LOCATION: New Orleans, Louisiana

Peltier, Nicolette (aka Lo, Mama, Mama Bear)   The matriarch of the Peltier clan, Nicolette, and her husband, Aubert, founded Sanctuary as a safe zone after the death of their sons Bastian and Gilbert. Nicolette vowed that no mother would ever know grief as long as her child was under a Peltier roof. She is caring until someone or something threatens the sanctity of her home and those she loves. It is then that you remember she is, in fact, a bear at heart. Nicolette represents the Ursulan patria as Katagaria Regis in the Omegrion.

WERE-FORM: bear
CURRENT LOCATION: New Orleans, Louisiana

Peltier, Quinn   The youngest—and most reticent—of the quadruplets, Quinn is an exceptionally talented carpenter and repairman. He makes all the furniture and is responsible for all the ornate woodwork at Sanctuary. His other handmade items have been sold to tourists and donated to shelters. He may be quiet and shy, but he's very good with his hands. Quinn also soundproofed the storeroom at Sanctuary, a feature that has come in handier than anyone could have imagined.

WERE-FORM: bear
CURRENT LOCATION: New Orleans, Louisiana

Peltier, Remi   Yet another sibling in the Peltier clan. Smooth-talking and quick to anger, Remi is not your average bear. He tends to fall in with the wrong crowds and loves to pick on Aimée (who often runs to Dev or Papa Bear for protection). He is forbidden to be a bouncer due to his temper. He can usually be found in the kitchen or back room.

WERE-FORM: bear
CURRENT LOCATION: New Orleans, Louisiana

Peltier, Serre   Twin to Griffe, Serre is a loafer and comedian who fills in at Sanctuary in whatever position he happens to be needed.

WERE-FORM: bear
CURRENT LOCATION: New Orleans, Louisiana

Petcu, Andrei   A Lykos Were-Hunter, Andrei is the brother of Francesca.

CURRENT LOCATION: Transylvania

Petcu, Francesca   Nickname: Frankie. A Lykos Were-Hunter, and best friend of Esperetta Danesti for more than four hundred years. Francesca's mother, Raluca, was Retta's nurse. Velkan Danesti originally sent Frankie to watch over his wife—they met in a rain-soaked Germany when Retta was stranded on her way to Paris, and Francesca shared her room with her.

HAIR/EYES: chestnut/light blue
WERE-FORM: chestnut she-wolf
CURRENT LOCATION: Transylvania

Petcu, Illie   (deceased) Illie was Raluca Petcu's unbonded mate. He was captured by a Taser and killed by the Order of the Dragon.

Petcu, Raluca   A Lykos Were-Hunter, Raluca is the mother of Andrei, Francesca, and Viktor. She worked as a servant in Vlad Tepeş's castle, performing the role of his daughter Esperetta's nurse. This tall, striking woman looks about forty. She shares her progeny's chestnut hair and blue eyes.

CURRENT LOCATION: Transylvania

Petcu, Viktor   A Lykos Were, Viktor is the older brother of Francesca.

CURRENT LOCATION: Transylvania

Petra   (deceased) A Katagari she-wolf, Petra was shunned by vane when she tried to sleep with him, and then he stopped her from sleeping with his brother Fang. She was killed by Bryani.

Petrakis, Arion   The Gerakian Arcadian Regis, Arion travels with a human sorcerer. The two of them are sure to find mischief at every available opportunity. He isn't married to one time period, and is often found traveling between them. Arion is a scoundrel and has never been known to pass up a willing female.

He has a long-standing rivalry with the Were-hawk Jasyn Kallinos, and has vowed to see him dead (as lifelong enemies are wont to do).

BORN: A.D. 812
BIRTHPLACE: Gwynedd, Wales

Pontis, Angel   Cousin of Dante Pontis and his brothers.

Pontis, Bonita   (deceased) The bonded mate of Donatello Pontis. Bonita accidentally killed her mate (and in doing so, herself) in the throes of passion. Their tale is often told as a warning to young Katagaria Were-panthers.

Pontis, Dante   A Katagari Were-panther, Dante is the eldest of a litter of eight. He has a wicked sense of humor, and as both a panther and man is an extremely laid-back (but lethal) creature. He owns Dante's Inferno in Twin Cities, Minnesota, a known sanctuary, where he follows his own set of rules. He has his own creed and code of behavior: Dark-Hunters, Were-Hunters, and gods be damned.

Dante killed his brother Salvatore, who betrayed them to the Daimons. He is the mate of Pandora Kouti, whom he met at

Dragon*Con in Atlanta. Dante represents his patria at the Omegrion as the Katagaria Panthiras Regis.

BORN: A.D. 1392
BIRTHPLACE: Florence, Italy
HEIGHT: six foot six
HAIR/EYES: black/clear blue
WERE-FORM: panther
CURRENT LOCATION: Twin Cities, Minnesota
FEATURED STORY: "Winter Born"

Pontis, Donatello   (deceased) The Pontis Were-panther brother who was accidentally killed by his bonded mate (Bonita) in the throes of passion.

Pontis, Gabriel   A Were-panther brother of Dante Pontis.

Pontis, Leonardo   Nickname: Leo. A Katagari Were-panther, Leo is the younger brother of Dante Pontis and is Mike's twin.

Pontis, Michaelangelo   Nickname: Mike. A Katagari Were-panther, Mike is the younger brother of Dante Pontis and is Leo's twin.

Pontis, Pandora   (née Kouti) This Arcadian Were-pantheress is the wife and mate of Dante Pontis, whom she met at Dragon*Con in Atlanta. Pandora belonged to a near-future Arcadian Panthiras patria whose women were subject to a bargain with an all-male Katagaria patria from the current time. Pandora was kidnapped from the future, and her older sister was killed by this pack.

Pandora wears her husband's signet ring, an object he uses as a homing beacon so that he will always be able to find his wife across space and time.

HAIR/EYES: brown/lavender
FEATURED STORY: "Winter Born"

Pontis, Romeo   A mated Katagari Were-panther. The older brother of Dante Pontis, Romeo is one of the most vicious of the panther pack. He has a particularly morbid sense of humor and lives for the thrill of the kill. His greatest pleasure in life is tormenting his younger brothers, especially Dante. Quick and lethal, he is a Strati to be reckoned with. Romeo works at Dante's Inferno most often as a bouncer, but he will double as a DJ from time to time.

Resist the urge to make fun of his name, or to quote Shakespeare in his presence. Your life will be all the longer for your prudence.

BORN: A.D. 1116
BIRTHPLACE: Venice, Italy
HEIGHT: six foot five
CURRENT LOCATION: Twin Cities, Minnesota

Portakalian, Justin A Were-panther, Justin is a bouncer, waiter, and bartender at Sanctuary. He's an ex-con with a chip on his shoulder. There's nothing like being a Katagari Were-Hunter in prison. It makes for some interesting stories. Only . . . you might not want to ask him to tell them if you've got a weak constitution.

HEIGHT: six foot six
HAIR/EYES: dark brown/hazel
CURRENT LOCATION: New Orleans, Louisiana

Regis The leader of a Were-Hunter pack who in essence acts as their king (or queen) and representative at the Omegrion.

Romano, Anelise A snow leopard Arcadian Were-Hunter, Anelise represents her patria at the Omegrion as the Niphetos Pardalia Regis.

Rytis The invisible stream of waves that move through everything in the natural world. These waves echo, flow, and occasionally buckle. Were- and Dream-Hunters use the Rytis to move through time and space. Many have equated the Rytis to Ley

Lines, though the Rytis is much less geographically stable and virtually impossible to map.

Sasha   A Katagari Were-Hunter, and best friend to the justice nymph Astrid. Sasha was barely a pup when his Lykos patria sided with the Egyptian goddess Bast in her war against Artemis, and so was judged innocent of his actions. Unfortunately, the Arcadians still want him dead because of his prior association with Slayers, and the Slayers want him dead because they think he betrayed his patria. Smart Sasha tries to stay out of it all by sticking close to Astrid's side.

Sasha helps Astrid when she is stricken blind during judgment—they communicate telepathically.

HAIR/EYES: pale blond/electric blue
WERE-FORM: white timber wolf

Scooby   Derogatory Lykos Katagaria term for a brainless, cowardly pup.

Sebastienne, Paris   One of the few Katagaria Slayers who travels with friends of a different patria, Paris is often found in the company of Trey, Ax, and Trion Xanatos. This Were-lion travels in human form, usually on a custom-built Harley. His one known weakness is full-bodied brunettes; it seems as though he is always being lured by one. Paris has left in his wake a long line of dead Sentinels, dark beauties, and broken hearts.

Paris represents his patria at the Omegrion as the Katagaria Litarian Regis.

BORN: 3162 B.C.
BIRTHPLACE: Athens, Greece

Stefan   A Strati leader, and Vane Kattalakis's mortal enemy. Stefan is Markus Kattalakis's second-in-command.

Stefanopoulos, Myles   The Katagaria Were-jaguar Regis. Myles represents the Balios patria in the Omegrion.

Stephanos, Lysander   Nickname: Sander. The Tigarian Katagaria Regis whose entire family was executed by a clan of Arcadians. He alone survived. Vowing vengeance on the ones
responsible, Lysander has sought these Arcadian butchers
throughout history. Like many of his vengeful brethren, he won't
stop until he has claimed them all.

Pronounced a Slayer the moment he entered puberty, he has
a death warrant on his life that is equal to Vane's, and in some
centuries even more. Because of his relentless pursuit of Arcadians, the Katagaria have offered rewards for his hide in hopes of
buying a truce from their enemies.

Lysander has a shoulder and bicep covered in a tattoo of a
heart pierced by a sword.

BORN: 6523 B.C.
BIRTHPLACE: Athens, Greece
HAIR/EYES: brown

Strati   The term used for Katagaria soldiers who seek out Arcadians to fight. Some Arcadians refer to all Strati as Slayers. The
Strati are the Katagaria equivalent of Sentinels, only without the
facial markings.

Much like their predatory ancestors, Strati will not engage an
enemy unprovoked. They will only kill to defend themselves,
their pack, or their territory.

-swain   Suffix for a male Were-Hunter. (Example: dragon-
swain, pantherswain, bearswain, and so on.)

-swan   Suffix for a female Were-Hunter. (Example: dragonswan, pantherswan, bearswan, and so on.)

Tessera   From the Greek word for "four", this is the term used
for a group of four Were-Hunters sent out to hunt others of their
kind. Of course, just to be contrary, a tessera can also have eight
members.

Theodorakopolous, Colton   Nickname: Colt. One of the more powerful modern Ursulan Arcadian Sentinels. Unlike many of his brethren, Colton doesn't have an ax to grind with the Katagaria. In fact, he owes his life to a few of them. Colt was orphaned at birth (his mother escaped a Slayer attack). He was harbored and raised at Sanctuary—the Peltiers were responsible for rescuing Colt and his mother, and then they fostered Colt after her death. He is the only child Mama Peltier has officially adopted. Colton has never forgotten what he owes this particular Katagaria clan, but he doesn't let that detract from his Sentinel duties.

Colt is the lead guitarist for the Howlers, the house band at Sanctuary. He normally hides his Sentinel markings with his powers.

BORN: A.D. 1875
BIRTHPLACE: St. Louis, Missouri
HAIR/EYES: black
CURRENT LOCATION: New Orleans, Louisiana

Thirio   The instinctual need inside Weres to bond and combine life forces during the consummation of a mating. During this basic, powerful animal thrall that overtakes a Were, the canine teeth grow to facilitate the bonding.

Tier   One of the fiercest of the Tigarian Katagaria. A known killer, Tier was even driven out of his own patria. He is merciless on the hunt and will not stop until he achieves whatever it is he seeks.

Women have been said to faint as soon as he turns his animalistic charm upon them. He keeps mostly to himself and is very quiet. He can often be found on the beach or wreaking havoc with the local Santaria cults. Mischievous and wild, he loves to toy with his prey before he devours it.

BORN: 565 B.C.
BIRTHPLACE: the Amazon Basin

Height: six foot four
Current Location: Rio de Janeiro, Brazil

Tigarian, Aristotle   Wren Tigarian's father, a white tiger Were-Hunter, who—despite popular opinion—did not actually murder Wren's mother. When Aristotle's own mother was dying of cancer, she gave her powers to him. Aristotle later bestowed these powers upon Maggie Goudeau, when she and Wren visited him from the future. For many years he perpetuated the lie about his death and lived in secret under the name Josiah Crane, so as not to interrupt the natural time flow.

Tigarian, Grayson   (deceased) An Arcadian Were-Hunter and Wren's uncle, Grayson was Zack's father. He was killed by his brother Aristotle.

Tigarian, Karina   (deceased) Last of the Katagari snow leopards, and mother of Wren Tigarian. A passionate and irrational woman, Karina hated her son. She and her lover were both killed by Aristotle.

Tigarian, Maggie   Born: Marguerite D'Aubert Goudeau. Nickname: Maggie. (*Hates* being called Margeaux.) Maggie was mated to Wren Tigarian as a gift from Nick Gautier through Savitar. She became a Were-tiger after Aristotle Tigarian bestowed upon her his mother's powers.

Maggie is the socialite daughter of a prominent U.S. senator. Her mother was a Cajun beauty (a former Miss Louisiana) who worked as a docent at the Audubon Zoo before her marriage—she later overdosed on antidepressants when her husband refused to divorce her.

Maggie was also a friend and study partner of Nick Gautier. Julian Alexander was her undergraduate advisor.

Born: August 6, 1981
Hair/Eyes: chestnut/brown
Were-Form: tiger

CURRENT LOCATION: New Orleans, Louisiana
FEATURED NOVEL: *Unleash the Night*

Tigarian, Wren   A Katagari Were-Hunter born in the wilds of Asia, Wren Tigarian is a man of few words. He is a *tigard*—a rare white tiger (father)/snow leopard (mother) hybrid mix that neither clan will tolerate. As a result, he can take either form at will. After his parents allegedly went mad and killed each other, Savitar brought the cub's half-dead carcass to Sanctuary to be protected . . . and to protect everyone else.

While he was at Sanctuary, Wren bussed tables and washed dishes, despite the fact that he was the heir to the Tigarian Technologies empire. As his mother was the last of the Katagaria snow leopards, Wren is Regis in the Omegrion for a Niphetos Pardalia patria of one. His father is the wealthy Aristotle Tigarian.

Wren has a tattoo on his left arm of a white tiger lurking in the tall grass. He weighs more than 800 pounds in animal form and, like many of his brethren, does not take Tylenol or eat chocolate. He is great friends with Marvin the Monkey, the mascot of Sanctuary.

HEIGHT: six foot three
HAIR/EYES: dark blond/turquoise
WERE-FORM: white tiger, snow leopard, or combination
CURRENT LOCATION: New Orleans, Louisiana
FEATURED NOVEL: *Unleash the Night*

Tigarian, Zack   The Were-tiger son of Grayson and cousin of Wren Tigarian. Zack was the one who called the charge of trelosa on Wren, saying that Wren was responsible for the death of his parents.

Timoria   Katagaria punishment.

Trelosa   A rabieslike madness that comes upon Were-Hunters when they hit puberty. Zack Tigarian accused Wren of killing his parents while under the influence of the trelosa.

Whelps   Young Were-Hunters who have reached puberty, and mastered their hormones, but have yet to harness all their powers.

Whitethunder, Carson   Arcadian Were-hawk; the only son of a Sioux shaman and a Gerakian Katagari. His mother died not long after his birth, and his father raised him alone. Once he fell into puberty, his father took him to Sanctuary so that the Peltiers could help him "adjust" to his newfound powers.

The cross-mixture of his blood has left him with a few strange tendencies that cause him to spend a lot of time alone. Hoping to better understand himself, he went to med and vet school. He ended up back at Sanctuary where he now helps both Arcadians and Katagaria as the resident vet and medical doctor. He hopes to one day find a way to bring peace to the two groups.

He takes a room upstairs above the club and is on duty pretty much 24/7. Carson often seeks the advice of Dr. Paul McTierney on tricky cases.

BORN: October 13, 1910
BIRTHPLACE: New Orleans, Louisiana
HEIGHT: six foot four
HAIR/EYES: black/hazel green
WERE-FORM: hawk
POWERS: astral projection

Wilder, Jace   Arcadian Were-cheetah, and Regis of the Helikias patria.

Xanatos, Trey/Ax/Trion   Some of the few Katagaria Slayers who travel with a friend, Trey/Ax/Trion (they are not actually the same person, but are in fact identical triplets) are often found in the company of Paris Sebastienne. These Were-tigers possess the ability to be in more than one place at a time.

BORN: 55 B.C.
BIRTHPLACE: Gaul

Dream-Hunters

Mr. Sandman, Your New Best Friend

Dreams provide a necessary outlet for everyone.
—Arikos

Origin of the Oneroi

Dream-Hunters (also known as the Oneroi) are the cursed children of the Greek gods of Sleep (Morpheus, Hypnos, Phobetor, Icelus, Phantasos, and Thanatos). Some are born of human mothers, but many are born of the Greek goddess Mist.

As long as one of a child's parents is an Oneroi, that child can inherit their powers and duties. They also inherit some residual emotions, emotions that are stripped from them very early on, usually by beating. More about that when we get to the curse.

Once a child has been embraced by its Dream-Hunter brethren, the distinction between branches of the family tree, however distant, becomes obsolete. All Oneroi consider one another brothers or sisters whether they actually share the same parents or not. They are taught by their siblings how to enter dreams, and the rules of what to do and what is forbidden. They learn how to fight the Skoti, and how to fight the war of raging emotions inside themselves after a visit with a vivid dreamer so that they don't become the next monster with a price on its head.

Dream-Hunters can be either male or female. Most have black hair and pale blue, almost colorless (and kind of glowy) eyes. They feel a bit like static electricity when touched, and transport from one place to another in a golden flash of light.

The Oneroi possess the power to create dreams, and control them. They direct the dream host to reveal his or her deepest desires, or to find solutions to the nagging little problems of the dreamer's everyday life. Without the Oneroi to steer dreams and inspire people, humans (and other such dreamers) would lose their minds.

It takes many years for a Dream-Hunter to master his powers. If the training of an Oneroi fails, and it cannot be beaten into him, then he is executed by order of the leaders of the Dream-Hunters.

It's not that the leaders are evil (they are not), or because they are cold (which they are). It's because they don't want to incur the wrath of the gods . . . again.

The curse of the Oneroi all started with a joke. Zeus thought the Dream-Hunters too powerful and arrogant, and not being known for his tact he said as much. But even gods have to sleep sometime. Gods, like everyone else on the planet, are vulnerable to the Oneroi when they are resting. And since Oneroi can travel carte blanche through the dreamworld, they know a lot of tricks the old gods don't.

The Fates enjoy being tempted, you know. Spices up the long days of eternity for them. And they can be vengeful bitches.

One of these mischievous Oneroi thought Zeus's statement more than a bit hypocritical, so he played a joke on old Thunder-butt (it's said that Hades, Hypnos, and Wink had a hand in this, too . . . but what roles they played exactly has never been made clear). This Dream-Hunter monkeyed with the god's mind and made him lust after a goat.

Which, you have to admit, is pretty darned amusing.

No harm, no foul. At least, that's what the Oneroi thought.

As you have learned by now, gods don't exactly have the best senses of humor. By simply performing that one not-so-innocent act, the Dream-Hunter had cursed himself and his brethren until the end of time.

Zeus—once he regained his composure—ordered his assassins, the Dolophoni, to round up all the Dream-Hunters. A small group was immediately killed outright, including the one who had played the trick. Another group was summarily tortured to a point just before death. Among that group were M'Ordant, M'Adoc, and D'Alerian.

The rest of the Oneroi's torture was a bit more subtle. Any non-Oneroi members of their families were killed. They were cursed to never again have emotions of any kind. Without humor or pride or jealousy, none would be tempted to try the same trick on any other god again. But with those emotions also went fear, hate, ambition, envy, compassion, and love.

Yes, it's all fun and games until someone loses their emotions. (Sorry, I couldn't resist that one.)

Since the inherent nature of the Oneroi had changed after the curse, their duties summarily changed as well. Instead of causing, creating, and playing in dreams willy-nilly, the Dream-Hunters became siphons.

The empty emotional containers that are the Dream-Hunters' bodies help humans (and others) by absorbing the excess emotions during sleep so that they might feel less stressed and more rested in the morning.

What's it like for them? Arikos once said that being in a dream was "like bathing in Jell-O. It feels kind of thick and at times can be overwhelming. You never know what you're going to find". A heady and sensual description indeed, but one limited to the external senses. They cannot love or hate or fear or care. They just *are*.

The only times the Oneroi can feel anything emotionally are those moments when they are helping in the dreams of humans. All that fear and love and passion are all-too-brief visitors in the cold vessel that is a Dream-Hunter's consciousness, like stolen souls in a Daimon. Emotions are like a drug for them; they crave what they cannot have.

Because of that, the Oneroi are sworn to never participate in the dreams, and to never visit the same human more than once. They are also sworn to never seduce a human during sleep to jump-start these passionate, heady emotions.

It's never easy to resist. Ever. A Dream-Hunter faces these temptations every single night, and every single night he must somehow force himself to resist them. It takes tremendous strength, unbelievable control, and a willpower I'm not sure even I possess.

The World of Dreams

*Betrayal is for those who have
something to gain.*
—Kratos

There are different kinds of dreams, and different realms for each of them. The Oneroi often travel between these dreams through the *strobilos*—a vast demesne like a hall with many chambers. The strobilos amplifies the powers of the Oneroi so that they can slip in and out of dreams unnoticed, manipulating them with superior ease, and siphoning emotions from their dream host without fear of any lasting physical or emotional damage to that host. The Oneroi may rest undisturbed in the strobilos, drifting in and out of dreams at will.

While in the strobilos, however, the actions of the Oneroi can be monitored by both their leaders and certain interested gods.

The idea is that the knowledge that they are never unwatched will serve to keep them in line.

The Oneroi know that the gods fear them, and the gods make a show of their powers by exacting control over the Dream-Hunters whenever the opportunity presents itself.

As a rule, Dream-Hunters do not prey on dreamers. But when a subject needs to be induced, there are several serums Dream-Hunters use to make a dream host drowsy. Lotus serum is the most popular, and idios more rare. Others have been known to use sleep mist (or dust) directly from the god Wink himself.

One of the other main duties of the Oneroi is the care of the psychological well-being of the Dark-Hunters. In fact, an entire branch of Oneroi are dedicated to this cause. The transition to what you are . . . what you've been through . . . it's hard. Even the toughest bully would crack under that kind of pressure. Many have.

It is in Artemis's best interest to have her soldiers remain hale and whole and unaffected by their past lives. They need to be able to set the sadness, hate, love, and pain behind them, and to channel those feelings into their war against the Daimons.

A Dream-Hunter can help a Dark-Hunter control those feelings. To ease them. To make them more manageable, and to make you more able to manage them. He can be your Yoda, for lack of a better comparison.

Since Oneroi can siphon pain, they are also given the task of speeding up the healing process of an injured Dark-Hunter. A Dark-Hunter heals while sleeping, and a Dream-Hunter's powers are unmatched in the dream realm. Voilà!

When a Dark-Hunter is given to a Dream-Hunter to care for, no one else is allowed to trespass on that Dark-Hunter's dreams without an invitation. And once a Dream-Hunter is assigned to you, it's for life. As condescending and annoying as a Dream-Hunter can be, it's a blessing really, so appreciate what you've got. Don't think you're the only one with a severely messed-up

How to Summon a Dream-Hunter

- Severe Pain. (They will feel it and be drawn to you.)
- Unconsciousness. (Dreaming is their deal, after all.)
- Get Emotional. (Sad? Angry? Orgasmic? A Skotios will find you . . .)
- Just call. (Do try to shy away from "Hey, Dork, I need you".)

- *Don't ask Ash. He's got better things to do.*
- *Don't eat to try and induce nightmares. Unless you're going for option one. . . .*

past. There were more Dark-Hunters before you, and there will be more after you.

If they were all well-adjusted individuals, they wouldn't *be* Dark-Hunters, now would they? Besides, Dream-Hunters with their steady, calm, Zenlike manner will always be a welcome change of pace from your over-opinionated, crazy, loud, hormonally imbalanced, know-it-all brat of a Squire. And they're definitely more rational and level-headed than most gods you'll ever come across.

Perhaps, at times, too rational.

Some say that while Zeus is a mighty god indeed, his control over an entire race of beings this powerful is not quite so endless and all-encompassing. There is a rumor that the emotions of the Oneroi are returning slowly after all this time, and growing stronger with every year that passes.

But if this is indeed true, it is not for a Dream-Hunter to ever tell.

Some things are better left unknown.

Sticks and Stones

Ah, man, not another one of you. Great.
Shoot me now and put me out of my misery.
—Nick Gautier

When the Oneroi were cursed, Zeus stripped them of their names, as well as any sense of individuality they might have had. For that reason, the legions of Dream-Hunters take their names based on the roles they serve in the dream realm.

The prefix to the Dream-Hunter names designates their role in the hierarchy:

M   The leaders. These enforcers work like a police force to keep the Oneroi from crossing the line . . . and pass judgment upon the ones that do. The current leaders of the Dream-Hunters are M'Ordant, M'Alerian/D'Alerian, and M'Adoc. They meet at the *Onethalamus,* the gathering place where all policies, peace treaties, and death warrants are fashioned.

V   Dream-Hunters who aid insomniacs, or who save humans from nightmares. (See V'Edrix, V'Arian.)

D   Dream-Hunters sent to help gods and other immortals. These are the ones most often recruited to help newly forged Dark-Hunters escape the nightmares of their past, and the transition to immortality. Once assigned to a Dark-Hunter, this Dream-Hunter will usually watch over them for their entire existence. (See D'Aria, D'Ravyk.)

Skoti

*Have you ever wanted something that you knew
was bad for you? Something that you ached for
so much that you could think of nothing else?*
—Wren

*Yes, which is why I always end up eating
the whole chocolate bar anyway.*
—Maggie

Also known as "energy vampires". some Dream-Hunters (usually the nightmare children of Phobetor) inevitably get seduced by the drug that is a human's emotions. They begin to instigate dreams, and alter them so as to exact more emotions from their dream hosts. Some will fall in love with their human subject, appearing as incubi or succubi. Once they build up a tolerance, they can siphon emotions and creativity for longer and longer periods of time, an act that inevitably ends in the death of the dream host.

These Dream-Hunters are called *Skoti*. (*Skotos* is the singular term.)

Just when you thought having boring dreams was a bad thing.

Most people dream in black-and-white, with lots of mist—that's not a big draw for them. Skoti are drawn to the rare dreamers who have vivid, colorful dreams.

Certain Skoti (*Phobotory Skoti*) get their kicks in nightmares, feeding off the unadulterated, paralytic fear that they can induce in their dream host. The heart-pounding adrenaline is like race car driving or skydiving for them. Extreme dreaming, if you will.

The down and dirty baddies are called *Erotikos Skoti*. They really do have one thing on their minds, and it's the one thing on their dreamer's mind, too. An Erotikos Skotos will induce and thrive in dreams built on the sexual fantasies of their dream host. Such a heightened state of emotion is exceptionally addictive to the Skoti, and exceptionally dangerous for the dreamer.

Barely more than demons, the Skoti are hunted down by their Oneroi brethren and punished for their crimes. Some Skoti are tolerated only to help drain humans of excess emotions. They are not allowed to spend too much time with one person, and are deemed uncontrollable if they fail to heed the warnings of the Oneroi leaders. They are given *one* warning before they are severely punished . . . or eliminated from existence.

Earthbound

Feel? Why would anyone in their right mind
wish for that? Feelings are for fools.
—Hades

In dreams, the Oneroi can only be fought by others of their kind. They are gods and have the full range of god-powers. And, much like the gods, both the Oneroi and Skoti can choose to take form in the human realm on earth.

When in human form they still lack emotions, but have all the powers inherent with their Oneroi blood. They are still gods and are very much omnipotent. They assume human form to "mark" a host, meaning they scope the host out and follow them with a psychic link that enables them to infiltrate dreams later. They can also manipulate and siphon while human, but they must be very careful to avoid detection.

There's another way a Dream-Hunter can become truly human: He or she must stop eating ambrosia and drinking the nectar of the gods. We all know the result of this, don't we? Not only will the Dream-Hunter lose his immortality, but he will also lose all of his powers. He won't just be human, he will be *mortal.*

It is a high price to pay for a Dream-Hunter—the highest price, some would say.

It is not a path that is taken lightly . . . or often.

Dream-Hunter Directory

It is exceptionally difficult to maintain a list of Dream-Hunters, since most go out of their way to remain undetected. You may dream of one, but was he real? Or just a figment of your imagination?

Below are some of the known Dream-Hunters, as well as a list of gods, demons, and terms relating to the dream realm. You never know when one of them might help you discern the difference between fantasy and . . . *fantasy*.

Alp   A German nightmare spirit often associated with vampires (for draining his victims of blood and/or energy) and with the werewolf in his mortal form. The Alp has ghastly taste in hats.

Arikos   Nickname: Arik. Son of Morpheus and Mist, and half-brother to M'Ordant. Arik was once one of the most powerful of the Oneroi. He was called V'Arikos—a name he came to hate after he learned some emotions, since it reminded him of varicose veins—and his mission was to hunt down and destroy all the Skoti he could find. Arik became a Skotos when fighting Solin in a human's dream—Solin turned his human victim on Arik in defense. Instead of destroying her, he tasted her lust. In the blink of an eye, Arik went from being a good guy to one of the worst Erotikos Skotos out there.

For thousands of years Arik walked the line of evil, trying to find another vivid and daring dreamer who could give him that fleeting sensation again. He found that person in Megeara Kafieri, and so became her dream lover.

He bartered Megeara's soul with Hades for the chance to visit earth as a living, breathing, and feeling human (who went by the name of Arikos Catranides) for fifteen days. After falling in love with Megeara and sacrificing his life to Hades for her, he became fully human.

BIRTHPLACE: Mount Olympus
FEATURED NOVEL: *The Dream-Hunter*

C'Azim   At one time the most honored of the Oneroi, C'Azim discovered the pleasures of mortal women. Since then, he has been rather insatiable with them. Though he still performs most of his Dream-Hunter duties, he is easily swayed by his hormones. An outrageous flirt, it is said that no woman, either mortal or immortal, can deny him. His touch is hot and powerful, his kiss deadly. To lay with him is to know the most heavenly bliss.

D'Alerian   Son of Zeus and D'Aria (one of the original Oneroi) and brother of Persephone, D'Alerian is a healer and helper to the Dark-Hunters. He is a straight man who never met a rule he didn't love. He has an aura of incredible proportions; his presence can be felt all the way to the marrow of your bones. His real name is Nikomedes (Neco as a nickname), and he is called M'Alerian by some.

Part of the Higher Pantheon, he keeps a constant vigil over the Dark-Hunters and is quick to step in with aid whenever one of them needs it. He can easily tell when a Daimon is messing with a human subconscious. He and Acheron are close friends; he was assigned to Kyrian Hunter when he first came into the service of Artemis.

D'Alerian has a soft heart, due to the loss of someone he once loved very dearly. Because of this, he called in a favor that Persephone owed him and had her intervene to help save the human Megeara Kafieri and her Dream-Hunter lover Arikos from Hades.

D'Aria   A known Dream-Hunter assigned to Wulf Tryggvason.

Day Dreamers   These are the Oneroi and Skoti who don't have to be near their host to command them. They are the most powerful of their kind.

D'Ravyk   Son of Icelus, D'Ravyk also helps the Dark-Hunters and the gods. One of the highest members of the pantheon, he is also one of the oldest of the Dream-Hunters. A Goody Two-shoes, he is often at odds with Arikos. He likes order; he spends a lot of time counseling younger Dream-Hunters against the dangers of cavorting with humans. He is extremely solitary by nature.

Dream-Walkers (Perparti)   Humans who can channel dreams. They can also act as Skoti or Oneroi.

Ensyneiditos   The conscious part of a person that can travel outside the body. This is the only way Acheron can ever see Apollymi (since he can't do it in the flesh).

Ephialtes   A Greek nightmare demon.

Erebus   The Greek god of Darkness. Erebus is the father of Wink, Hypnos, and Thanatos.

Hypnos   Greek god who holds dominion over all the gods of sleep. Son of Nyx and Erebus and twin of Thanatos, Hypnos oversees the physical punishments of the dream gods. And he is harsh.

Icelus   A son of Hypnos and one of the Oneroi, Icelus creates human shapes in dreams. He is the father of some of the more erotically addicted Dream-Hunters.

Idios   A rare serum made by the Oneroi that enables someone else to become one with the dreamer. Idios is a dark red liquid. It is possessed by only M'Adoc, M'Ordant, and D'Alerian.

Incubus   A male demon or Erotikos Skotos that seduces—and sometimes impregnates—a female dream host. Excessive exposure to an incubus (or its female counterpart, the succubus), can drain a human dream host to the point of death.

Incubi have been blamed for many "unexplained" pregnancies over the centuries. Many of the Greek gods—Zeus and Apollo in particular—have fathered a child on a woman or forty in this fashion.

Kallitechnis   A Dream Master. Can move through anyone's dreams: past, future, and beyond.

K'Allon   K'Allon is a creature of complete sensual arts. It is said he is the father of desire and lust. To see him is to crave him; to feel his touch is to be rocked and shattered. When he is near, women are said to be blinded by his beauty. They forget any and everything except his gorgeous form.

K'Allon picks his lovers at random and has a fondness for soft, full-figured women. His appetites are robust, and he will easily play with his lover from dusk to dawn. If he comes to you, be prepared for a night you will never forget. And should he fixate on you, then prepare to lose yourself to pleasures unimaginable. Not that I know from experience or anything.

Kratos   A Skotos who claims to be able to bring a soul out of eternal rest and return it to the land of the living. Kratos was only very recently an Oneroi, but Artemis's handmaiden Satara summoned him in her dreams and turned him Skoti. She seduced him with her body and made him crave emotions like a drug. Now he plays Satara's lapdog and does her bidding.

HEIGHT: six foot four

Krysti'Ana   A Skotos who takes the form of a giant snake with a woman's upper body. In human form, she is a large brunette who goes by the name Chrissy Phelps. She posed as Erin McDaniels's friend and coworker so that she might feed off her.

Kytara   Nickname: Tara. A Skotos Dream-Huntress. Another great mystery of the night, Kytara was killed by gallu demons when Kessar used the Tablet of Destiny to drain her awesome powers.

Liderc   A demon lover (from Transylvania) who takes the form of a dead loved one to seduce its dream host, leaving the dreamer sick. The Liderc has the ability to enter a house through chimneys and keyholes. It can sprinkle flames from its fingertips, leaving ash and soot around its victim.

Lilim   The demon children of Lilith.

Lilith   In many religions, Lilith is the first wife of Adam, a demon succubus, and the mother of all demons. Her children are known as the lilim.

Lotus Serum   A dangerous sedative. Some go insane from it, and some become so addicted they choose to never wake from their dreams. It gives some humans exceptionally bad headaches.

Mab   Shakespeare's tiny fairy Queen, Mab rides through the dreams of humans on her chariot and grants them their heart's desires . . . or brings their worst fears to life.

M'Adoc   Son of Phantasos, M'Adoc is one of the Enforcers who watches over both the Oneroi and the Skoti. When a Skotos or Dream-Hunter steps over the line, they answer to him. He is quick to issue orders, but seldom takes them. M'Adoc is the Oneroi of last resort. He abhors profanity, but has no problem executing his "nuisances". When he comes after a Dream-Hunter, that Hunter knows he is going to pay. M'Adoc takes the jobs no one else wants to do. And he's happy about it . . . which is more than a little disturbing.

M'Adoc tried to kill the human Megeara Kafieri for what she knew of the secrets of the Oneroi, but he was stopped by M'Ordant and D'Alerian (they trapped him in a diktyon). M'Adoc then killed Arikos but didn't bury him, so that he couldn't pay Charon and cross over into Hades.

M'Adoc was taken away to learn compassion. He was sent to tend to the Dark-Hunter Zarek in Alaska as his punishment.

HEIGHT: seven feet

M'Alerian   (See D'Alerian.)

Mara/Mare   Female wraith believed to cause nightmares (from Scandinavia). She was also said to ride horses in the dead of night as she rode her men, leaving them both sweaty and with tangled hair.

Mist   Amorphous consort of the Sleep gods, Mist has birthed thousands of children. Not the most maternal of mothers, she turned the raising of her sons and daughters over to Hypnos and the nymphs who serve her.

HAIR/EYES: black/white, glowing

M'Ordant   Son of Phantasos and brother of V'Aidan, M'Ordant is another of the Dream Police (despite the fact that he looks more like a Boy Scout). M'Ordant watches over both the Oneroi and the Skoti. As far as the Enforcers go, he is hard-nosed and down to business. Still, he has a certain degree of compassion that is forbidden to his kind. It was M'Ordant who took Erin McDaniels to see V'Aidan in Tartarus.

Morpheus   Greek god of Dreams, father of many Oneroi, and the son of Hypnos. Morpheus is responsible for shaping dreams, or giving shape to the beings that inhabit dreams. His name means "he who forms, or molds" (from the Greek *morphe*).

Nikos   Nikos is human and a Skotios of extreme sexuality. He moves like a predator through crowds and is never too busy to pass time with a willing female. Sensual and hot, he is plagued in his mortal life by women who want him. At night, he often finds them in their sleep and shows them exactly the fantasies that they crave. His legend is legion. He walks the night searching for the one woman whose touch can bind him, the one woman who will bring peace to his wounded heart and love to his lonely existence.

Nocnitsa   Night Hag (from Eastern Europe). The Nocnitsa is an elderly woman who torments the dreams of sleeping children. Long ago it was said that the Nocnitsa could not bear the touch of iron, so many mothers would leave a knife in the crib with their children.

Nytmares   Atlantean female spirits who run through dreams and teach the dreamer lessons he or she needs to know.

Oneirocritica   Written by the Roman Artemidorus Daldianus, the *Oneirocritica* is considered the first book on dream interpretation. The idea was that each dream and its symbols are unique to the dreamer—that the memories and feelings that a person associates to an object in their waking life will translate over into the dreamworld.

Oneiromancy   Dream divination; the ability to predict the future by interpreting dreams and their symbols as portents.

Onethalamus   Meeting hall in the dream realm where the leaders of the Oneroi meet to discuss problems, share secrets, and pass judgment. The Onethalamus has witnessed and holds all the secrets of the Dream-Hunters . . . including the one they're still trying desperately to keep.

Orasia   Atlantean goddess of Sleep.

Phantasos   Son of Hypnos and creator of nonsentient dream objects. Phantasos is the father of the more cerebral Dream-Hunters. His children are most often the Oneroi who police the Dream-Hunters. His name means "apparition".

Phantosis   The shadow realm between conscious and subconscious.

Phobetor   Son of Hypnos, and Greek god of animal shapes. Phobetor is the father of the nightmare Dream-Hunters. His name means "frightening".

Rec'Sord   A Skotos who posed in the mortal realm as Erin McDaniels's boyfriend Rick Sword, a psychologist who specialized in sleep disorders.

Seric   Restless and wicked, Seric's specialty is exotic locations. He loves to pick a woman and take her to her most forbidden fantasy. He finds his pleasure in the giving of pleasure and has a particular fondness for women who have suffered broken hearts. He was cursed to an earthly existence and tends to frequent the most unlikely locations where he can find his prey, so that he might catch them off guard. Libraries and bookstores tend to be his favored spots. He especially prefers women who read romance novels, since they tend to have a much more robust imagination. Though he appears human by the light of day, at night he really is a god.

Siphon   Act of infiltrating dreams to feed off another's emotions.

Solin   A human of extraordinary talents. It wasn't until puberty that he discovered he was the demigod son of a peasant human mother and the dream god Phobetor. Because of his heritage, he escaped the no-emotions curse that plagues his siblings.

Even so, he grew up harshly. He was sold into slavery as a child. When his powers manifested during adolescence, the Oneroi started hunting for him. He is one of the few Skoti who has ever warranted a death sentence.

Solin lives on earth by day (as Solin Catranides, the multibillionaire playboy), and runs amuck in human dreams at night. Seductive and quiet, it is said his eyes alone are enough to make a woman reach ecstasy. Those who have felt his touch have been driven to madness in search of his return.

A cousin of Arikos, Solin thinks that humans are no better than gods. There are only a few gods Solin tolerates, though he has been known to help the Chthonians from time to time.

Strobilos   The vast black nothingness between dreaming and waking that has no sound or color. It is used by the Oneroi to locate dreamers.

Succubus   Demon or Erotikos Skotos that takes the form of a human to seduce a male dream host. The succubae draw their energy from the dream host during intercourse. In some legends succubae also retain semen from the male host, then transform into incubi and use it to impregnate a female dream host.

V'Aidan   A Skotos who fell in love with the human Erin McDaniels. He was allowed by Hypnos to be born into the human world so that he could be with Erin.

Featured Story: "Phantom Lover"

Vanishing Isle   Island at the edge of the world where Greek sailors believed they would go when they died. You can see it for a few minutes at sunup and sundown, but it is unreachable. The Vanishing Isle is where most of the dream gods reside.

V'Arian   A son of Icelus, V'Arian is one of the Monitors for human sleep. He protects humans from the Skoti who give them nightmares. He is fascinated by human behavior and studies it closely. There are those who fear he may one day turn Renegade, but so far he has done his job as required.

V'Edrix   A son of Icelus, V'Edrix is also one of the Monitors for human sleep. He was one of the first of his kind, and feels an extra responsibility for the humans he watches over. He prefers to work with children and with women who have suffered trauma. There are some who claim he also works with certain Rogue Dark-Hunters to punish the human nightmare instigators, but there is no proof to this rumor. He keeps himself away from most of his Dream-Hunter brethren.

Wink   A minor Greek god, Wink is the son of Nyx and Erebus and V'Aidan's great-uncle. A puckish character, Wink is what led to the belief of the Sandman. He is sent by the gods of Sleep to induce slumber. Most claim he does so by sprinkling a magic dust into their eyes. Children are most often fond of Wink, who is said to love them best of all since they are innocent and most deserving of untroubled rest.

A chronic prankster to both the Oneroi and Skoti, Wink is often found playing tricks on them. He may be one of the oldest gods, but he has the personality of a thirteen-year-old boy. He can be found hanging out with the dead from time to time "for a laugh".

Wink's dust or mist is often used by Dream-Hunters to make a human drowsy, or to exert control over a human.

Xypher   A vicious Phobotory Skotos Renegade who thrives on fear. He used to hunt down humans and terrorize them until they went mad from it. M'Ordant, D'Alerian, and M'Adoc were forced to kill him for his wicked ways, and he was damned to Tartarus for all eternity. Hades made him human for a month in exchange for helping Katra and Sin recapture the Dimme.

Zakar   A Sumerian god of Sleep. He is the brother to their god Sin.

Squires

Can't Live with Them, Can't Live Without Them

I am technically human, though my multitude of siblings would deny it. And barring the pasties, I'm really not some kind of sicko.
—Otto Carvaletti

Shield-Bearers

When the Dark-Hunters were created back in 7382 B.C., Artemis made a pact with Acheron that she would provide for them everything they would need in order for them to maintain their focus on killing Daimons.

Acheron returned from that meeting with Artemis to the cave where the first three Dark-Hunters hid. With him he brought two men, because every good knight needs a man-at-arms. Armor and weapons are expensive and unwieldy, after all. Who do you suppose looks after all that when the knight is off killing things?

Exactly.

Originally, the men were called Shield-Bearers, much like those who served the warrior knights of old. Later, they came to be known as Squires.

The Squires are the helpmates and companions of Dark-

Hunters in many of the same ways medieval Squires were expected to aid their knights. Something of a cross between a servant and an employee (they serve Artemis, just like the Dark-Hunters, and they are compensated well for their troubles), they keep watch over their Dark-Hunters and provide everything they need, especially in the daylight hours.

In the beginning, after their ranks were assembled by Acheron, a Squire's job was to stand guard over the crypts where their charges slept. Today they perform a few more mundane duties, not the least of which is legally acquiring and maintaining both land and property for the unique men and women they serve who died a very, very long time ago.

Squires are bound to kill any human who poses a threat to a Dark-Hunter by exposing his or her existence. (They are not necessarily the ones who do the killing, but they are required to pass the information along to someone who will.) They are forbidden to reveal anything embarrassing about a Dark-Hunter to whom they are in service (not that it ever stopped Otto or Nick), or anything that might endanger them.

As you can see, there is a lot of gray area when it comes to Squires. Ultimately, however, they are essential to the survival of the Dark-Hunters, and their loyalty is unvarying, unyielding, and eternal. You can trust that with your life; you may one day need to.

It is up to the Dark-Hunters to fight the battles—Squires are not meant to engage Daimons. Their duty is to protect their Dark-Hunters. It helps a lot if they're alive to do that. They also (normally) do not have psychic abilities, or supernatural powers of any kind.

The rank of Squire in the ancient world was often hereditary. Similarly, Dark-Hunter Squires are either the children of other Squires or they are recruited by other Squires and Dark-Hunters. Many a Squire has been made of a too-smart-for-her-own-britches youth who couldn't keep her nose out of trouble and wouldn't take no for an answer.

Some of the best Squire families have descended from those whippersnappers.

Unlike their squire namesakes, Dark-Hunter Squires are not the apprentices of the Dark-Hunters. Think about it—who in their right mind would say, "Yes, please, I hope someone kills my family and friends and betrays me in a fashion so unforgivable that I will trade my soul to become an immortal superpower soldier fighting vampires until the end of time."?

Seriously.

And no, Nick Gautier is not—and doubtfully ever was—in his right mind.

Squire Council

What we deal with is bigger than spiders.
It's bigger than you and me.
—Leo Kirby

The Squire Council is a select and secretive group of men and women who oversee the activities of the other Squires. They make the payroll and give out money to any Squire who wishes to set up a business front for their Dark-Hunters. They have a database of all the networked Squires, their hand and retinal imprints, and their dental records. It's quite a massive amount of information—while there may be thousands of Dark-Hunters, there are tens of thousands of Squires behind them, making the world go 'round.

The Squire Council is also responsible for looking after the human families of Dark-Hunters after they have sworn their oath to Artemis and crossed over. Knowing that fact has set many a Dark-Hunter's mind at ease.

Squire Branches

The Squires have a whole detailed organization
that's kind of like the Hotel California.
You can check out anytime you like,
but you can never leave.
—Nick Gautier

Today, not every Squire is assigned to a Dark-Hunter, nor does every Squire want one. They have an elaborate network of affiliates that can quickly get anything a Dark-Hunter or another Squire needs. The Squire Council has on their books lawyers, doctors, bankers, pilots, almost anyone to do anything you could possibly think of. They also found and run establishments such as hospitals, restaurants, and libraries that appear to serve humans as a front, but in reality were put in place solely to serve the Dark-Hunters and their assistants.

In order to maintain this elaborate ruse, the Squire Council designated that the league of Squires be broken into various branches.

Some Squires can be classified under two branches—for instance, a Squire can be both a Blue Blood and a Blood Rite. (It is actually quite rare to have a Blood Rite Squire who is not descended from a long line of Squires before him.) Similarly, all Blood Rite Squires are Theti Squires, but not all Thetis have spiderweb tattoos. Confused yet? Good, that's why I'm here. It's all about to become clear again, so take that Tylenol (not that it'll work on you), and come right back.

Some Squire classifications are mutually exclusive. One cannot be both a Dorean and an Assigned Squire, for example. You either have a Dark-Hunter, or you don't. There's no two ways about that one.

The branches of the Squires are:

Barnacle/Echo Squire A Squire who is assigned to a particular Dark-Hunter, usually living in the same house and very often the legal mortal owner of the property. This Squire attends to all the day-to-day monotony of running the household, so that the Dark-Hunter can concentrate on killing Daimons. (And you just remind your Squire of that the next time she acts out.) This Squire (and his or her family) is the most at risk, since the Daimons know there is an inevitable emotional attachment between a Dark-Hunter and his or her assigned Squire.

They often fetch for the Hunter as well. They are aides and personal assistants. They live with the Dark-Hunter and help to create an illusion that there's nothing unusual going on with the occupants of a house. "Barnacle Chip" is a slang term used for someone who was recruited to be a Squire, as opposed to someone who was born into an established family.

Blood Rite Squires Squires called out to perform blood hunts to terminate any Rogue Dark-Hunters, or to execute humans (including other Squires) who betray their world. They are all marked with a spiderweb tattoo on their hands, usually on the skin between the thumb and forefinger or over the knuckles. The Blood Rites are a subbranch of the Theti Squires.

Blue Blood Squires Squires who hail from a multigenerational Squire family. If his last name is Addams or Carvaletti, you can bet your bippy he's probably a Squire.

Dorean Squire A sort of free agent. A Dorean Squire has no attachment to any particular Dark-Hunter; he is a protector of all. These Squires often set up businesses that support the Dark-Hunters in their work in some way, specializing in goods such as weapons, computers, and cars. Doctors, pilots, police officers, and judges fall into this category. The Dorean Squires have also enlisted bankers and lawyers who know all about the Dark-Hunter world, and who work to keep up the outward appearance of normality.

The Squire Oath

In the light of day, I am all that protects my Dark-Hunter from death and persecution. I am the eyes, the ears, and the soul of my chosen one and I will die before I let any harm befall him.

It is my duty to maintain a haven for my Dark-Hunter. To keep his residence clean and safe. I will do as asked without question, without complaint until the Fates see fit to separate us.

I am a Squire, the human counterpart of my Dark-Hunter, and it is my oath that I will never allow harm to befall my Dark-Hunter on my watch. I will be there when he needs me and will give myself freely to anything he requires.

I am all that stands between him and the world that would see him dead. I, alone, am his link to humanity and I, alone, will be with him when he needs me most.

I will never speak publicly of my Dark-Hunter or of their world. All things of them, their lives, their pasts, their abilities, and existence are secret.

I take this oath freely, without reservation or under any duress. I understand that once made, it is absolutely unbreakable. To breach my oath will call down the Wraiths of Hades upon my head, and I will pay for my treachery with my life. No one betrays the Dark-Hunters with impunity.

So says the goddess Artemis, and so she accepts my eternal service to her and all her Dark-Hunters.

Oracle Squires   Squires who confer with the gods, especially the Fates, to gather information that is helpful to the Dark-Hunters. The most prominent Oracles are the Lekti, who keep the Book of Prophecy where all important events in human history are predicted. It is said even the end of the world is chronicled within its pages. They fall outside the control of the Squire Council and are led by the Delphinian (or Oracle of Delphi).

Talpinas   Originated in the Dark Ages, the Talpinas were a clan of Squires whose sole purpose was to sate the carnal needs of the Dark-Hunters. Talpinas were banned by Artemis after one of her Dark-Hunters fancied himself in love with a Talpina, and she didn't pass the test. The Talpinas are the origin of Ash's "Never touch your Squire" law.

Tech Squires   Squires who are involved in research and technological fields. They are the ones who conceive and create special toys and who enable Dark-Hunters to communicate with one another. These are the Squires who handle the intricate workings of the www.Dark-Hunter.com Web site.

Theti Squires   The Squire police, the Thetis make sure all the Squires obey the law. They are also the ones sent out to deal with any civilian who finds out about the Dark-Hunters. Unlike Blood Rites, layman Theti Squires are not allowed to kill. They are sent in first to clean up the situation. If they are ineffective, then the Blood Rites are called in.

The Squire Oath

Oh gee, golly, goodie, Mr. Leo!
Can I have my eyes gouged out, too?
—Susan Michaels

Somewhere, the Squire Council has a book of all these contracts to Artemis, signed in blood by every Squire that has ever lived . . . and died. Remember, Squires don't ever really "quit"—a Squire's oath is both unbreakable and eternal.

You can relate.

Squire Directory

Again, this is not a list of all the Squires in the world that ever were, are, or shall be—you'd need the Squire's Handbook for that (dusty, enormous tome that it is). This is just a sampling of folks you might run into on your travels . . . or ones you might want to call when you're in need of absolutely anything. And don't be afraid to call on any of them at any time; keeping you alive to fight another day is what they're there for.

An assigned Squire can also put you in touch with his or her Dark-Hunter, when necessary.

Addams, Alicia   Daughter of Patricia Addams, Alicia is sister to Brynna, Jack, Jessica, and Tad.

BLUE BLOOD SQUIRE

Addams, Brynna   Brynna is an eighth-generation Squire to Xander St. James, and very often his angel of mercy. Handmaiden to the goddess, she occasionally works as an Oracle. Brynna's father Squires for Treig Olavsson.

Brynna has a great sense of humor, as well as the ability to remain calm in a crisis. She's most often found on the Squires' Web site.

BLUE BLOOD SQUIRE
BORN: September 12, 1976
BIRTHPLACE: Sioux City, Iowa
DARK-HUNTER: Xander St. James

Addams, Daphne   Helps maintain the Dark-Hunter.com Web site. She's Brynna's cousin.

BLUE BLOOD SQUIRE

Addams, Jack   Son of Patricia Addams, Jack is brother to Alicia, Brynna, Jessica, and Tad.

BLUE BLOOD SQUIRE

Addams, Jamie   Cousin to the other Addams.

BLUE BLOOD SQUIRE
DARK-HUNTER: Blade

Addams, Jessica   Daughter of Patricia Addams, Jessica is sister to Alicia, Brynna, Jack, and Tad.

BLUE BLOOD/BLOOD RITE SQUIRE

Addams, Patricia   (deceased) Matriarch of one of the most prominent Squire families in Seattle (mother of Alicia, Brynna, Jack, Jessica, and Tad). Maintained an enormous computer-filled Squire warehouse facility in Seattle, with a deli-coffee shop in front to keep up its innocent appearance. Patricia was attacked by a Daimon and killed in 2006.

Addams, Sara   Sister to Jamie.

DOREAN SQUIRE
DARK-HUNTRESS: Corbin

Addams, Tad   Brynna's older brother, Tad set up and runs the ISP for the Dark-Hunter Web site. You'll often find him there, hanging out with Otto Carvaletti. Oh, and the man's brain functions like a computer. If you care anything about keeping your money, never, ever play poker with Tad.

BLUE BLOOD SQUIRE

Bambi   Orphaned when her Squire parents were killed by Daimons, Bambi was raised by the Squire Council. She's not particularly computer-savvy, but Bambi certainly knows which end of a gun is which. Her greatest hope is to one day be chosen as an Oracle.

DOREAN SQUIRE

Bennet, Tate   Tall, African-American Parish coroner and Dorean Squire. Tate and his ambulance are often called to the aid of Dark-Hunters in a pinch ... most often when they need to take refuge from the morning sunlight in one of Tate's body bags.

DOREAN SQUIRE
CURRENT LOCATION: New Orleans, Louisiana

Blackstone, Jamie　A first-generation Squire raised by an alcoholic father (his mother died when he was very young), Jamie ran away from home at fourteen and made the fortunate mistake of trying to mug the Dark-Hunter Kell. Kell fostered Jamie with a family of Squires, and then offered him the position when his own Squire retired.

BORN: August 17, 1977
BIRTHPLACE: Texas
DARK-HUNTER: Kell

Brinks, Jeff　Former Squire of Rafael Santiago, Jeff is a college student in Columbus, Mississippi. A budding fiction writer, he wrote a story ("The Night-Searchers") based on the legends of the Dark-Hunters, and had it published in the well-known speculative fiction magazine *Escape Velocity*. This action compromised his Squire vows and got him into all sorts of trouble with the Council. The Squire Celena was sent after Jeff to kill him, but Rafael managed to stop her ... by falling in love with her.

BLUE BLOOD SQUIRE
CURRENT LOCATION: Columbus, Mississippi

Callahan, Mike　Helicopter pilot ... at least, he was until Zarek blew it up.

DOREAN SQUIRE

Carmichael, Justin　One of the group of Blood Rite Squires that went to Alaska in order to hunt Zarek.

BLOOD RITE/DOREAN SQUIRE
BIRTHPLACE: New York, N.Y.

Carvaletti, Otto   Half Italian mafia, half Blue Blood–Blood Rite Squire, Otto earned his Ph.D. from Princeton in film studies. (He's cute, but he's a contrary bugger.) Otto's grandfather was the Squire Council Chair before Brendan.

Otto was assigned to Valerius in New Orleans, where he took up the persona of loudly dressed lout just to annoy his boss. (He should have been awarded a Ph.D. in that, too.) Otto has the unique talent of being able to insult your mother in twelve different languages. He even makes up some of his own; for instance, he delights in calling Valerius "Penicula".

We joke that Otto doesn't have a lot of close friends, but it's truer than you'd think. I think it's the intimidation factor—the superintelligence more so than the mafia—but that's just my own personal theory. You're welcome to decide for yourself, if you think you can keep up with him.

When it comes to his duties, however, Otto has no sense of humor, and even less patience. His day job is to keep watch over the safety of the Dark-Hunter Internet services. You're likely to find him online, hanging out with Kyl.

BLUE BLOOD/BLOOD RITE/DOREAN SQUIRE
BORN: August 30, 1972
BIRTHPLACE: Woodbridge, New Jersey
HEIGHT: six foot five
HAIR/EYES: black/dark brown

Celena   The former Squire of Ephani, Eamon, and Sara. A native of Trinidad, Celena has a weakness for stiletto corset boots (and so do the boys, let me tell you). She is immensely efficient, loves lists, and never tells lies—after losing so many Dark-Hunters, she's convinced she has bad karma and won't dare tempt the Fates more than she already has.

She will break her very strict self-imposed rules only for Rafael Santiago, whose soul she had Acheron retrieve from Artemis. She passed the test and returned Rafael's soul, freeing him from his

Dark-Hunter bond so that they could be together for the rest of their lives.

Celena was drafted by the Squire Council to kill Jeff Brinks (Rafael's Squire at the time) for publishing his story based on the Dark-Hunters.

BLOOD RITE SQUIRE
HAIR/EYES: brown/dark brown

Delphinian   The Oracle of Delphi. Leader of the Oracle Squires.

Erikkson, Christopher Lars   Nickname: Chris. Wulf Tryggvason's Squire, and a direct descendent of Wulf's brother.

Because he is a blood relative, Chris falls through the loophole Acheron created in Wulf's unfortunate curse. He can remember the existence of Wulf, though folks like his mother—who married into the family—will keep on forgetting. (If you need a laugh, call Mrs. Erikkson sometime and ask her about her son's boss.)

Some member of the Tryggvason family has always been Wulf's Squire for this reason. Unfortunately, Chris is an only child.

Chris is a brilliant student—okay, technically he's a teacher's pet with perfect scores—who shared a few classes with Cassandra Peters (before she went and married his Dark-Hunter uncle). Not real smooth in the social skills department, Nick Gautier was Chris's only real friend.

Chris's claim to fame is a story you'll hear circulating around the Dark-Hunter watering holes. I'll fill you in, but be sure to have someone tell it to you with their own personal flair. In a desperate attempt to help his nephew "go forth and multiply", Wulf Tryggvason flew Britney Spears in for Chris's twenty-first birthday. Rumor has it they played Trivial Pursuit all night. Chris won. Britney ate all the birthday cake.

Born: April 21, 1981
Birthplace: St. Paul, Minnesota
Height: six feet
Hair/Eyes: black/blue
Dark-Hunter: Wulf Tryggvason

Gautier, Nicholas Ambrosius   Nick. Nick, Nick, Nick. (Sigh.)

Bastard son of a convict (who died in Angola during a prison riot), and a teenage exotic dancer on Bourbon Street (Cherise Gautier), Nick was raised in the back room of his mother's club and ran wild as a child. He was pulled off the streets by the Dark-Hunter Kyrian. It didn't take him long to become a brilliant prelaw student at Loyola and a technogeek computer whiz. According to Tad Addams, Nick could hack into anything.

Nick was Kyrian's Squire and best man at his wedding, drinking buddies with Tabitha Devereaux, and—despite his smart-mouthed, mule-headed, charming-as-hell self—the closest thing to a best friend Acheron ever had. After Kyrian's return to mortality, Nick became Talon's unofficial, part-time Squire.

It all sort of went to pot the night Nick made the worst decision of his life and slept with Simi ... though to his credit, he didn't know what she meant to Ash at the time. Ash went so crazy when he found out that he inadvertently cursed Nick by saying, "If I were you, I'd kill myself to save me the trouble of doing it later."

When Nick found his beloved mother after she had been murdered by the Desiderius-possessed Ulric, he took his own life so that Artemis would be forced to make him a Dark-Hunter and allow him his vengeance. Artemis—who cannot make a Dark-Hunter from a suicide—felt she had no right to Nick's soul, so she handed it over to Acheron.

Nick bears his bow-and-arrow mark on his face and neck, making it impossible to conceal (though it goes quite well with his Blood Rite tattoo). After Acheron gave Nick to Savitar to train,

Savitar handed him over to Ravyn Kontis. Angry at the world, Nick ran off and *really* went to the dark side. He made a pact with Stryker and drank his blood, an act that gave him silver eyes and godlike powers.

Like the world didn't have enough to worry about.

BORN: September 12, 1978
BIRTHPLACE: New Orleans, Louisiana
HEIGHT: six foot four
HAIR/EYES: dark brown/hazel blue (turned silver)
AGE AT DEATH: twenty-seven
POWERS: godlike

Greg   Squire who saw his Dark-Hunter burned to death in a holding cell.

DARK-HUNTER: Troy (deceased)

Kirby, Allen   A multigenerational Squire from Toronto, and a complete smart-ass. (That seems to be a Squire prerequisite, doesn't it?) Brother to Leo.

BLUE BLOOD SQUIRE

Kirby, Leo   Attended college with Susan Michaels; later became her boss at the *Daily Inquisitor*. Leo holds the office of Squire Regis of Seattle, and is in charge of the Theti Squire branch. He also sports a spiderweb Blood Rite tattoo on his left hand. Leo is always more receptive to a bearer of Starbucks.

SQUIRE REGIS
HAIR/EYES: black/gray
CURRENT LOCATION: Seattle, Washington

Lekti   Oracle Squires who keep the Book of Prophecy, where all important events in human history are predicted. It is said that even the end of the world is chronicled within its pages.

Liza   Liza is the extremely talented dollmaker who owns Dream Dolls and Accessories in New Orleans. She was Xander's Squire (pre-Brynna) and an Oracle for thirty-five years.

Liza is the master weapons designer famous for "Starla," an angel doll with three-inch blades that shot out of her feet, given as a gift to Amanda Devereaux that later killed Desiderius . . . the first time. In her spare time, she also likes to make jewelry and other innocent items (the "Accessories") equally as lethal. She's a touch deaf, so do yourself a favor—look at Liza and speak clearly when addressing her.

She also makes a great cup of tea.

DOREAN SQUIRE
HEIGHT: five feet (on a good day)
HAIR/EYES: white/brown
CURRENT LOCATION: New Orleans, Louisiana

Mallory, Keller   The former Squire of Dangereuse St. Richard. Be on your toes around Keller—he's a fast talker.

Poitiers, Kyl   Third-generation Squire by his mother and fifth generation on his father's side, Kyl hangs out a lot with Otto Carvaletti. He was thrilled to become a Blood Rite Squire, and he enjoys his job *waaaaay* too much.

BLOOD RITE/DOREAN SQUIRE
BORN: March 14, 1974
BIRTHPLACE: Christian, Mississippi

Rob   The former Squire of the Rogue Dark-Hunter Kyros, Rob has family in Nashville, Tennessee.

HEIGHT: five foot seven
HAIR/EYES: brown

Samuel, Carl   A former classmate of Tad Addams at Iowa

State, Carl is quite the computer nerd. He hangs out on the Dark-Hunter bbs with Tad a lot. So when you visit, make sure to say "Hi" to Carl.

DOREAN SQUIRE
BORN: September 4, 1975
BIRTHPLACE: Cedar Falls, Iowa

Sharon   Sharon is the former Squire of Streigar, a Dark-Hunter who was trapped by humans and exposed to daylight.

Simms, Andy   Jess Brady's Squire from Reno. Andy's father was Jess's Squire before him.

HEIGHT: six feet
HAIR/EYES: black/brown
CURRENT LOCATION: Reno, Nevada
DARK-HUNTER: Sundown

St. Germaine, Alec   A first-generation Squire who was caught hacking into the Dark-Hunter computer system. Alec was given a choice: Work with Tad and Carl, or die. Guess which one he picked, smart boy.

DOREAN SQUIRE
BORN: January 3, 1981
BIRTHPLACE: Dulac, Louisiana

St. James, Eric   Once a "vampire hunter" and snitch for the Dark-Hunters, Eric became a Barnacle Squire for Valerius when he first arrived in New Orleans. He is now a Dorean Squire, serving any Dark-Hunter who might need him.

More dangerous than all of those put together, Eric used to date Tabitha Devereaux. He's now happily married . . . to someone else.

DOREAN SQUIRE
HEIGHT: five foot eleven

Winstead, Tyler   Squire from Milwaukee. Tyler is what we like
to call intense.

DOREAN SQUIRE
CURRENT LOCATION: Milwaukee, Wisconsin

How to Roast a Daimon

*Apollites and the Origin and Weaknesses
of Daimons*

> It's messy and it's heartbreaking, but
> at the same time, it's a thrill ride.
> —Alexion

Birth and Death of the Apollites

Zeus and Apollo were walking through Thebes. (They may have walked into a bar . . . but that's not the point. Sounds good though, doesn't it?) Zeus looked down upon his puppy-eyed worshippers and commented on the perfection of the human race. Like every son who wants to one-up his father, Apollo scoffed, bragging that he could do better with one hand tied behind his back. To prove his point, he found a nymph to bear his more-perfect children, children who would hold the fate of the world in their hands. It was as true then as it is now—absolute power corrupts absolutely.

Sure, Apollo's had liaisons before, but he royally screwed it up with this one.

Made from his own flesh and blood, he dubbed the new race Apollite and gave them superior strength and psychic abilities. In three days, the first four Apollites were born, blond and beautiful and with psychic abilities. Three days later, they were adults. Three days after that, they were ready to take over the world.

Zeus wasn't having any of that nonsense. So he banned them from the earth. 'Cause he can do that sort of thing.

He banished the Apollites to Atlantis, where they brooded and stewed, intermarrying with the Atlantean natives. They were an aggressive race, ever pursuing their hunger for world conquest. The Apollites and Atlanteans intermarried, mixing blood until they truly became a race of people whose powers were unmatched. Apollo did not dissuade them. He looked forward to the day he would sit on Olympus as Supreme God.

In 10,500 B.C., the Apollites sent the beautiful virgin Clieto to Delphi as an offering to Apollo. The god fell in love with her, and she gave birth to ten of his children: five sets of twins. Clieto and her children were sent back to Atlantis, to intermarry with the Atlantean royal family and, inevitably, secure the rule of Atlantis by Apollo. Through Atlantis, Apollo meant to cast out Zeus and take his rightful place as ruler of the heavens and the earth.

After all, that's how Zeus did it. And his father before him . . . Apollo was just following the family tradition at this point.

Apollo himself fathered the first son of every Atlantean queen, hoping that each child would be the one chosen to bring about the downfall of the Atlantean gods. Each year, the Oracles turned him away.

(Now, this part gets confusing, so pay attention. It's a bit like the shell game. *Baby, baby, who's got the baby.* . . . Yeah, I've never been good at that one either.)

In 9548 B.C., Apollo fathered another son on the Atlantean queen, seducing her in the guise of her dead husband as a phantom in a dream. Talk about one seriously potent dream. Voilà: baby number one: Stryker.

The same year, the dreaded queen of the Atlantean gods, Apollymi, found that she was not barren, as had been originally supposed—she was pregnant with her first child. A child, the

Fates declared, who would bring about the end of their pantheon.

Enter baby number two: Apostolos.

Well, Archon wasn't ready to schedule the apocalypse just yet. His child or not, he demanded that his wife slay the baby upon its birth for the good of the world.

Right. Like Apollymi was going to let that happen.

She gave birth to her son prematurely, in secret, and hid him away. Lucky baby number two. When the time came to present Archon with the baby, Apollymi gave him a baby made of stone wrapped in swaddling.

Archon was furious. He knew his wife had hidden her baby . . . no doubt in the womb of a mortal woman. (Human wombs are apparently an exceptionally convenient place for gods needing to hide a cursed baby without a moment's notice.)

Which brings us back to baby numero uno: Stryker.

Archon knew the Atlantean queen was pregnant, so he demanded that her baby be slain as well.

You know, women don't take really well to executive orders regarding the death of their children.

By now, the queen had figured out that the baby she carried was Apollo's son. She knew that Apollo would never let his son be killed, especially by the Atlantean gods. She kept that smug thought close to her heart all throughout her labor. Only . . . the moment after she gave birth to her son, he was slain before her eyes.

What the Atlantean queen didn't know was that Apollo had pulled his own switcheroo—with the help of Artemis, Apollo had placed his unborn child inside the womb of one of his priestesses at Delphi.

The child the Atlantean queen had given birth to was baby number three.

Poor baby number three. He didn't live long enough to be a problem and the poor human queen wasn't told about the switch.

The Atlantean queen hated Apollo for abandoning her and her now-deceased child . . . and with good reason. A widow, she also resented the fact that Apollo never came back to her bed to get her pregnant again. She steeped in that bitterness, letting it infect her and poison her soul. Letting it breed vengeance. Letting the dish get nice and cold before she served it to Apollo on a silver platter.

Based on Apollo's gigolo history, she knew it was only a matter of time.

In 9529 B.C., nineteen years later, the Greeks gave it a go and tried to woo Apollo to their cause. They knew fighting against the Apollites was a lost cause, so to help win favor with Apollo and hopefully gain his backing they sent to him Ryssa, the most beautiful woman ever born. Ryssa instantly charmed the god and won his heart. Having the same weaknesses all deities seem to have, Apollo succumbed to her beauty and sowed his ever-fertile god seed. Ryssa bore him a son, and the tide of war changed in favor of the Greeks.

The Atlantean queen immediately ordered the death of Ryssa and her son, instructing her minions to not hold back in their brutality, to make it look as if wild animals had torn the woman and child to shreds.

They did their job, perhaps a little too well.

And so Apollo destroyed Atlantis (at least that's what Apollo says).

His beloved sister Artemis managed to stop him before he destroyed all the Apollites (and with them, the world), so instead he cursed his wayward children. He named them the wild animals that had slaughtered his mistress and son, giving them characteristics befitting such beasts (the fangs and eyes of predators) and forcing them to feed on one another's blood every few days in order to survive. He banished them from his domain, the sun, as he could no longer bear to look upon them and be reminded of their treachery.

To this day, Apollites only live to the age of twenty-seven: three times three times three, the age Ryssa was at her death. On the last day they die an excruciatingly painful death, slowly disintegrating to dust until the sun finally sets.

Absolute Power Corrupts Absolutely

Cowards aren't the only ones who die a thousand deaths. Sometimes heroes do too.

—Sin

Apollo overlooked one tiny little detail when he cursed his children—and that was that he had cursed *all* of them, including the infamous baby number one, tucked away all safe at Delphi.

Words have power. And, like Eddie Vedder says: Once spoken, they can't be taken back.

Apollo should have also considered this on his son's wedding day, which occurred before Apollo cursed his son's people. "In your hands you hold my future," he said. "Your blood is mine, and it is through you and your future children that I live." Too bad he didn't go to his own Oracle before he made that promise, huh? If he had, he'd have known that by making that particular pledge of loyalty, Apollo had just damned himself to extinction.

When his son's bloodline dies out, so will Apollo . . . and with him the sun itself, the earth, and all who dwell here.

Oops.

Cassandra Peters Tryggvason is a direct descendent of the son of Apollo (Stryker), and through her, her son Erik. If you ever find yourself in a situation to do so, you must protect these two people at all costs. They are worth more than your life and mine put together.

Not to be clichéd, but the fate of the world actually does depend on it.

Today, many Apollites blend in seamlessly with the human world, while others live in segregated communes. There are no records of all existing Apollite groups, but there are known Apollite communities in major cities all over the world, among them Athens, Buenos Aires, Helsinki, Hong Kong, London, Paris, Rio, Tokyo, and Montreal. In America, they can be found in New York, Seattle, Los Angeles, Las Vegas, Miami, and of course, New Orleans. (It is said that Apollites and Daimons stay away from Washington, D.C., due to the undesirable overpopulation of soulless politicians . . . but this may just be a rumor.) Daimons are often welcomed into these communes.

The Arcadians and Katagaria will always tolerate their cousin Apollites in their sanctuaries, but never Daimons. Their brethren they can control, but Daimons always mean trouble since it will invariably cause Dark-Hunters to come and Daimons tend to eat their paying clientele—it's just not good business sense.

Apollites are territorial, and their emblems may vary, but there are a few common themes. Most involve the sun (and therefore Apollo) in some form or fashion. Teardrops are also used to denote the loss of loved ones. These can appear as tattoos, banners, or signs. When an Apollite enters a community, they must swear a blood oath to uphold the laws and beliefs of that community for as long as they choose to reside there.

We certainly don't begrudge them their communities—the Apollite life is often lonely and always short. They have ventured far and wide over the long years to find safe lands for their children and brethren, and we respect that. Many Apollite children are orphaned and forced to live in small groups, or alone among humans. Many do not know their history, and do not find out until it is far too late.

It's a depressing proposition any way you slice it.

They may not all have blond hair (another rumor Daimons enjoy perpetuating), but they do have certain similar physical characteristics that are easy to spot if you're looking for them.

Full-blooded Apollites cannot be in sunlight. They will burst into dust if they are. Halfbloods are born with varying degrees of sunlight intolerance, but it's not something sunblock can cure. Most are so sensitive that they spend most—if not all—of their life underground.

Due to their shortened life span, Apollites today mature at an extremely advanced rate. (Congratulate me, I'm trying really hard not to make a Chia Pet analogy.)

Apollites reach adulthood at age eleven, and often marry between the ages of twelve and fifteen. (At an Apollite wedding, the bride is usually given away by a sponsor, since the parents are probably dead.)

They gestate their babies in about twenty weeks—roughly half the time of normal humans.

They all still die at twenty-seven. Halfbloods may live longer.

The only way for a full-blooded Apollite to survive past that age is to turn Daimon.

Daimons

*At worst, we just have a stomachache
from the blood.*
—Stryker

Daimons (what modern-day humans would call "vampires") cheat the twenty-seven-year death sentence by taking human souls into their bodies. Once an Apollite has a foreign soul, it turns them into something other than they were, something evil and uncaring. Any Apollite that takes a human soul into his or her body is instantly classified a Daimon. There's no real gray area there.

I suppose it's a bit like being pregnant—either you are, or you're not.

This, too, goes back to Apollymi—she was the one who adopted Stryker, Apollo's accidentally ill-fated son, and taught him how to take souls into his body in order to elongate his life. It was a lesson Stryker gladly shared with others of his race, legions of others who became Apollymi's grateful and willing servants.

As long as they maintain a soul, they live. But the human soul fades, so Daimons must feed every few weeks. The stronger a soul is, the longer it lasts, but even the strongest of souls can only last at most five to six months. The only soul that does not wane is that of an unborn child—it can sustain a body until that body dies.

Not surprisingly, Daimons prize the death of a child or pregnant woman above all else.

Apollites are not born instinctively knowing how to take a soul into their body. There are certain things that have to be learned. For instance, there is a coagulating gel in Apollite saliva, which is why they must continue to suck after opening a wound. (And let me tell you—you don't want an Apollite to spit in your eye. Hoo-boy. Kiss your vision good-bye after that one.) It's a significant education. A newly turned Apollite has to be trained, and so must find a Daimon willing to mentor them.

When a Daimon takes a soul, it takes all the powers with it, which is why it is very dangerous for a Were-Hunter to fall prey to a Daimon. However, the Daimon population does warn its brethren to be wary of the Weres, since they tend to have large, powerful families with long lives and long memories . . . who can also hunt in daylight.

If a soul is eaten by Daimons and it dies within his body, that soul is lost forever. And yes, some of us are constantly aware of how incredibly many are lost. I know for a fact that whenever a Daimon takes a soul, it screams . . . and Ash can hear it.

Think about that the next time you consider letting a Daimon out of your sight alive. If you kill them before the soul dies, the soul is freed and is then able to go to its eternal rest.

Daimons and vampires are not exactly synonymous. There are four kinds of vampires: soul-suckers, bloodsuckers, energy- or dream-suckers, and Slayers. (Slayers destroy simply for the sake of destruction.) Similarly, there are also different types of Daimons— they are listed in the following glossary. Beware of Spathi Daimons especially; they are the warrior Daimons that can and will put the most hurt on you. Even worse, you don't kill a Spathi Daimon. You release his essence, but if one of his brethren or children want to bring him back, they can. And have.

The one element all Daimons have in common is the shadowy "birthmark" that forms in the center of their chests when they cross over. This mark is where all the souls they have consumed gather. If punctured, it will release the captured souls and end the Daimon's life.

Which is pretty much what we're going for here.

Daimons can also die from exposure to sunlight, or from blood loss—like, say, if you ripped out one's jugular. (Ah, the things we learn from trial and error.) Dark-Hunter blood is poisonous to Daimons. Blood is important. Blood is life.

But it's best to always go for a Daimon's heart.

Strike at its most vulnerable spot.

That's Dark-Hunter to You

The bad guys don't knock.
—Romeo Pontis

Daimons aren't exactly going to seek you out, so you have to know where to find them. Luckily, newly formed Daimons aren't too bright (it's that whole "we're only twenty-seven and have limited world experience" thing), and tend to follow established feeding patterns and behavior. Unluckily, humans aren't much brighter and still tend to fall for some of the oldest tricks in the book.

Tips on How to Spot a Daimon

Sure Bets

- They look twenty-seven
- Blond roots
- Inkblot on chest
- Can't dance
- Mesmeric gaze, scoping the people around them—like a tiger eyeing a steak
- They know who you are and run as soon as you appear

Definite, but Not Definable

- Fangs
- Pasty complexion
- Smart-ass comments
- Tall
- Travel in even-numbered groups
- Irrationally scared of bees
- Teardrop tattoos
- Apollite tattoos (pictured here)

I know. Sad, but true.

(And hey, no offense if you used to be one . . .)

Long-haired Daimons with supermodel good looks tend to hang out with the Goth crowd. Think about it . . . what better place to blend in than with a bunch of other fanged, pasty-complexioned young people? Goth chicks think Daimon teeth are hot. Daimons think Goth chicks are like potato chips.

They can't eat just one.

One way to spot a Daimon in a Goth crowd is his superb diction—a Goth with custom-made vampire teeth won't have had the years of practice getting his tongue around them that a Daimon will. (How long did it take *you* to get around that particular impediment?)

Apollites are usually quite tall—a god like Apollo wouldn't have created a race of short people to take over the world, would he? Daimons use that gift to loom over their prey, giving them an immediate false sense of power, and making them more intimidating.

They also have that mesmeric gaze that made Dracula so sexy and popular in the old Hammer movies. Chicks totally dig that, apparently, too. Don't ask me why. Must be to do with the "brooding" part of the whole "dark and brooding" thing. They have a variety of psychic abilities, but like Dark-Hunters, they vary. You won't know what you're dealing with until you face them.

Another way to spot a Daimon in a Goth club is—and don't laugh—they can't dance. Seriously. Apollites have no problem in this arena. It's as if as soon as they cross over, they lose all sense of rhythm. (I think it might have something to do with them literally not having any soul.) Whatever the reason, it's a valid one to look out for.

Sometimes simple is best.

And yes, Daimons can enter clubs. In fact, they tend to own the clubs rather than dance in them. They can also come and go as they please from malls and other such public areas. Otherwise, they are indeed forbidden to enter private dwellings without an invitation. (Though chances are that scrumptious little Goth girl is probably going to invite the big bad Daimon in . . . unless she's seen him dance.) Hey, there's a reason punks invented slam dancing. Even a Daimon can do that.

Daimons won't drink the blood of the dead, and they are forbidden to feed on their Apollite brethren. That doesn't, of course, mean that there aren't Daimons who do . . . but they are hunted even more viciously by their own kind. Dead with a death wish, if you will.

Apollites are also very handy for spotting Daimons. Blood calls to blood, I suppose.

Watch your own reputation—a Dark-Hunter is the personification of Satan for the Apollites. He's the boogeyman, the monster under the bed, and the thing that will eat you if you don't clean your room or mind your mother. As for Acheron, well, he's the Angel of Death and the Grim Reaper and everything else all rolled into one. Apollites are born and bred in fear of the Dark-Hunters, so it is their natural instinct to hide and protect themselves from them.

From you.

If they do not live in established clans or communities, Apollites and Daimons have still been known to take up residence in crypts and catacombs. If they are surrounded by bodiless souls, they have a quick outlet to a pick-me-up when needed. They also have a pretty foolproof way of warding off Dark-Hunters.

Like killing two birds with one soul.

They travel in groups. Usually in even numbers. Kill one and the odd number will make them spaz—that is a joke by the way. We can only wish it were the truth. If they have a female with them, they will protect her at all cost if they are old school. If they're not, they might very well throw her at you as a shield, hoping you won't hit a girl. I know your mom taught you better, but in this case, hit her. Your life will depend on it.

Daimons use bolt-holes, or laminas, to travel between dimensions. These bolt-holes drop them in the banquet hall of Kalosis, which is why it is wise for a Dark-Hunter to never follow a Daimon through one. Daimons *must* step through a portal when one opens . . . which is a good thing to know if you happen to possess that particular ability.

During Mardi Gras of 2003, the threshold between Kalosis and the mortal world was very thin. Dark-Hunters were brought in from all over the globe to keep the situation under control. Some of them stayed. Some of them returned to the cities where they were stationed. Some of them left their otherwise immortal coil.

Such things happen when chaos takes a hand.

Either way, the last such occurrence was in the 1400s, and the next will be in the 2800s sometime. If you're just joining us now, that means you shouldn't be too worried about this one. (We hope.) Wait, did I say that out loud? Forget you heard it.

Not that you shouldn't be worried about an apocalypse in general, of course—you never know when the next god is going to have the next kid cursed by the Fates. Just don't worry overly much about Mardi Gras. Visit New Orleans and have a coffee and a beignet for me. Off a few Daimons. Enjoy yourself.

You do have the rest of that miserably long life to live, after all.

Oh—one more thing, the answer is no. No, no matter what you've heard, no matter how reliable your source may be, Daimons can*not* fly. Promise.

Cross my cold little heart. Unless Kyrian throws them off the hood of his speeding Lamborghini. Or you throw them off a building. While this can be highly entertaining, please don't as it will only tick the Daimon off and not kill him. He'll only die if by some fortunate act of some god (and they never do anything when it's actually convenient for you) he lands on something that pierces his mark.

One last thing: Daimons are afraid of bees. Since Apollo's son is a beekeeper, bee stings are lethal to them. I have no idea when you would use this information or how, but there you have it.

Daimon Directory

Here is a list of known Daimons, their branches, and the terms they use.

Learn it well.

Akelos/Agkelos   The Akelos are a branch of Daimons who find it hard to take the lives of "innocent" humans, so they only prey on criminals and predators. This sounds like a good deal on the surface, but the venom of the corrupt souls can overtake the Daimon and turn him or her into one very, very nasty customer. (See Trelos.) Their leader's name is Karlos.

Allegra   One of Stryker's four Spathi commanders.

Amaranda   Apollite wife of the Dark-Hunter Cael, Amaranda bears a bow-and-arrow tattoo on the small of her back entwined with a rose as a symbol of their love. She also has Spathi teardrop tattoos on her hand. Cael's nickname for her is Sunshine.

Amaranda accidentally turned Daimon after killing the Daimon who attacked her husband. She then saved Cael's life by forcing him to feed on the blood of a Daimon, turning him into . . . gods only know what.

Anaimikos   A Daimon who only feeds from other Daimons in order to survive.

Apati   These are the "fake" Spathi Daimons. Dark-Hunters (and many Apollites) can't differentiate between these and the true Spathi warriors. Most of the Apati are found living in and around human cities. They are tough, but not nearly as lethal as the real thing. Their high leader is Christof.

Arista   Member of the Illuminati.

Arod   One of Stryker's four Spathi commanders.

Athenians   This large community of Apollites has branches that are mostly found in and around the Apollites' native home-land of Greece. People and places friendly to this community are marked by various sun symbols.

Bloody Dungeon   Club in Transylvania where Daimons fre-quently pick up tourists wanting to meet "real" vampires . . . and where they're most likely to run into Velkan Danesti.

Bolt-holes   Doorways that open when a Daimon is in trouble. The Daimons have no control over them. (See Lamina.)

Buffites   Nickname for human vampire slayers. While they really do exist, they don't normally last long in a fight. They will, however, attack you as they can't tell the difference between you and the Daimons. Sucks (sorry for the pun), doesn't it? Here's the really sucky part. Since they're human, you can't attack back. You're supposed to protect them even while they're trying to stake you.

Callyx   Apollite husband of Dirce who became an incarnation of Thanatos. After he was defeated, Callyx was given the chance (by Acheron) to be reborn as human so that he might be with his wife. (See Thanatos.)

Carmillas   Women looking for Daimons to turn them into immortal vampires. Also called "Daimon Bait" or "Incredible Morons".

Chloe   Apollite bride whose wedding reception was crashed by the Dark-Hunter Rafael and the Squire Celena.

Cliff   Amanda Devereaux Hunter's annoying, half-Apollite ex-fiancé. A nice, quiet, average-looking data entry clerk on the sur-face, he broke off his engagement with Amanda after meeting her eccentric family . . . and then later betrayed her to Desiderius. Slimeball isn't a strong enough word.

Cult of Pollux A group of Apollites who take an oath to die exactly as Apollo intended for them to die—slowly, on the day of their twenty-seventh birthday. Members of the Cult of Pollux do not commit ritual suicide or become Daimon. Not well liked by other groups, cult members are usually found in remote areas.

It should be noted that every Apollite in the colony of Elysia has taken an oath to uphold the Cult of Pollux.

Davyn Member of the Illuminati who was made second-in-command to Stryker after the death of Trates. Davyn was once a close friend of Stryker's son Urian.

Dawn Surfer Slang for a Daimon exposed to sunlight. Known to the Dark-Hunters as "Daimon Flambé".

Day-Slayer Apollite myth of a Daimon-Apollite that can walk in sunlight. It is believed that one day the Day-Slayer will come and unite all the Daimons, so that they can take their rightful (according to Apollo) place as supreme rulers of the earth. (See Thanatos.)

Deadmen Walking Humans who serve Daimons usually because they have been promised immortality. They're also called really stupid.

Delphinians Daimon Oracles. Found throughout the world, it is believed they can summon the bolt-holes at will. You can recognize them by the dolphin tattoo or jewelry they all carry.

Desiderius Nickname: Desi. Demigod son of Bacchus (Dionysus) and an Apollite woman, Desiderius was a Spathi Daimon with a grudge against the Devereaux family. His Apollite wife (Eleanor) died at the age of twenty-seven.

Desiderius was originally killed by Kyrian and Amanda Hunter. Unfortunately, due to his Spathi nature, he spent some time as a noncorporeal ghost haunting everybody.

Later, Stryker awarded Desiderius the ability to reincarnate. 'Cause some people just can't have enough of a bad thing.

He finally wound up taking over the body of the Dark-Hunter Ulric, where he wreaked havoc on a major killing spree, taking the lives of Kyrian and Amanda Hunter, Tia Devereaux, the Dark-Hunter Kassim, and Cherise Gautier. Ulric/Desi was finally stabbed and decapitated by Valerius Magnus and Tabitha Devereaux.

Dikisi   Also called Vengeance Daimons, the Dikisi specifically target humans who have preyed on Apollites, as well as Dark-Hunters and any who help or serve them. They are governed by a series of leaders, and only the strongest of them is capable of leadership. If a leader is perceived as weak, he is overthrown and killed by his next in command.

Dirce   When a previous incarnation of Thanatos destroyed Taberleigh (the village where Zarek lived), Zarek fought his way to the Apollite village where Thanatos sought asylum, determined to kill him. In the battle, Thanatos threw an Apollite in front of him whom Zarek unintentionally killed—that was Dirce. Dirce's husband, Callyx, sought his own vengeance and became the new Thanatos (after Ash killed the one who attacked Taberleigh).

Dirce was reborn into the mortal world as a human named Allison Grant; a dance major sophomore at Ohio State University. After his defeat, Ash gave Thanatos/Callyx the opportunity to be reborn as a human, so that he might be with his former wife.

Doulos   Human servants of Apollites or Daimons. The doulosi guard and protect the Daimons from being discovered or hunted by humans. Their blood can tide a Daimon over if they are desperate, but they are only killed when they have betrayed their masters or are no longer necessary. Most of the doulosi believe their masters have the ability to turn them into Daimons, and that by doing so they will obtain immortality. I'm telling you, these people watch too many Hammer flicks.

Draco Believed to be the oldest Daimon alive, it is said that Draco commands his own Katagaria pack—a rare sight for sure. Legend has it that he is Apostolos, son of Apollymi and the missing heir to Atlantis. He, like Acheron, also travels with a demon that he commands.

Dyana Stryker's Apollite daughter and sister to Urian, Dyana died on her twenty-seventh birthday, when she refused to turn Daimon.

Eleanor The Apollite wife of Desiderius who died at the age of twenty-seven when she refused to turn Daimon.

Elysia One of the oldest Apollite communities in North America, Elysia is hidden beneath a mountain. Urian, named protector of the city, showed the inhabitants how to build it.

Expire Slang term for killing a Daimon.

Fabio/Cato Derogatory term for a Daimon, stemming from the fact that they are all tall, blond, and good-looking.

Gatopoulous, Damien The Daimon manager of Sin's casino in Las Vegas. He's as sarcastic a match for Katra Agrotera as you'll ever see. And if you want to stay on Sin's good side, fight the instinct to kill Damien if you ever cross his path. Sin would be highly offended and since he's not really a Dark-Hunter, he could put a major hurt on you.

Happy Hunting Ground Apollite-Daimon bar in Seattle, Washington. There is a black dragon silhouette flying against a yellow sun on the club's sign—this symbol is the international welcome mat for Apollites and Daimons. It's also the home of Cael, who patrols it. Stay away should you ever find yourself in Seattle.

Heilig, Ben   Daimon son of Paul Heilig, Seattle Chief of Police, and brother to Derrick.

Heilig, Derrick   Daimon son of Paul Heilig, Seattle Chief of Police, and brother to Ben. Derrick was killed by the Apollite Amaranda.

I am the Light of the Lyre   "I am the Light of the Lyre and I walk in his grace" is the phrase used by Daimons and Apollites seeking shelter from another Daimon or Apollite. The "Light of the Lyre" refers to their ancestors' kinship to Apollo.

Icarus   A known Daimon.

Illuminati   The thirty or forty oldest and most powerful of the Spathi Daimons, and the last of the Atlanteans. The Illuminati are the bodyguards of Apollymi, and they are led by Stryker. Then again, *all* Spathi are led by Stryker. He has a god complex (sorry, couldn't resist that crack).

Inkblot   Derogatory term for Daimons, stemming from the strange black mark that all Daimons develop on their chests at the moment they cross over, the mark where the souls they have stolen collect. This spot is where a dagger or other sharp weapon must penetrate in order to kill the Daimon.

Iroas   Iroas means "hero" in the Apollite language. A Daimon hero is an Apollite who can find it in himself to defy Apollo and his "minions". This term also refers to anyone who crosses over from Apollite to Daimon—the ultimate defiance.

Kalasian   The Kalasian are Apollite angels of mercy. Found all over, they usually live among the humans, but are willing to aid any Apollite they find. Many of the Kalasian are located in the Arcadian or Katagaria sanctuaries.

Karones   A community of Apollites found in areas across North America, usually Canada and the northern United States.

Unlike most Daimons, members of the Karones tend to frequent cooler climates.

Kathoros   Said to be even more evil than the Spathi, Kathoros Daimons are rare. At one time they were believed to have been the servants of the Atlantean war god Misos. Like the Arcadian Sentinels, one half of a Kathoros Daimon's face is tattooed, and legend says they shave their heads.

Katoteros   The Atlantean term for "heaven". and currently the home realm of Acheron Parthenopaeus. All Apollites and Daimons dream of being able to reclaim their right to rest in Katoteros.

Katoteros.com   Apollite-Daimon Web site that teaches about the Apollite history and way of life and warns the Daimons about specific Dark-Hunters. (Yeah, we've got their number.) It is made to look like a Greek history site, but there are password-protected areas. Don't worry, we've got a team of Squires assigned to cracking those. It's only a matter of time.

Kerri   Apollite sister of Amaranda. Kerri was killed by one of Paul Heilig's Daimon sons.

Lakis, Maia   Apollite doctor and member of the Cult of Pollux who helped Cassandra Tryggvason give birth to her son Erik while in Elysia. Dr. Lakis died naturally very soon after, at age twenty-seven.

Lamina   Atlantean term for "haven". Laminas are portals between Kalosis and the human world, often used by Spathi Daimons to escape Dark-Hunters. They are also commonly referred to as "bolt-holes".

The term *lamina* also applies to any Were-Hunter sanctuary, since both Apollites and Daimons are safe from Dark-Hunters there. There is more information on these kinds of laminas in the section on Were-Hunters.

Mavrovian   A community of Apollites whose branches are located in the warmer climates. Mavrovians can often be found in and around the Mediterranean. They are exceptionally secretive. Many of them carry the mark of the lyre.

Ryssa   Ryssa was the princess given to Apollo by the Greeks. She was one of his favorite mistresses. At the time, Ryssa was declared the most beautiful woman in the world.

She and her son (whom Apollo fathered) were brutally murdered by servants of the jealous Apollite queen, the act that caused Apollo to curse all Apollites, damning them for eternity and creating the Daimons.

Peters, Nia   Cassandra's sister and Jefferson Peters's half-Apollite daughter. Along with her sisters, Nia was one of the last direct descendents of Apollo. She died alongside her mother when Spathi Daimons blew up their car.

Peters, Phoebe   Cassandra's sister and Jefferson Peters's half-Apollite daughter. Along with her sisters, Phoebe was also one of the last direct descendents of Apollo. She was rescued from the Spathi car bomb that killed her mother and sister Nia. Phoebe was turned Daimon by her savior (and later husband), Urian. She remained an Animakos Daimon until she died in Elysia, saving Cassandra and her newborn son from Stryker.

Rigas   Much like a Were-Hunter Regis, Rigas are the leaders of certain branches of Daimons who travel in packs. Daimons in that pack must swear ultimate fealty to their Rigas. Once that oath is taken, it is eternal. The only way out is death.

Scuds   Slang term for young Daimons out to prove themselves worthy. They are headstrong and belligerent, and they tend to talk big (bigger than normal). They should be slightly easier to kill. *Should* be. Don't show them any mercy, just to be on the safe side.

Shanus The Supreme Councilor of Elysia.

Sirius One of Stryker's four Spathi commanders.

Spathi The Spathi are elite and evil Warrior Daimons. They are Apollymi's guards and pets. Spathis can be reincarnated after they die, as their disembodied essence will remain intact. The true Spathi can be identified by the mark of a yellow sun that holds a black dragon in its center. Stryker is their leader.

Strykerius (aka Stryker) Also known as the Daimon king. Stryker is the adopted son of Apollymi, and the only Spathi allowed in her presence. The direct son of Apollo, Stryker was one of the first Apollites cursed. Because of this, he hates his father passionately. Wouldn't you?

It was through his adoptive mother's teachings that Stryker learned the art of harvesting souls to elongate his own life—a secret he happily shared with his Apollite brethren. He was the first Daimon, and he is the commander of their legions.

You may notice that Stryker shares Acheron's silver god-blessed eyes, but he was not born with them. Stryker got those eyes only after he scorned his father Apollo. The details after that as we know them are kind of sketchy.

Ever vigilant, Stryker also holds a grudge against Acheron, and vows to rid the world of everything and everyone Ash holds dear. Essentially, Stryker feels as if he's been betrayed by the whole world, and he has vowed to see his father, Apollymi, and Acheron fall at any cost. He's one bad mama-jama and he makes no bones about it, but despite his rage he is forbidden to harm the Abadonna (Katra) or the Elekti (Acheron).

Stryker may be a ruthless Daimon, but he does have a code of honor. He is the leader of the Illuminati and father of Urian (the only person Stryker ever loved). Of course, that didn't stop Stryker from slitting Urian's throat when he discovered his son's betrayal and leaving him for dead.

Beware: Stryker also has the ability to transform into a large, black dragon.

HEIGHT: six foot eight
HAIR/EYES: ebony/silver

Summoning, The   The name for a Daimon homing beacon the Day-Slayer can use to summon Daimons and Apollites to conference, or for war.

Terrence   Daimon brother-in-law of Paul Heilig, Seattle Chief of Police.

Tiber   One of Stryker's four Spathi commanders.

Trates   Stryker's second-in-command. While in Seattle, Trates was stabbed in the back and killed by Paul Heilig in 2006.

Trelos   The Trelos are insane Daimons that even other Daimons hunt and kill. Trelos start out as Akelos who have taken so many criminal and evil souls that they have destroyed their very own nature and sense of self. They no longer have control of their bodies, and they will kill anyone they come into contact with, Apollite, human, or Daimon, whether they need to feed or not. They have no leader.

Tryggvason, Cassandra Elaine   (née Peters) Half-human/half-Apollite and the last of Apollo's direct bloodline, Cassandra is the daughter of Jefferson Peters (human), and sister to Nia and Phoebe. She is a graduate of the University of Minnesota.

In order to survive unmolested as a human, Cassandra had her teeth filed down at the age of ten, and received bimonthly blood transfusions. She wears a small signet ring on her right hand that her mother gave to her before she died—a ring the Atlantean kings used when they were married. She also has five pink teardrops tattooed on her palm that form a flower's petals, in honor of her mother and sisters.

Cassandra was married to Wulf Tryggvason while seeking asylum in Elysia. She was brought back to life (after mutually feeding off her husband, as advised, and then dying, which was unforeseen) by Acheron. When he revived her, Ash also revoked from her and her progeny the daylight curse of the Apollites. She is the mother of Erik Tryggvason.

HEIGHT: six foot one
HAIR/EYES: strawberry blonde/hazel-green
POWERS: latent telepathy

Tryggvason, Erik Jefferson Son of Wulf and Cassandra Tryggvason, and therefore also a direct descendent of Apollo. Both he and his mother *must* be protected at all cost.

Tselios, Theo, Dr. Apollite-Daimon veterinarian who captured the Dark-Hunter/Were-Hunter Ravyn Kontis in feline form and trapped him in a Seattle animal shelter. Dr. Tselios was later killed by Stryker.

Urian Stryker's last surviving son, Urian was the first child ever to be naturally born a cursed Apollite. He was at one time second-in-command of the Illuminati. Urian saved Phoebe Peters (whom he later married) from the explosion that killed her mother and sister Nia.

Acheron saved Urian when his father slit his throat for treachery, reincarnating him and turning him into something other than Daimon or Apollite . . . as only Ash can do.

BORN: 9526 B.C.
BIRTHPLACE: Delphi

Van Helsings Slang term for human vampire slayers.

Zolan Stryker's third-in-command.

Great Gods All Mighty

Dealing with Demons, Demigods, Deities, and All Other Things Immortal

So, can I eat the redheaded goddess now?
—Simi

The Wrath of the Gods

They're sensitive, emotionally volatile, and prone to violent outbursts. No, it's not your ex-girlfriend with PMS ... meet the gods (who are like an ex-girlfriend with PMS that can read every thought in your head). You treat them much the same way: Compliment them generously, shower them with gifts, and keep a safe distance. Only do it more so with the gods, because (unless you were very unfortunate) your ex-girlfriend isn't going to turn you into a spider or curse you until the end of time.

Remember that nifty double bow-and-arrow mark you got from a certain goddess after your Act of Vengeance? You know where I'm coming from.

Demigods are the sons or daughters of gods, the product of a dalliance with a nymph or human (it happens more than you think). Demons are the "animals" (and no, they won't excuse that expression, so don't you ever repeat it) of the immortal world.

Some are merely pets, protectors, and playthings, but some are intelligent enough to have thwarted the gods themselves.

Any way you slice it, it's important to remember one thing: If it's immortal, it has the ability to make your life more of a living hell than it already is. Yes, you've got superpowers and would be able to hold your own . . . for a while. Just don't.

Summoning Gods

Cupid, you worthless bastard, I summon you
to human form.
—Julian Alexander

The proper way to summon a god is to say the following: *"[Name of god], I summon you to human form"* . . . or some close variation thereof.

Please know what you're getting yourself into before you summon a god. Refresh your memory by reading the proper summon again. Be *reeeeally,* really sure this is what you want to do.

Also keep in mind that all the gods (save Artemis, of course) are forbidden to help the Dark-Hunters. And really don't count on her coming with a cavalry either. You are a soldier of Artemis, her pet if you will (or if you don't, up to you), and the rest of the gods will keep a safe distance from you because of that.

However, just because they're *forbidden* to help you doesn't mean they *won't.* You try to forbid a god something. Go ahead. Let me know how that turns out for you.

If you're summoning a god to ask a favor from them, remember that you can't get something for nothing—especially with these folks. Compassion isn't one of their biggest traits. You better have something to barter with, something good, or they'll come up with something they want that you might not be prepared to give (very often a soul, and not always yours). And once they have their hearts set on something, that's the way the deal goes down or not at all. Tread carefully, and be prepared.

Power of the Gods

Sweetie, in our world, fair's got nothing to do with anything. He who has the greatest power wins. It's why we're all willing to kill each other off without flinching.
—Solin

Thunderbolts, immortality, resurrection—who wouldn't want god-powers? Watch yourself on Mount Olympus though; the big guys can instantly sense when someone is using an unauthorized or unfamiliar power. It's the best security system in the world.

Gods always want the best, and must always have the best of anything and everything. Better than humans; better than other gods. Gods, like all immortals, can't have addictions. Despite their love for caffeine and their fondness for spirits that have nothing to do with souls, they won't get a buzz, nor will they get drunk. (Hard to say never, though, since Dionysus has a way about him that tends to get around those rules . . . but I digress.) Of course, you don't need to be drunk to be bold, arrogant, or stupid. So why bother? Save yourself the calories.

Anyone with a god's blood in them has that god's protection, as well as immortality. Blood is important. And be careful—you never know who you'll run into at the grocery store whose ancestor is a god. Ask Cassandra Tryggvason (descendent of Apollo), or Sunshine Runningwolf (granddaughter of the Morrígan). Anyone who is a god, or has even the tiniest bit of god blood, has a certain aura and scent that can be discerned by a sensitive individual. Learn to be sensitive in a killer kind of way.

It is also important to note that if a god is defeated by another god, a chunk of the loser's powers is absorbed by the victor. Not quite *all* the powers, of course, and we're talking true and utter defeat here, not just plain old competition. (If that were true, Athena would be goddess of the Sea as many times as she's kicked Poseidon's water-pruned butt over the years.) Any time a major god is killed, their powers are released back into the universe. If no one absorbs them, they can easily detonate like a nuclear bomb . . . especially if the dying god was born of the sun or the moon. (Acheron Parthenopaeus, anyone?)

As far as the Chthonians are concerned, the only person capable of killing a Chthonian is another Chthonian. If the person talking to you has really funky eyes, stay on their good side.

God-powers can also be obtained by consuming ambrosia, as in the case of Valerius Magnus or Zarek of Moesia.

Holy Moly

Well it isn't every day we fish a nearly naked
god out of the sea, now is it?
—Thia

There are indeed more things in heaven and earth than are dreamt of in our philosophy . . . or contained within these meager pages. There are a great many books on the different gods and their pantheons, be they Greek, Roman, Norse, or Egyptian. For further reading, I suggest starting with *Bulfinch's Mythology*, or Edith Hamilton's *Mythology*. But please remember that these are cursory guides and by no means are the end-all, be-all information on the gods. The ancient scribes took a lot of liberty when writing about their superbeings and much of that is contradictory. Case in point, in some myths Artemis is a virgin. In others, she's the lover of not only Orion, but also her brother Apollo. Still, Bulfinch and Hamilton are a good starting point.

Where you go from there is up to you.

The gods and goddesses appear in this guide by their Greek names (when applicable), along with their Roman name in parentheses. Their totem symbols—including animals, birds, and trees—are listed beneath their description.

Aeacus Former Greek king of the island of Aegina, Aeacus was famous for his sense of righteousness and his ruling of his people with a steady hand. To honor him, he was appointed one of the judges of the dead in Hades. Aeacus oversees the souls of those of European descent.

Aengus/Angus Irish god of Love and Youth; the product of the god Dagda's affair with a married woman. In order to hide their fling, Dagda made the sun stand still for nine months . . . so Aengus was technically conceived and born in one day. He fell in love with a girl (Caer) he saw in his dreams. After searching the world for her he found her trapped in the body of a swan, so he turned himself into a swan to be with her.

Agapa Love is blind. That current universal truth finds its origin in Agapa, the Atlantean goddess of Love. Unlike her Greek counterpart Aphrodite, Agapa is virginal. The embodiment of pure love, she has never allowed anyone to touch her. She is also the goddess of Childbirth and Hearth and Home. It is said that she was born the moment Archon first looked at his half-sister Apollymi. His heart swelled to ten times its normal size and out of it popped Agapa (Love) and Chara (Joy).

HAIR: red

Agrona Celtic goddess of War and Strife.

Agrotera, Katra Nickname: Kat. Daughter of Acheron Parthenopaeus, Katra was handmaiden to both her mother Artemis and her grandmother Apollymi. (Artemis released Katra from her service as handmaiden so that Apollymi could help

Acheron.) She served as bodyguard to Cassandra Peters. She also worked with Eneas Kafieri in his search for Atlantis, and later with his daughter Megeara.

Raised on Olympus, Katra used to sneak into Athena's temple and play with the owls. She is known as the Abadonna. "Agrotera" is also one of the Greek names for Artemis, meaning "strength" or "huntress". Katra is as quick and deadly with her body as she is with her wit. She lives to taunt any male she can find, especially Stryker.

Katra's powers, derived from both the sun and the moon, are second only to Acheron. (She was once forbidden to be near or touch her father, as he was blind to those closest to him, but she was always his unknown protector.) At sixteen, she became able to invoke Apollymi's powers as well. She is also a "conduit," through which godlike powers can be transferred. On the downside, her healing powers only work on other people. She can feel emotions, but cannot trace their root. And the longer she is away from either the sun or the moon, the weaker she becomes.

She has a small sfora from her father with Acheron's DNA in it that she wears around her neck; it was this sfora that she used to help imprison the Dimme. She has a bow-and-arrow tattoo just above her left hip, and a tattoo on her stomach of a sun. Some say it's the mark of the Destroyer; others believe it's the mark of Apostolos. More than likely, it's both.

Kat has incredible weaknesses for New York at Christmas, flannel pajamas, chocolate, and her Dark-Hunter, Sin. After Katra was bitten by a gallu demon, Acheron blood-bonded his daughter to Sin in order to save her. She must drink from him every so often to survive.

HEIGHT: six foot four
HAIR/EYES: blonde/green
FEATURED NOVEL: *Devil May Cry*

Alastor Demon who sometimes works with the Were-Hunters to cause mischief. Conjured by Vane Kattalakis's mother, Bryani, Alastor brought Bride McTierney back in time to Dark Age Britain. Has dark purple skin, flaming red hair and eyes, twisted feet, and large teeth.

Alecto One of the Furies. (See Erinyes.) Whereas Nemesis seeks vengeance on crimes committed in anger against the gods, Alecto seeks vengeance on crimes committed in anger against man. She is the Fury in charge of increasing anger.

Alera One of the Dolophoni. She has bright red hair.

Alexander, Julian (aka Julian of Macedon, Augustus Julius Punitor [Julian the Great Punisher]), Champion of Greece, Macedonia, Thebes, Punjab, and Conjara. Demigod son of Aphrodite and Diokles of Sparta, Julian was dipped in the river Styx (like Achilles) so that he would be invulnerable. Pretty much the sexiest thing to walk the planet (and I'm not even into blonds). Julian was cast out of Olympus by Zeus only hours after his birth.

Reared in the manner of his Spartan brethren, he knew no love of any kind. His childhood was harsh and unforgiving. As a man, he fought his way to the top and became the most feared Macedonian general of his time. He was the original commanding officer of Kyrian of Thrace.

He fathered two children, Atolycus and Callista, by his mad wife Penelope. She later killed them both, before committing suicide, when she found out that Julian had tricked her into loving him by shooting her with one of Eros's arrows.

Julian was cursed—trapped inside a book—at age thirty-two (149 B.C.) by his brother Priapus, after having sex with one of Priapus's prized virgins. Julian was forced to be the monthlong love slave of any woman who conjured him. He was rescued from the book in 2002 by his now-wife Dr. Grace Alexander.

He currently resides in New Orleans with his family, and is a professor of history and the classics at Loyola and Tulane as well as being an Oracle. He is a ridiculously inept driver.

Born: 182 B.C.
Birthplace: Sparta, Greece
Height: six foot three
Hair/Eyes: blond/blue
Featured Novel: *Fantasy Lover*

Anatum   Ancient Sumerian goddess of Creation and wife of Anu. She was the first victim of the gallu demons—Anu caged her after she tried to bite him in his sleep. Sin and his daughter Ishtar destroyed Anatum; Ishtar absorbed her powers to replace her in the pantheon.

Anemoi (Venti)   Gods of the Winds: Boreas (North), Notus (South), Eurus (East), and Zephyros (West).

Annwn   The Underworld in Welsh mythology, or "land of departed souls". Also called Annwfn. Annwn is ruled by Arawn, Lord of the Underworld.

Anu   Ancient Sumerian god who created the gallu to combat the Sumerian pantheon's enemies. (Specifically, they were created to battle against the Charonte demons.) He was ultimately killed by them. Some of his powers were locked up in the Tablet of Destiny.

Aphrodite (Venus)   Greek goddess of Love, Beauty, and Sexual Rapture. Mother of Priapus, Eros, Julian, Anteros, Hymenaios, and Aeneas (among others). Daughter of Uranus. (Not, as is commonly thought, Zeus and Dione. Blame Homer.) Aphrodite is the wife of Hephaestus, but remains promiscuous, and has taken many lovers. She is often referred to as Kypris, Vanessa, or Cytherea.

Hair/Eyes: blonde/blue
Bird: dove, swan
Animal: dolphin
Tree: pomegranate, lime

Apollo   Greek god of Light, often called Phoebus. He is also the god of Music, Prophecy, Medicine, Plague, Poetry, Dance, and many others. The son of Zeus and Leto, and twin to Artemis. One of the only men allowed to set foot in the temple of Artemis (Ash is the other one).

One of Apollo's famous love affairs involved his infatuation with the nymph Daphne, a passion invoked by Eros in revenge for Apollo's mocking. Daphne did not share the god's love and so she ran from Apollo's embrace, finally transforming into a laurel tree to escape him.

Another love affair involved the infamous Cassandra, who spurned Apollo after learning the art of his prophecy. In his anger Apollo cursed Cassandra, so that no one who heard her prophecies would ever believe her.

Apollo killed Acheron when Ryssa was slain. He also claims that it was he who trapped Apollymi in Kalosis, since he was the greater god.

As you can see, Apollo is pretty full of himself.

BIRD: swan
ANIMAL: wolf, dolphin
TREE: laurel
SYMBOL: tripod (prophecy), lyre (music)

Apollymi   The Atlantean goddess of Life, Vengeance, Death, and Wisdom, Apollymi is the daughter of Chaos and Zenobi (the Atlantean north wind). She holds many epitaphs including: the Destroyer, the Bringer, the Giver, Biosia (Life), Thanata (Death), Magosa (Wisdom), and Fonia (the Killer). Her name is also the Atlantean word meaning "soul".

Capricious and vain, she is the most powerful of all the Atlantean gods and can only be controlled by her half-brother and husband Archon. She travels in the wind and can strike down her victims in an instant. It is said those who are about to die by her hand can glimpse her blond hair swirling in the mist a second before they die; at the instant of their death, the last vision they hold is her merciless pale eyes.

A goddess of contradictions (I'm sure she's a Gemini), Apollymi tends to be loving and kind in one breath and then brutal and cold in the next. No one is safe from her wrath, so Archon imprisoned her in Kalosis, where she can see the human world and other gods, but not affect them. She was sent to this realm while her natural son lived, and when he died, she escaped and went on a killing spree. The Greek gods put her back but no one knows how . . . or if they do, they're not telling.

There are various legends that tell of her release. Some claim it is only by the sacrificial blood of an Atlantean that she can be freed, while others claim it is strictly the hand of her lost son Apostolos that can free her. Because of her imprisonment, she alone escaped death when Atlantis was destroyed. Now she sits in her prison, awaiting her release so that she can wreak her havoc across the earth and bring about Telikos—the end of the world as we know it.

She calls to the sensitive humans of the world, those with Atlantean in their blood, begging them to discover the sacred seal and release her from imprisonment. Her cry is like a beacon, interpreted by many as a mad obsession for the discovery of Atlantis. This call was heard by Megeara Kafieri, and other members of her family.

Apollymi protects and uses the Spathi Daimons as her army, keeping a group of around thirty Illuminati as her guards, in addition to Charontes and ceredons. She enjoys finishing off her victims with an iron hammer.

HAIR/EYES: white blonde/silver

Apostolos (Acheron) Son of Apollymi, also known as the Messenger. Amorphous and ever-changing, Apostolos was conceived by Apollymi during a night of divine sex with Archon. He is the harbinger that will bring about Telikos—the destruction of the world.

Apostolos was destined to be his mother's heart, and to aid her in her destructive ways. But when the Fates told Archon that Apostolos would be the destruction of the Atlantean pantheon, Archon demanded Apollymi kill the fetus in order to protect all of them. Apollymi refused. She hid her fetus away from the other gods and when they demanded his life, she offered them a stone baby instead.

Angered by her actions, the gods feared what she would do once her son grew to manhood. Combining their powers, they imprisoned Apollymi and cursed Apostolos to die. It is believed that he perished with Atlantis, yet there are others who claim the baby survived and was taken to Europe and hidden away. Some claim he is the mysterious founder of the region known as Basque. Arikos is positive Apostolos is alive and that he speaks to his mother, calming her down when she's extremely irate and threatening to destroy the world. (In reality, Apostolos is Acheron, but you're not supposed to know that. Don't worry, you'll forget that soon enough.)

Only black flowers grow in Apollymi's garden in memory of her son.

Arachne   The famous and unfortunate young woman who challenged Athena to a weaving contest. Either no one told Arachne that Athena never loses, or Arachne was too vain to care. Her loss. Literally. Arachne hung herself in shame, but Athena revived her . . . and turned her into a spider, destined to weave for all time.

Archon   Also called "Kosmetas", which means "orderer". Atlantean counterpart to Zeus. He is the son of Chaos and Fegkia (Splendor), and mate of Apollymi.

It is said that Fysia spun strands of Archon's hair to form Atlantis, and that she used her blood to fertilize the earth (and to create the blood-red Fysian lilies that could only thrive in Atlantean soil). Overwhelmed by the beauty of the continent his sister had created, Archon wept. As his tears fell, the race of the Atlanteans sprang up.

Archon held many epithets: Kosmetas (Orderer), Soter (Savior), and Theokos (the Divine One). He was a god of extreme patience and kindness. The exact opposite of his wife Apollymi, he was said to be the balance that she needed so that the order of the universe could be adequately maintained. He adored his wife and, unlike the other gods, was never faithless to her (at least that's the story *he* tells). He watched over his children and people with benediction and care. When Zeus banished the Apollite race to Atlantis, Archon welcomed them in, thereby causing perpetual strife between the Atlantean gods and the Greek.

However, Archon's wrath, when incurred, was every bit as ruthless as that of Apollymi. When the Deridians attacked Atlantis and sacked Kanosis (the capital city of Atlantis), he struck their country with his mighty thorn-hammer and destroyed every man, woman, and child who bore their blood.

He also ordered the death of Apostolos and trapped Apollymi in Kalosis. There are those who say that Apostolos, if ever found, holds the ability to raise his father from the dead and to return Archon to his throne.

As a point of interest: Archon did not like many, but he liked Simi.

Ares (Mars)　Greek god of War; the son of Zeus and Hera. Born in Thrace. Ares is not exactly what you would call a benevolent god . . . after all, not even his parents like him. He is a mercenary, fighting for any side no matter what the cause, reveling in the sound of battle, delighting in danger.

The Romans, who glorified war and battle, liked Mars (Roman for Ares) much better than the Greeks liked Ares (Homer had the *cojones* to call him a coward). He was never to them the mean, whining deity of the *Iliad*, but a magnificent and invincible warrior.

Ares has been defeated in battle by his sister Athena (twice), Heracles (Hercules), and the sons of Aloeus.

BIRD: vulture
ANIMAL: dog

Ariman   Ancient Phoenician god who visited Atlantis while it was being destroyed and is now stuck in human form. Not to be confused with the god that follows.

Ariman   Ancient Persian god, not to be confused with the deitically challenged Ariman in the above listing.

Aristaeus   Demigod of Hunting, Husbandry, and Beekeeping. Protector of cattle and fruit trees. Son of Apollo and the nymph Cyrene.

Artemis (Diana)   Daughter of Zeus and Leto, and twin to Apollo. Greek goddess of the Hunt, the Moon, Virginity, Childbirth, and Wild Animals; creator of the Dark-Hunters. She, like Apollymi, is a study in contradictions. A very possessive goddess, she does not easily give up what is hers. The Dark-Hunters are decidedly hers.

Also known as Amarynthia, Diana, or Cynthia (she is sometimes confused with Bastet and Selene . . . though trust me, after that bow-and-arrow mark, you're not going to confuse her with anybody). Common epitaphs are: Potnia Theron (mistress of wild animals), Kourotrophos (nurse of youths), Locheia (helper in childbirth), and Agrotera (huntress). Her bows are made for her by Hephaestus.

When Apollo called upon Artemis for help with his cursed Apollites, Artemis turned to the Atlantean hero Acheron. She convinced him to help her hunt down and destroy the Daimons. At least . . . that's how the story goes. No one's really sure what the truth is behind Ash and Artie. But if you do look at her in a certain light, you can see her fangs.

And watch out for the crazy talk—our beloved goddess is not the most adept at colloquial slang. (My favorite is still when she says, "You're baked bread!" instead of "You're toast!" Kind of loses its edge, doesn't it?)

HAIR: red
SYMBOL: double bow and arrow

Asag   The demon who was used by Enlil to create the gallu demons. Sin's brother Zakar battled him once; during the fight Zakar absorbed some of Asag's powers, thus making him resistant to the bite of the gallu.

Asclepius   Greek god of Healing. Son of Apollo and Coronis.

Asteros   The Atlantean god of Heavenly Light: stars, comets, and fire. The eldest son of Chaos (who birthed the universe) and Fegkia (Splendor), Asteros was born to give light to the heavens. His tale is a version of the Greek myth of Prometheus: It is said that Asteros looked down out of his golden chariot one night and saw the Atlantean people huddled in the dark. Taking pity on the humans, he reached up into the sky and took a handful of stars and gave them to the people and showed them how to make fire—their own version of heavenly light.

Astral Blast (See Godbolt.)

Astrid   Daughter of Themis, and youngest sister to the Fates. She is a justice nymph, an impartial judge sent down to earth to rule on possible Rogue Dark-Hunters. Since her eyesight becomes forfeit when she is sent to judge someone (in order to remain impartial), she turns to her Were-Hunter friend Sasha during these times for protection.

Astrid is married to Zarek of Moesia (bless her patient soul), the first Dark-Hunter she ever judged who lived. Her favorite book, given to her by Acheron, is *The Little Prince*.

HEIGHT: six feet

HAIR/EYES: honey blonde/pale blue
FEATURED NOVEL: *Dance with the Devil*

Athena (Minerva) Virgin goddess of Wisdom and War; daughter of Zeus. She was the first to teach the science of numbers and all ancient women's arts, such as cooking, weaving, and spinning. She never loses a battle, and does not bear arms in times of peace. But watch out, she often borrows weapons from her father, including but not limited to: the aegis, the buckler, and thunderbolts.

Athena's mother was Metis, a woman who spurned Zeus's advances much as Daphne fled from Apollo. But Zeus was not as easily dissuaded as his son. Once she was pregnant, it was prophesied that the second child of Metis would overthrow Zeus . . . so he swallowed her whole. (Gods are so melodramatic.) Zeus later ran to Hephaestus with a splitting headache (sorry, I couldn't resist). The smith opened Zeus's head with a blow from his ax, and out popped Athena, fully grown and in full dress armor.

Athena was fond of many Greek heroes and assisted them in their quests, helping many of the Greek superheroes attain their goals. Those she helped included Perseus, Jason, Cadmus, Odysseus, and Heracles. While she could be tough, Athena was a modest, generous, and benevolent goddess. The Greeks built the Parthenon as a temple to her. Athens is also named in her honor.

Athena is lovely and wonderful, yes, but don't ever let your guard down around her. Despite her benevolence, even Pallas Athena has succumbed to moments of petty godliness. (See Arachne.) Above all, never forget: *Athena always wins*.

HAIR/EYES: curly black/blue
BIRD: owl
TREE: olive
SYMBOL: aegis, helmet, shield, spear

Atlantia   Ancient Atlantean goddess; the eldest sister of Archon. Her name means "graceful beauty". Atlantis was named after her.

Atlantis   An ancient island civilization with an advanced culture, and its own pantheon of gods. It sank into the Aegean Sea more than eleven thousand years ago, legends say, at the hands of a vengeful Apollo.

Atropos   Nickname: Atty. Eldest of the Fates. Responsible for cutting the threads of lives. Atropos is the smallest of the Fates in stature, but the most feared. Atropos and Ash do not get along (really, none of the Moirae can stand him).

Badb   Irish goddess of War often known to take the form of a crow or a wolf. Badb was the sister of Macha and the Morrigán. She also was reported to have prophesied the end of the world.

Basi   The Atlantean goddess of Excess and Intoxication, Basi is the daughter of Epithymia (Desire) and Misos (War). She is said to have been conceived the night her father won a major battle against the Greek pantheon. Drunk on his own power, he ravished Epithymia. (In some more popular versions, it was Epithymia who ravished him.)
   Completely hedonistic, Basi takes numerous lovers and is seldom seen sober. She is a mischievous goddess who loves to create havoc in mortal lives. Basi is often blamed for illicit affairs and for greed.

Bast   Egyptian goddess whose name means "devourer". The protector of Egypt, she is often depicted as a fierce lion. Bast was originally a goddess of the Sun (serving Ra), but was later changed by the Greeks to a goddess of the Moon: the source of her enmity with Artemis.

Blood-Bond   The vampiristic (and very sexual) bond between two people where one has to drink from the other in order to survive. There is a blood-bond between Acheron and Artemis, as well as between Sin and Katra Agrotera.

Boreas (Aquilo)   God of the North Wind, who brings the deadly winter. He also saved Athens from attack by the Persian King Xerxes. Fond of horses, Boreas lived in Thrace.

Bran   Also known as "Bran Fendigaid" or "Bran the Blessed" in Celtic mythology, Bran was the son of the sea god. He can bestow upon souls the right to be reborn into the human world.

BIRD: raven

Brigid   Daughter of the Irish god Dagda, and keeper of the sacred flame. Her powers and aspects are much like that of the Greek goddess Athena.

Calliope   Chief of the Muses. The Muse of Epic Song. A great friend of both Meatloaf and Celine Dion.

Camulus   Black-haired Gaulish god of War, forced into retirement. Runs with Ares, Kel, and Ara.

Caradoc   Charonte demon.

HEIGHT: four feet
TRUE FORM: black wings, yellow eyes, skin marbled black and dark green

Cassiopeia   Constellation; queen of Ethiopia and mother of Andromeda. In her vanity and pride, she boasted that she and her daughter were more beautiful than the sea nymphs, thus incurring the wrath of Poseidon. To thwart his curse, Cassiopeia chained Andromeda to a rock as a sacrifice, but she was saved by the hero Perseus. Poseidon's punishment for Cassiopeia was to place her in the heavens, upside down on her throne in disgrace for all to see forevermore.

Catubodua Gaulish goddess of Victory, often synonymous with Badb.

Cerberus Three-headed snake-tailed dog who guards the gates of the Underworld. He keeps the living from entering, and the dead from leaving. And he does a good job . . . when he's not drugged or magicked by someone who's cleverer than his master.

Ceredons Creatures with the head of a dog, the body of a dragon, and the tail of a scorpion. Protectors of Apollymi. They are forbidden to leave her realm (at least, they're *supposed* to be).

Chara The Atlantean goddess of Joy. It is said that Chara and her sister Agapa were born the moment Archon first looked at his half-sister Apollymi. His heart swelled to ten times its normal size and out of it popped Love (Agapa) and Joy (Chara).

Chara was the most favored child of Archon, and all the gods loved her. She was often seen in Atlantean murals walking or standing between Isorro and Basi.

As with many of her brethren, Chara could be capricious, giving pleasure one minute and then taking it away the next. The Atlantean people often sacrificed to her in the hope of keeping her goodwill and ensuring that they would prosper and be happy.

Charon The son of Erebus and Nyx, Charon is the ferryman of Hades, who takes the departed from one side of the river Styx to the other. He appears as an old man with a beard and dark brown clothes.

Ancient Greeks were buried with a coin under the tongue—or over both eyelids—so that their souls would have currency to pay the toll. It is custom to show Charon the coin, but not to pay him until he has delivered you to the other side. If you cannot pay, you are doomed to wait on the banks for one hundred years. If you pay Charon before you have crossed, he will dump you in the river, where you will suffer in eternal misery.

Not that Charon gets out much, really, so one wonders what exactly he *does* with all that money. . . .

Charonte Demon Ancient demon race the Olympian gods feared, but the Atlantean gods managed to tame. They can bond to gods, Hunters, and humans as companions. Once bonded, they can rest in the form of a tattoo on their bonded's body. Charontes are the über-id, they love to shop, kill, and eat everything. Easy to annoy, dangerous when angry, and big-time fun to party with.

You do not, however, want to be killed by a Charonte. Charontes do not just destroy the body of their victim. They also destroy the *ousia*—the life force that exists beyond the body or soul. A Charonte can be killed by an Atlantean dagger.

Charontes normally sleep with their feet in the air (usually propped up against a wall), and they snore *very* loudly.

Chloe Female statue that guards the temple of Demeter on Olympus.

Chthonians The god-killers. A long-ago race of men and women who banded together as policemen for the gods. They were the check-and-balance system for the universe . . . until they turned on one another for reasons known only to themselves. Now the handful who have survived watch over mankind with a bitter eye and with no real leader. Because of their hostility toward one another, the earth has been divided among them for safekeeping. They are highly territorial.

Chthonic Pertaining to very, very ancient Greek gods of the earth, or spirits of the Underworld. Some chthonic cults practiced ritual sacrifice. Most of the chthonic gods and goddesses were often associated with fertility.

Circe Sorceress goddess from the island of Aeaea, famous for her exploits with the hero Odysseus. Circe turned his men into pigs after they gluttonously ate her food, but Odysseus had been warned by Hermes and had protected himself from her poisons.

Circe fell in love with Odysseus, then turned the pigs back into men and helped him on his quest home to his wife . . . but not before she slept with him first and bore him three sons.

Clio   Muse of History.

Clotho   Nickname: Cloie. The youngest Fate. In charge of destinies; she spins the threads of lives.

Cronus   Greek god of Time.

Cuchulainn   The Hercules of Irish mythology, it was said that Cuchulainn could never be defeated in battle. He wielded a spear called the Gae Bolga.

Dagda   Supreme benevolent god in Irish mythology, also known as the High King. He wields a club that can kill nine men with one blow, and has a magic cauldron that can feed an army from its contents.

Deimos   Nickname: Demon. One of the Dolophoni; dark-haired son of Alecto and twin to Phobos. He was strangled by Sin when he would not recant his death hunt for the Dark-Hunter. (He still carries the scar.) He finally ended up sparing Sin's life, because Sin put the welfare of an innocent human above both his own and Katra's.

HAIR/EYES: various/blue

Demeter   Greek goddess of the Harvest, Fertility, and Society. Daughter of Cronus and Rhea and sister of Zeus, she is the mother of Persephone, who became the sometime consort of Hades, the god of the Underworld. When her daughter is above-ground with her, things blossom and grow (spring and summer). When she is belowground with Hades, the earth withers and dies (autumn and winter). Demeter has also been referred to as Auxesia, Deo, Chloe, and Sito. The Romans equated her with their goddess Ceres.

Demeter's solution to every problem is time spent in the garden.

Demios   Greek god of Dread.

Dikastis   The Atlantean god of Justice, born after Isorro (Moderation) seduced the nymph Merina (Thought). Like his father, Dikastis is a deity of balance and prudence. Cold and unfeeling, he never allows his emotions to rule him. He is able to see straight into the hearts of mankind and gods, and to judge them instantly. Even the gods fear him, for no one can hide from the eerie eyes of justice. He is known to send out Dikisi (Vengeance) to punish wrongdoers as well as Amobia (Reward) for those who do good deeds. At banquets in the great hall of Chrysafi (the home of the gods), he sits to the right side of Archon.

Dike   Daughter of Themis and Zeus, Greek goddess of Justice and Humanity.

Diktyon   One of Artemis's hunting nets. A diktyon can capture and hold a Dark-Hunter. It will also negate all powers, even those of a god.

Dimme   Anu and Enlil's final revenge. The Dimme are seven female Sumerian demons unlike anything even I can imagine. They are uncontrollable, even for the gods. They were locked away in a cell that, unfortunately, has a time release that weakens every few millennia. If the Sumerian gods are still alive, they reseal the seven demon sisters and life goes on as normal. But should something happen to the pantheon and there be no more Sumerian gods to reseal their tomb, the Dimme are unleashed on the world to destroy it and whatever pantheon is in charge. The Dimme were the Sumerians' last laugh against whoever killed them.

Dionysus (Bacchus)   Nickname: Dion. Cousin of Eros and Julian. Greek god of Wine and Excess; son of Zeus and the mortal woman Semele, who was burnt to death upon seeing the true form of her lover. (Later Dionysus brought Semele up from the Underworld, gave her the name Thyone, and ascended with his mother to Mount Olympus, where she was made immortal by Zeus.)

There was much chaos on Mount Olympus surrounding the birth of Dionysus; the pomegranate tree sprang from where Dionysus's blood fell to the earth. Most great Greek plays were written to honor Dionysus during his festival every spring.

Forced into retirement, Dionysus now amuses himself as a corporate raider. He usually appears as a tall man with short hair and a neat goatee. Like many of his divine brethren, he is not a very good driver, especially when it comes to Mardi Gras floats.

HAIR: brown

Dolophoni   Children of the Furies and assassins of the gods. Both male and female, they were the ones who originally gathered the Oneroi together for Zeus to punish. Their weapons are made by Hephaestus, in order to cause the most harm . . . and to kill other gods. Once they have been set on a death hunt, the order cannot be recanted. They don't really have a set of rules; you just hope they abide by everyone else's. It can be said, though, that they only kill for a reason justifiable to Themis. If they kill needlessly, they are executed. The Dolophoni can ultimately be controlled by the Furies.

Eda   Atlantean earth goddess. Archon's sister.

Elysian Fields   Also called the Elysian Plains, this was the final resting place of the souls of heroes. It is the only part of Hades's Underworld realm where good souls go to live out their eternity in paradise. They have everything their heart desires, and they can be reincarnated, if they so choose.

Enlil   Ancient Sumerian god—and father of Sin—who possessed the Tablet of Destiny. Enlil was empathetic with the gallu, and reasoned with Anu that they not be destroyed.

Enyo (Bellona)   Goddess of War. The Romans often worshipped her and Mars (Ares) in the same temples.

Eos (Aurora)   Titan goddess of the Dawn, and sister of Helios and Selene.

Epithymia   The Atlantean goddess of Desire, of unknown origin. Some claim she is sister to Agapa, in other tales she was born parthenogenetically, like Athena, from either Agapa or Archon. Beautiful beyond description, she can make all desires come true. To see her is to want her, to touch her is to be blessed by having your wishes granted.

Erato   Muse of Erotic Poetry.

Erebos   One of the Dolophoni, Erebos had spiked green hair, sunglasses, a spiked staff, tattooed arms, pierced ears and lip, and fangs. He was killed by Arikos.

Erebus   Greek god of Darkness. Father of Wink.

Erinyes (Furies)   The three goddesses of Vengeance, said to be born from the blood of the ancient god Uranus when he was castrated by his son Cronus. They often appear dressed in black leather with black hair and lipstick. They have fangs, dark eyes, and snakes in their hair. (See Alecto, Megeara, Tisiphone.) They are the older sisters of the Meliae, and they draw from the power of the entire Greek pantheon to kill.

   The Furies are also referred to as the Eumenides—meaning "kind ones"—because they are vindictive, but fair.

Eris (Discordia)   Greek goddess of Discord. Sister to Ares, she often accompanies him on the battlefield. Eris has a knack for starting wars by spreading rumors and fueling petty jealousies. She is as beautiful as Aphrodite, and the most evil of any god.

   One of the more famous Eris stories is that of the golden apple—when Zeus did not invite her to a party because of her troublemaking reputation, she inscribed a golden apple with the words "To the Prettiest" on it, and tossed it into the room. Hera, Athena, and Aphrodite immediately started fighting over it. Zeus decided to leave the decision up to a Trojan shepherd. Each of the goddesses tempted him, but it was Aphrodite who offered him what he could not refuse: the most beautiful woman in the world. So Aphrodite got her apple . . . and Paris got Helen of Troy.

HAIR: curly black

Eros (Cupid)   God of Lust and Love. son of Ares and Aphrodite, and brother to Julian and Priapus. He appears in public as a biker with a youthful face and goatee. Can often be found playing pool at Sanctuary with his wife, Psyche. (See Psyche.) He wears his bow on a necklace, and carries a dagger forged by Hephaestus.

Eros's bow wields two kinds of arrows: golden with dove feathers, and lead with owl feathers. The golden arrow causes the victim to fall in love. The lead arrow poisons the desire of a person and turns them away from their intended. It should be noted, however, that the lead arrow can only kill lust and infatuation. It cannot touch the love of soul mates.

The Romans use the image of Cupid as a symbol for life and death. The Greeks used Eros as a symbol for love and beauty.

BIRTHPLACE: Mount Olympus
HEIGHT: six foot seven

Eurus (Vulturnus)   Greek god of the East Wind. Generally thought of as unlucky.

Euryale   A gorgon who tries to steer Megeara Kafieri off her path out of Hades.

Eurydice   A nymph; the wife of Orpheus who died when bitten by a snake. Orpheus had the chance to save Eurydice from Hades, but he did not pass the challenge and was doomed to live without her.

Euterpe   Muse of Lyric Song.

Fates (Moirae, Parcae)   Daughters of Themis: Clotho, Lachesis, and Atropos. Together they spin the threads of lives, weave their destinies, and cut the threads to end the lives. (Not surprisingly, they have a nasty way of dealing with people who alter history.) There is a great deal of debate over whether or not the Fates work for Zeus or with him . . . like any such debate, it depends on whom you ask. (See Clotho, Lachesis, Atropos.)

Ferandia   Ancient Atlantean with a tale similar to that of Orpheus and Eurydice.

Four Realms   Time, Space, Earth, Dreams. These are what the Pyramid of Protection guard. There is only a small group of individuals who can walk all four.

Freya/Frigga   Norse goddess who hand selects warriors for Valhalla. In her own hall, she has a harem. It is Norse custom to be married on a Friday (the day named after her) in her honor.

She and Rafael Santiago had a thing once. At least, that's what I heard.

HAIR: strawberry blonde

Fysia   The daughter of Eda (Earth) and Chaos, Fysia is the Atlantean goddess of Nature. She was born when Chaos covered the earth and spread his seeds along her shores. One of the oldest of the gods, Fysia is both gentle and violent. She has the power to change herself into anything, and it is believed that the seasons come from her ever-shifting forms. In the spring, she is a child, loving and sweet. In summer, a youth who frolics. In autumn, a grown woman who nurtures. In winter, she is an old shrew who punishes those who haven't made preparations for her cold months.

Gaia   Ancient Greek goddess, the second born after Chaos. Gaia was all-powerful and gave birth to the Titans, including Cronus, the father of Zeus. She is the Earth.

Gallu   Ancient Sumerian demons created to combat the Sumerian pantheon's enemies. (Specifically, they were created to battle against the Charonte demons.) The horrible demon Asag was used as the donator father in their creation.

The gallu can turn humans into one of them with a bite. They have two rows of razor-sharp teeth and unlike Daimons can walk in daylight. If you can catch it early enough, you can cauterize the bite wound and stop the poison from spreading through your body.

The poison in their bite could infect even gods and make them demons as well. Daimons can also become gallu . . . and faster too, since Daimon metabolism is so high. (A Daimon gallu does not die with a pierced heart *or* head.) A gallu Daimon is serious shit.

The only way to kill a gallu is to behead the creature (hit it right between the eyes or sever the spine) and burn its body. (They explode . . . and stink when they do.) It is the only way to completely destroy the bite poison and to keep them from regenerating.

Sin, Zakar, and Sin's daughter Ishtar imprisoned the Dimme and the gallu millennia ago. However, after the death of the Sumerian pantheon, the gallu began working their way free of their prison. They became smarter and more organized.

Mirrors show the gallu for what they are. They won't go near them. Nor can gallu infiltrate the dreams of someone they've never met; they must have physical contact first. It should be noted that you cannot kill a gallu in the dream realm. Lucky for us, they can't kill us either.

The gallu are quite prolific. After sex, one female can lay two dozen fertilized eggs. (They were born from eggs, so that they would survive if the mother was killed. The eggs are nearly indestructible.) Their venom is weak when they're young, and their victims will not turn right away.

Godbolt (aka: Astral Blast) A bolt of lightning from out of the hand of a god or demigod. It takes a Dark-Hunter quite a long while to heal after being hit by one of these puppies.

Goibniu Irish smith god of Art, along with his brothers Creidhne and Luchtaine. His weapons were always lethal, and he brewed a beer that made the drinker immortal. Hail Ale!

Gorgon Gorgons guard the barrier between the Outerworld and the Underworld. They are women with green, scaly snake's skin, red eyes that glow, fangs, and breath like toxic waste. Only men turn to stone when looking at Gorgons (not gods or Shades).

Hades (Aides, Pluto) Zeus's brother and god of the Underworld. He is also known as the god of Wealth, for the precious metals to be found buried within the earth. Not an easy fellow to warm up to (which could be why they named an icy planet after him), but Hades is always just. He just doesn't suffer fools. Period.

He has no temples, and any statues or images created in his honor are extremely rare. Once a body entered the Underworld, that person was forbidden to leave. (One of the only known survivors was Orpheus, who escaped with his life . . . but only his life and not that of his recently departed wife.)

Hades abducted Persephone, daughter of Demeter and Zeus. He permitted her no food or drink, in order to persuade her to marry him. Hades was forced to let her go, but first he tricked her into eating pomegranate seeds, which bound her to him for a few months out of the year. Some myths say that she fell in love with him and ate the seeds so that her parents would be forced to allow her to return.

Hades is always open to a good bargain because he hates the other gods so much (and the feeling is mutual). He has no fear of anyone or anything, and enjoys torturing the souls in the Underworld when his wife is gone. His main chamber room is the only part of his realm open to outsiders. There he sits on a throne made from the bones of Titans, clad in his black leather armor.

HAIR: black

Hayar Bedyr   The Forsaken Moon (Sumerian). The title of Sin's brother Zakar. (See Zakar.)

Hecate   Goddess of Wilderness and Childbirth (Thrace). Zeus has always had a soft spot for Hecate. Sometimes called the Queen of Ghosts, today she is known as the goddess of Witchcraft and Wicca.

Hel   Daughter of the trickster god Loki, and ruler of the Underworld in Germanic literature. It is said of Hel that she is half human and half rotting corpse, she eats human flesh, and she smells. And those were the nicer comments about her.

Helen   Daughter of Zeus and Leda; queen of Sparta. Also known as the famous beauty Helen of Troy. She had many suitors, not the least of which was Paris, the prince of Troy . . . the affair that caused the Trojan War.

Helios   Greek god of the Sun (often identified with Apollo).

Hephaestus (Vulcan)   The misshapen blacksmith god of Fire and husband of Aphrodite. Hephaestus made the dagger worn by Eros, as well as his arrows. He also created the chains to hold Julian while Grace attempted to break his curse. (Only a god or a key can open chains forged by Hephaestus.) He was responsible for Athena's shield, the chariot of the Sun god Helios, and the weapons of the Dolophoni.

Legend has it that Hephaestus was born crippled, so his mother Hera cast him from Mount Olympus (don't hold it against her—the Spartans did that kind of thing all the time back then). He landed on the island of Limnos, where he was cared for by its inhabitants. In revenge, Hephaestus forged Hera a beautiful golden throne . . . that entrapped her. Hephaestus only let her out when she promised him Aphrodite's hand in marriage. (And after Dionysus got him *reeeeally* stinkin' drunk.)

He is known to sport a beard, and walk with the aid of a stick or cane.

Hera   Queen of Olympus, daughter of Cronus and Rhea, and wife and sister to Zeus (don't ask). Hera has a full-time job staying jealous of Zeus's affairs, and her fury is legendary. She is often worshipped as a goddess of Marriage and Birth. She recently had a reputed affair with a well-known N.Y. cover model, which might have remained a secret had Eris—the goddess of Discord—not ratted her out to Zeus.

BIRD: peacock, crow
ANIMAL: cow
SYMBOL: pomegranate

Heracles/Hercules   Demigod son of Zeus and Alcmene and the greatest of the Greek heroes. He was known for his strength, courage, and wit. Many know the tales of the Twelve Labors he was set to perform, the last of which involved capturing Cerberus, the three-headed guardian dogzilla of Hades.

Hermes (Mercury)   Son of Zeus and Maia, daughter of Atlas. Born in a cave on Mount Cyllene in Arcadia, Hermes is sometimes referred to as Atlantiades or Cyllenius. He is the fastest of the gods, and his position was messenger to Zeus and all the other gods. He was the Divine Herald, the solemn guide who knew the road to hell and would lead the souls of the dead down to the Underworld, after Thanatos (Death) did his job.

Hermes is also the Greek god of Commerce and the Market, as well as the patron of all gymnastic games. He is believed to be the inventor of sacrifice, and so protects all sacrificial animals.

Hermes is cunning, shrewd, and a master thief. Watch this guy . . . or not. If he means to have something, he'll find a way of having it, to be sure. He plays a part in most of the myths you hear about; he's got his fingers in every pie.

The heralds' staff (called *kerykeion* in Greek) was given to Hermes by Apollo. The white ribbons surrounding the staff were changed into two serpents by later artists.

He's always in a hurry, so no one's really sure what he looks like, apart from a blur of a man whooshing by.

SYMBOL: winged hat and sandals, heralds' staff

Hestia   Goddess of the Home, Hearth, and Family.

SYMBOL: the eternal flame

Honos   God of Chivalry in Roman mythology.

Hypnos   Greek god who holds dominion over all the gods of Sleep. Son of Nyx and Erebus, and twin of Thanatos. He oversees the physical punishments of the dream gods, who are whipped when they don't stay in line.

Icelus   Son of Hypnos and one of the Oneroi. Icelus creates human shapes in dreams, and is father of some of the more erotically addicted Dream-Hunters. They live for sex and drift from dream to dream, seeking new partners.

Ichor   A mineral found in the blood of the gods that makes them immortal. (Artemis originally injected Zarek with ichor to give him his Dark-Hunter powers, because she did not want to touch him.)

Ilios   Atlantean god of the Sun, conceived when Asteros seduced Epithymia. Their passion was such that two balls of fire were placed inside the womb of Epithymia. In one day, she birthed the Sun (Ilios) and the Moon (Nyktos).

The twins were taken from their mother and placed in the sky so that Asteros could share his domain with them. He split rulership of the sky between his sons, giving Ilios control of the day and Nyktos control of the night. It is said the two brothers often embrace each other as they pass, thus giving the times when both the sun and the moon are visible to those who reside on earth. Those are the days dreaded by all Dark-Hunters.

Ilithvia   Greek goddess of Childbirth. (Spellings of her name vary.)

Iris   Greek goddess of the Rainbow.

Ishtar   Daughter of Sin but not by blood . . . or so his unfaithful wife told him. Very shy and wary of strangers, Ishtar loved animals and playing in fountains as a girl. After she and Sin destroyed Anatum, Ishtar absorbed her powers and replaced her in the Sumerian pantheon. She was ultimately killed by the gallu and buried—along with the Rod of Time—in a tomb concealed by ever-changing sands and guarded by a spell that hid it from mortal eyes.

Isle of Padesios   Region in Katoteros where Ash allows the Shades a facsimile of paradise.

Isorro   The Atlantean god of Moderation and Temperance, of Wisdom and Harmony. Isorro is the eldest son of Archon. He was said to be the chief mediator between his parents and the intercessor between the gods and mankind.

Kalosis   Atlantean hell where Apollymi is imprisoned, and where once sat the palace of Misos. Kalosis is also home of the Spathi Daimons, and is accessible to Daimons through bolt-holes and laminas. No Dark-Hunters can enter, and few Were-Hunters survive long after visiting this realm of perpetual darkness.

Katoteros   Atlantean word for "heaven". Katoteros is a small netherworld between dimensions where the ancient gods once lived, and where Acheron currently makes his home. Apollites and Daimons dream of being able to reclaim their right to rest here.

Kerir   Sumerian apocalypse, brought about by the freeing of the seven Dimme.

Kessar   The leader of the gallu demons, whose brother Sin and Katra killed while helping Zakar escape. In retaliation, Kessar attempted to form an alliance with the Dimme and unite the gallu against the gods. When that didn't work, he teamed up with our favorite Daimon, Stryker. After all, the enemy of his enemy . . .

HAIR/EYES: caramel blond/blood-red

Kori   A handmaiden of Artemis. All the koris live in Artemis's temple in Olympus.

Kyklonas   One of the ceredons guarding Apollymi's temple in Kalosis. His name means "tornado".

Lachesis   Nickname: Lacy. The middle Fate. Responsible for weaving the pattern of fate.

Lera   As justice nymph, Astrid's half-sister was called in to judge those who had fought against Artemis during the war with Bast. Lera found all guilty except the Were-Hunter pup Sasha, who was deemed too young to be held accountable.

Loki   Norse trickster god. Lover of Morginne, and onetime possessor of the soul of Wulf Tryggvason. In order to swap Morginne's and Wulf's souls, Loki used a thistle from the Norns (that lets someone swap souls for a day), and then made it permanent with his blood. That Loki, he's a clever bastard.

Lyta   Greek nymph who was two halves of one person. She made herself and everyone else miserable, until a Greek soldier came along and joined her two halves.

Macha   Irish goddess of War and Kingship. Macha was sister to Badb and the Morrigán.

Marking Medallion   When a god bestows this medallion upon a human, no one above, on, or below the earth can kill them without making that god very, *very* angry.

Marsyas   A satyr who discovered the first flute after Athena invented it and then discarded it. (Eros almost died laughing at the face she made when she played it, and teased her about it mercilessly.) Marsyas then challenged Apollo to a music contest (you'd think he would have learned from Arachne). Apollo won, of course, but instead of transforming Marsyas into something ugly or monstrous, he just flayed him alive.

Megeara   One of the Furies. (See Erinyes.) She is the root of jealousy and envy, and causes people to commit crimes such as adultery. Her name is the root of the Spanish word for "woman". (Not that I'm implying anything; I'm just tellin' it like it is.)

Meliae   Sisters to the Erinyes, the Meliae sprang from the same blood spilled when Cronus castrated Uranus. They are nymphs of the ash tree, and a lesser version of the Fates.

Melpomene   Muse of Tragedy.

Metus   Greek god of Fear.

Minos   Son of Zeus and Europa, brother of Rhadamanthus, and former king of Crete. Namesake of the Minoan civilization. He is the judge of the Greek souls that enter Hades, and the tiebreaker when Rhadamanthus and Aeacus differ over a ruling.

Misos   The Atlantean god of War and Death, Misos is the son of Fegkia and Chaos. His chief aides are Pali (Strife) and Diafonia (Discord), who are said to run about in battle and confuse and outrage soldiers and commanders to incite more bloodshed. During times of peace, they take on the form of humans in order to stir up mayhem and trouble between nations.

Misos's violence was such that Archon banished him to the

lower regions and made him ruler of the Underworld, where he lives with his wife Thnita (Mortality). When a civilian dies, their daughter Zena is sent to lead them to the Underworld, while soldiers are escorted by their son Stratiotis. Children are given their own special guide, Paidi, who is the youngest of their offspring. Paidi is said to take the form of a winged pony who carries the children to Telios (paradise) where they are given into the hands of adults who will love and nurture them until they can be reborn as mortals.

Their realm is guarded by the multiheaded dragon Prostateva, a woman cursed by Apollymi when she claimed to be more beautiful than the queen of the gods. No living human can cross the path of Prostateva. Any who try are eaten alive by her.

Mist Amorphous consort of the Sleep gods, Mist has birthed thousands of children. Not the most maternal of mothers, she turned the raising of her sons and daughters over to Hypnos and to the nymphs who serve her.

HAIR/EYES: black/white, glowing

Mnemosyne Daughter of Gaia. She is the ancient Greek goddess of Memory and the mother of the nine Muses, by Zeus.

Mnimi Greek goddess of Latent Memory, daughter of the Greek goddess Dike and the Atlantean god Dikastis, it is said Mnimi was born to make sure people remembered what they did so that they could learn from their mistakes. Imprisoned in her youth by Ares, who wanted people to forget so that they would be eager to war against each other, she was released when Pandora opened her box.

Mnimi most often serves Hades, and helps to punish evildoers by reminding them of their crimes. She is the conscience and judge of many.

HAIR/EYES: dark red/green, swirling

Morpheus   Greek god of Dreams. Father of many Oneroi, and son of Hypnos. Morpheus is responsible for shaping dreams, or giving shape to the beings who inhabit dreams. His name means "he who forms, or molds" (from the Greek *morphe*).

Morrigán   Celtic Raven goddess of War, and grandmother of Sunshine Runningwolf (aka Grandma Morgan). Her name means "Great Queen" or "Nightmare Queen". In myth, she is often equated with Alecto of the Furies. Other times she embodies all three aspects, including Badb, Macha, and sometimes Nemain.

She can sometimes be seen washing the clothes of men about to die in battle, effectively choosing who lives and who dies.

BIRD: carrion crow, raven
ANIMAL: cow

Mount Olympus   Home of the Greek gods. The twelve most powerful gods are: Zeus; Poseidon; Hera; Demeter; Artemis; Apollo; Athena; Hephaestus; Ares; Aphrodite; Hermes; and Hestia. Dionysus, the youngest of the gods, is sometimes lumped in with these twelve, and sometimes not. The weather on Olympus is always perfect, not too hot or too cold, with a blue sky overseeing lush, green mountains.

Muses   The nine daughters of Zeus and Mnemosyne: Calliope; Euterpe; Clio; Erato; Melpomene; Polyhymnia; Terpsichore; Thalia; and Urania. They are all patrons and inspirations of the various arts.

Nabium   A tall, dark-haired gallu demon.

Nemesis   Greek goddess of Indignation and Retribution, who punishes excessive pride, evil deeds, undeserved happiness or good fortune, and the absence of moderation. A feared and revered goddess, she measures out both happiness and unhappiness. She is an assistant of Zeus, along with Dike and Themis.

Nemesis is sometimes depicted as having wings, and is as beautiful as (some say more than) Aphrodite.

One of the classic stories of Nemesis is the downfall of Narcissus, who was too in love with himself to notice the attentions of the nymph Echo (who eventually withered away until nothing was left but her voice). Nemesis condemned Narcissus to spend the rest of his days admiring himself in a pool of water, where he eventually took root and transformed into a flower.

TREE: apple
SYMBOL: wheel, ship's rudder

Neti   Former gatekeeper to the Sumerian underworld, Neti is now a gallu demon who works beside Kessar as his right-hand man.

Nike   Winged goddess of Victory. Often found at Athena's side. A favorite of Zeus.

Notus (Auster)   God of the South Wind who brings the summer storms.

Nyktos   Atlantean god of the Moon, son of Asteros and Epithymia. Their passion was such that two balls of fire were placed inside the womb of Epithymia and in one day, she birthed the sun (Ilios) and the moon (Nyktos). The twins were placed in the sky so that Asteros could share his domain with them. He split rulership of the sky between his sons, giving Ilios control of the day and Nyktos control of the night.

Nyx   Ancient Greek goddess of Night, and mother to many of the other gods and goddesses.

Obulos   Greek coins or Persian danace that the dead must pay Charon for passage across to the Underworld.

Odin   Chief god in Norse mythology. He symbolizes Creation,

Wisdom, and Inspiration as well as Fury, War, and Death. He was also in charge of the valkyries.

Oracle   Anyone who communes with the gods. Warning: Oracles are a bit like cats. Never go to one if you're looking for a straight answer.

Orasia   Atlantean goddess of Sleep.

Orion   "The Hunter". A famous constellation in the night sky. The story goes that Artemis fell in love with Orion so deeply that she forgot to illuminate the night sky and it all went dark. Jealous and hating the fact that his sister was in love with a mere mortal, Apollo dared Artemis to hit a tiny speck on the waves with her bow—which, of course, she did. That speck was Orion. Grief-stricken, Artemis placed the image of her beloved in the night sky forevermore in remembrance.

Another version of the story is that Artemis killed Orion because he raped one of her handmaidens, and then placed his image in the sky as a warning of her wrath.

Orpheus   Son of the muse Calliope, and famous for his mastery of the lyre. Attempted to rescue his beloved wife, Eurydice, from Hades after she died from a snake bite. He sang his woes to Hades and Persephone, who took pity on him and presented him with a chance to win back his love. The challenge was that Orpheus must walk out of Hades and not turn around for any reason until he had exited the Underworld. Unfortunately, Orpheus could not resist, and turned back just in time to see Eurydice vanish from his sight forever.

Ousia   The part of a person that exists beyond the body or the soul. The life force.

Pallor   Greek god of Terror.

Pandora   The first woman, created by Zeus as a punishment for Prometheus having given fire to the humans. She was given gifts from all the gods: beauty, musical talent, cunning, boldness, charm . . . and curiosity (thank you, Hera). She was also given a storage jar or box that she was instructed not to open under any circumstance. She did, of course, thus releasing all the misfortunes of mankind into a world that had previously existed in peace.

Parriton   A young Charonte demon.

Pasiphaë   Daughter of Helios, sister of Circe, and onetime queen of Crete (married to Minos). She had several children, among them both Ariadne and the legendary Minotaur (which is what happens when you get cursed by Poseidon).

Persephone (Proserpina)   Nickname: Seph. Daughter of Zeus and Demeter, and goddess of the Underworld. (See Hades.) She loves her husband and resents her mother for keeping her from Hades for nine months out of the year. She *reeeeally* hates gardening. Persephone is kind and dainty, petite and shy. Her throne in the Underworld is made of gold, with cushions the color of blood. She is sometimes referred to as the Iron Queen.

HAIR: blond

Phantasos   Greek god. Son of Hypnos, and creator of nonsentient dream objects (his name means "apparition"). Phantasos is the father of the more cerebral Dream-Hunters. His children are most often the Oneroi who police the Dream-Hunters.

Phobetor   Son of Hypnos, and Greek god of animal shapes. Father of the nightmare Dream-Hunters. His name means "frightening".

Phobos   One of the Dolophoni; son of Alecto and twin to Deimos.

HAIR: brown

Pleiades   The seven daughters of the Titan Atlas, companions of Artemis, and teachers of Dionysus. They are Maia (mother of Hermes); Electra; Taygete; Alcyone; Celaeno; Sterope; and Merope (wife of Sisyphus). They were hunted by Orion, so Zeus changed them into doves and then into a cluster of stars, which Orion eternally pursues across the night sky.

Polyhymnia   Muse of Sacred Song.

Poseidon (Neptune)   Greek god of the Sea, son of the Titan Cronus and Rhea, second in power only to Zeus himself. He lives in his palace beneath the sea, and is transported around in his golden chariot drawn by white horses. Poseidon is married to the Nereid Amphitrite, who suffers her husband's affairs about as well as Hera does.

Poseidon and Athena are constantly at odds. He once fought Athena for the patronage of Athens—Poseidon brought a fountain to the Acropolis (albeit a saltwater one), and Athena brought the olive tree. The men voted for Poseidon, and the women for Athena. As luck would have it, the women outnumbered the men by one.

Poseidon is known for his anger (like many of his brethren), and is a very, very sore loser. He flooded Athens, and deprived the women of their right to vote in the future.

Animal: bull, horse
Symbol: trident

Priapus   Greek and Roman fertility god, protector of gardens and domestic animals and fruits. Son of Aphrodite and Dionysus. Brother to Julian and Eros. Carved images of Priapus, with large ithyphallic genitals, were placed in fields and gardens to ensure fruitfulness and protection. He was imported into Rome from Lampascus, where Pausanias reported he was supreme among all gods. (The Roman Priapus was far more popular than his Greek version.)

Priapus cursed Julian by trapping him inside a book in 149 B.C. for deflowering one of his virgins, and then was cursed into the same book himself by Aphrodite in 2002 for what he did to Julian. Ironic, don't you think?

Priestess Medallion   Worn by the Atlantean priestesses of Apollymi. Whenever a priestess was in danger, she would put the small, coin-sized medallion in her mouth. Apollymi would then protect the priestess by imbuing the woman with her strength, her power, and sometimes even her overwhelming presence. An ancient priestess medallion is currently worn by Megeara Kafieri.

Prometheus   Titan who brought fire to the humans and got his liver eaten out for all eternity in return. Remember? We mentioned Prometheus back there at the beginning. Poor guy.

Psyche   Goddess of Souls and Soul Mates, and wife of Eros. Youngest of three daughters. Much like Snow White's mother, Aphrodite became jealous of the beauty held by Psyche as a mortal. She bade Eros to shoot her with his arrow and force her to fall in love with the ugliest man on earth. Eros fell in love with her, of course, and would visit her as an invisible spirit. One night, while Eros slept, Psyche peeked in on her lover to see his true identity. When she did, hot oil from her lamp spilled on him, and he awoke and fled. It was Zeus who brought them back together and gave his consent for them to marry.

When seen in the mortal world today, Psyche often takes the form of a tall, beautiful biker chick.

HAIR: blonde
ANIMAL: butterfly

Pterygsaurus   A small, winged dragonlike creature. There are always six pterygsauri in Acheron's throne room. Or were. Xirena has found them to be quite tasty.

Ravanah   A female demon who eats the flesh of other

demons. When there are no demons to be had, Ravanah eats the flesh of infants and pregnant women. Even the gallu demon Kessar is afraid of her, and rightly so.

Rhadamanthus Son of Zeus and Europa, and brother to Minos. One of the judges of the dead in Hades, Rhadamanthus oversees those deceased of Asian descent.

Rod of Time The Rod of Time looks like a dagger with a crooked blade. A magical Sumerian implement, the rod is a vital piece of the lock on the imprisoned Dimme. It was Zakar who stashed the rod in Ishtar's tomb for his twin brother Sin to find when the time came. As only a Sumerian was meant to wield the rod, when Acheron touched it (and ultimately bled upon it), it broke the lock on the Dimme's cage. Sin, Zakar, and Katra Agrotera used Kat's sfora to recapture six of the seven Dimme.

Sabine A Charonte demon, one of Apollymi's personal guard (favored). Sabine has green hair and eyes, yellow skin, and deep orange horns and wings.

Saga Norse goddess of Poetry.

Satara A daughter of Apollo, Satara is the younger half-sister of Stryker. A handmaiden of Artemis (and not too happy about the prospect), she's loyal only to herself and hates Acheron with a passion. In fact, she hates most people and gods with a passion. But she does share one thing with Acheron: ever-changing hair color. While around Artemis, her hair is a deep auburn, but whenever she visits her half-brother Stryker, her hair is blond. On earth, it can be any shade she wants.

Once Nick drank Stryker's blood and turned Daimon, Satara was able to feel Nick's emotions through their shared blood. She played a trick on Nick, telling him that the Skotos Kratos would bring his mother back to life if he kidnapped Marissa Hunter and brought her to Kalosis.

Savitar   Even more mysterious than Acheron; as if such a thing were possible. Well, it is. Savitar is rumored to be the one who trained Ash in his Dark-Hunter powers, and who taught him how to bring back the dead without using blood. Some say he was born human, while others deny there's anything human about him at all. Truly, Savitar is a being unto himself. More powerful than Zeus and more wise than Solomon, he keeps his own company and prefers it that way. Even gods will not speak Savitar's name, for fear of drawing his attention. Covered in tattoos, Savitar is the most powerful and deadly surfer dude you'll ever meet.

Savitar oversees the Omegrion (though none of the Were-Hunters can remember how this came about). Nick was sent to him by Acheron for training, and later Savitar handed him over to Ravyn Kontis.

BIRTHPLACE: Eritara
HEIGHT: six foot eight
HAIR/EYES: dark brown/lavender

Scylla   A nymph who incurred the wrath of Circe for being fairer than she. Circe poisoned Scylla's bathwater (poison being Circe's modus operandi) and transformed her into a hideous sea monster with twelve feet and six heads, each with three rows of teeth. Legend has it that she was slain by Heracles, but that her father restored her to life.

Selene (Luna)   Greek goddess of the Moon, whose place in the pantheon was eventually taken over by Artemis.

Sfora   Atlantean scrying globe that people in Katoteros can use to watch events in other realms. Sometimes those who are being viewed can sense that Big Brother is watching. The sfora can see into the past, present, and future.

Simi   Means "baby" in Charonte. Real name: Xiamara, after her mother. Simi is Acheron's Charonte demon companion, given to him when she was a small child, and can manifest herself as a human or demon. She rests as an ever-changing tattoo on Ash's body, and is only allowed to leave this form at Ash's bidding. The only time she is allowed to leave his body without permission is when Ash is in danger. In human form, Simi's hair color always mirrors that of Ash. In demon form, the darker the color of her wings and eyes, the more upset she is. Whenever Simi is part of Ash, she cannot hear or see anything unless Ash gives her an order, but she can feel his emotions.

Though she is thousands of years old, she is equivalent to a human eighteen-year-old. She shops and parties like one, too. A complete cutie who loves extra-crispy barbecue, movies, Travis Fimmel (don't we all?), and QVC (where she is called "Miss Simi") . . . and who thinks everyone looks better with horns. If you value your life, don't ever, *ever*, say no to her. If she doesn't eat you for breakfast, Ash just might. Of course, not saying no is what got Nick into trouble in the first place. . . .

Simi has no concept of right or wrong. She is also allergic to rubber—it makes her sick. She may need to be reminded of this, so don't forget. She enjoys eating Diamonique. She likes her humans well-done.

BIRTHPLACE: Katoteros
HEIGHT: three feet, but it can vary
TRUE FORM: long yellow hair, white eyes rimmed with red, dark blue and black wings, black horns, and long, pointy ears

Strife   Son of Eris, goddess of Discord.

Styxx   Prince of Didymos, and Acheron's human twin brother. He was damned by Artemis to a six-by-six cell in Tartarus, but Ash had mercy upon him, and exiled him to paradise (even after Styxx plotted against him).

Due to his constant complaining about how the grass was

always greener, Mnimi gave Styxx the gift of understanding, so that he could see what life was like from Ash's point of view.

Sword of Cronus   Julian Alexander's sword. Only those with the blood of Cronus may touch the sword without being burned. Julian also has a shield bearing a bronze relief of Athena and her owl and the words "Death before Dishonor".

Symfora   Atlantean goddess of Death, Sorrow, and Woe. Daughter of Nyktos and Basi, to see the beautiful Symfora is to weep instantly. She walks beside mankind and is attracted to those who are self-pitying—so much so that she often visits even more sorrow upon them just to feed off their morbidity. In battle, she walks beside her grandfather Misos, and is often seen weeping by those who are dying. She appears to them as their loved ones.

Tablet of Destiny   The Sumerian *Tuppi Shimati*. Whatever god holds possession of the tablet can render another god powerless. It can also be used to strip a god of his or her powers entirely, thereby allowing the possessor to kill any god. The Tablet of Destiny does not affect the powers of demons.

Tartarus   The dark and pain-filled Greek version of hell, where Hades banishes the evil souls he wishes to torture. Only souls completely incapable of love can stay in Tartarus. This dark and woeful place is as far beneath the earth as heaven is above the earth. The entire area is lined with caverns and holding cells where screams of agony echo, begging for mercy. The occupants are seldom in a state to be recognized by even their own mothers, and the caverns are laid out like an intricate labyrinth. Around Tartarus runs a fence of bronze with gates that Poseidon fixed in such a way as to offer no escape. It is here that the Titans, whom Zeus and his siblings defeated, are forever confined.

Teiresias   One of the most well-known Oracles of Greece. Teiresias was blinded by Athena when he accidentally laid eyes upon

Her Radiance while taking a bath. Instead of killing him for what was clearly an accident Athena turned his sight inward, turning his punishment into a sort of gift.

Telikos   Armageddon.

Terpsichore   Muse of Dance.

Thalia   Muse of Comedy.

Thanatos   Artemis's assassin; a Dark-Hunter executioner. Also known as the Day-Slayer. Thanatos is death incarnate. Even his name means "death". Originally an Apollite chosen for Artemis's personal guard, Thanatos is neither Apollite nor Daimon, but has fangs. He can walk in daylight, and heals instantly. He knows no vulnerability . . . unless you stab the crescent moon located between his shoulder blades—something only Ash has ever been known to do.

When Acheron killed the Thanatos who slaughtered Zarek's village of Taberleigh, Artemis swore to never remake him. Only she did . . . to kill Zarek. The Apollite she chose was Callyx, the man whose wife Zarek had inadvertently killed. Artemis created this Thanatos, and kept him in a tiny cell until she needed him.

It was Acheron who defeated this Thanatos yet again—only this time, he offered to make Callyx human, so that he might be reborn and live with his wife again.

Thasos   Atlantean personification of Death who fashioned the throne for Misos while he ruled Kalosis.

Themis (Justitia)   Daughter of Uranus and Gaia, and Greek goddess of Justice. Themis is the personification of the divine right order of things as sanctioned by custom and law. She has oracular powers (it is said that she built the Oracle at Delphi). She is the mother of the Horae and the Moirae (the Fates). She is also the mother of Astrid.

HAIR: curly red

Theocropolis   Where Zeus holds court over all the Olympian gods.

Thor   The Norse god of Thunder; son of Odin and Jord. He travels in a chariot drawn by two goats that he eats when he is hungry. He revives their carcasses and brings them back to life when he wants to travel again. He has a hammer that will always return to him, a belt that gives him superstrength, and a special pair of iron gloves that help him lift the hammer. He uses these weapons in his seemingly endless battles against the race of giants.

HAIR: red

Tisiphone   One of the Furies. (See Erinyes.) Oversees the punishment of crimes of murder. In some legends, Tisiphone guards the gates of Tartarus.

Tree of Life   Tree that blooms only in the garden of Apollymi. It alone can break the ypnsi.

Triton   Son of Poseidon. Half-man and half-fish. He blows on his seashell to announce Poseidon's arrival.

Tuppi Shimati   Sumerian Tablet of Destiny. (See Tablet of Destiny.)

Tyberius, Zebulon   Nickname: ZT. Chthonian whose territory is Greece and the surrounding areas. He tolerates few gods, or their servants, treading on his turf. No one knows where he was born (more than 25,000 years ago), they only know that he has enough powers to kill a god in a single act.

ZT keeps permanent watch on Katra Agrotera anytime she's on earth. He watches for when she steps out of line. ZT has a scar from his hairline to his neck.

HAIR/EYES: dark blond/violet

Urania   Muse of Astronomy.

Valkyries   In Norse mythology, the valkyries were the beautiful battle maidens under Odin's command. It was the valkyries who chose which great warriors would die in battle and sit at Odin's table in Valhalla.

Vanishing Isle   Island at the edge of the world where Greek sailors believed they would go when they died. You can see it for a few minutes at sunup and sundown, but it is unreachable. The Vanishing Isle is where most of the dream gods reside.

Wink   A minor Greek god, son of Nyx and Erebus. A puckish character, Wink is what led to the belief in the Sandman. He is sent by the gods of sleep to induce slumber, and most claim he does so by sprinkling a magic dust into their eyes. Children are most fond of Wink, who is said to love them best of all since they are innocent and most deserving of untroubled rest.

A chronic prankster to both the Oneroi and Skoti, Wink is often found playing tricks on them. He may be one of the oldest gods, but he has the personality of a thirteen-year-old boy. He hangs out with the dead from time to time "for a laugh".

Wink's mist is often used by Dream-Hunters to make a human drowsy, or to exert control over one.

HAIR/EYES: brown/gray

Xedrix   Charonte demon. Apollymi's personal guard. Xedrix does not bow to Stryker.

TRUE FORM: black horns, blue hair, blood-red wings, yellow eyes, navy-blue skin

Xiamara   Charonte demon (deceased). Mother of Simi and Xirena. Simi's namesake.

Xirena   Eldest hatchling of Xiamara and Pistriphe, fiercest of the Charonte demons, and sister to Simi. Xirena is bonded to

Aléxion. As a human, Xirena tends to look more than a little bit like Apollymi. Which is disturbing in many, many ways.

TRUE FORM: black horns, lips, and hair, red wings, yellow eyes, skin marbled red and black

Ydor Atlantean god of the Oceans and Water, Ydor is the brother of Chaos. At one time, they split the universe between them, but due to trickery, Chaos was able to harness the power of Ydor and trap him between the thighs of Eda (Earth).

Not that it was difficult to trap Ydor between the thighs of a woman: The god's sexual appetites and conquests were legion. It is said that every lake, river, and stream is proof of his dalliance with a nymph. In some legends, he is believed to be the father of mankind (man needs water to live). Ydor was the patron god of all Atlantean port cities, and he worked with Archon to protect their people.

Ypnsi Sacred sleep that Orasia had once dispensed from the halls of Katoteros. The only antidote comes from the Tree of Life that grows in Apollymi's garden in Kalosis. Also, the only known item that can neutralize Acheron. And for your own sake, forget you know that.

Zakar Sumerian twin brother of the Dark-Hunter Sin. He is known as *Hayar Bedr*, the Forsaken Moon. After their father killed the eldest of the triplets because of a prophecy, Sin hid Zakar away in the dream realm. Zakar once battled the demon Asag, the donator father used to create the gallu. During the fight Zakar absorbed some of Asag's powers, thus making him resistant to the bite of the gallu.

Along with Sin and Sin's daughter Ishtar, Zakar imprisoned the Dimme until their impending escape in 2007. This time around, it was he, Sin, and Katra Agrotera who managed to contain six of the seven demons.

Zakar was captured in his sleep and held for a time as a gallu demon blood slave. He was found by Kat, Sin, Simi, and Xirena pinned to a stone by swords through his body and bite marks all over his neck from the gallu. His eyes were seared shut, his eardrums were pierced, and his powers were stripped. (Katra healed him.) Zakar should have had resistance to the gallu, but because he had been fed on for centuries, he may have become a gallu as well.

The gallu demon Kessar forced Sin to come to him by embedding the lock to hold the Dimme in Zakar's chest. Acheron saved him after it was removed.

Zebulon   A Chthonian who, as a child, was persecuted to the point of being tied to a stake and set on fire. As a result, he doesn't think much of people and even less of gods. He's a renegade and no one is ever sure whose side he's on. He has no patience, and a morbid sense of humor.

He hates being called Zeb. If you want to shorten his name, he'll answer to ZT, or Supreme Ruler of the Universe. The latter stands a better chance of not getting you killed.

Zephyros (Favonious)   God of the West Wind, the gentlest wind, and the messenger of spring. He was the brother and husband (don't ask) of Iris.

Zeus (Jupiter)   Youngest son of Cronus and Rhea, and ruler of Mount Olympus. God of Sky and Thunder. Because of a prophecy that Cronus would birth a child who would overthrow him (much like he did his father), Cronus swallowed all of his children when Rhea presented him with the babes. After giving birth to Zeus, Rhea presented Cronus with a stone, which he swallowed, thinking it was his son.

Zeus was raised on the Greek island of Crete (where his cave still remains). When he was a young man, he challenged Cronus and forced him to . . . well . . . vomit up all his siblings. He then defeated his father, banishing him and the rest of the Titans to Tartarus. Afterward, Zeus and his brothers drew straws to see which aspects of the world they would rule over. Zeus got the sky, Poseidon the ocean, and Hades the Underworld.

Zeus sowed his godly seed far and wide, for better or worse, and had many, many offspring. To list them all would take another whole book.

BIRD: golden eagle

TREE: oak, olive

Zurvan   Ancient Persian god of Time and Space. Also known as Cas.

Civilians

Your Raison d'Être

Life's too short . . . well, maybe not for you,
but for the rest of us mortals it is.
—Tabitha Devereaux

The gods created humans, and without them the Dark-Hunters would have no purpose. Without humans, the Were-Hunters would not exist, and the Dream-Hunters would starve to death. They are stubborn and unpredictable, their imaginations have no boundaries, and their capacity for every emotion between love and hate is infinite. There are six billion of them on this planet, and each one has the potential to be something amazing.

They are the humans, the mortals (or, mostly mortals). Inherently good or inherently evil, they are what makes this beautiful little green-and-blue planet worthwhile.

Some of them have developed powers that rival the gods, and some are merely spectators of the game that is being played out before them. But each individual one is important in his or her own way.

Stay alert: That next human you save from a Daimon may hold the fate of the world in their hands.

Aara   Queen of the ancient Greek island of Didymos. Aara is the wife of Icarion, and mother of Acheron and Styxx.

Achilles   Handsome hero of the Trojan War, Achilles was the son of King Peleus and the sea nymph Thetis. His mother tried to make him immortal by dipping him in the river Styx as a babe, but she forgot that she was holding him by the backs of his heels . . . making this his most vulnerable spot. Achilles was later killed by Paris, prince of Troy and lover of the famous Helen, queen of Sparta.

Agrippina   A lowborn slave who served in the Magnus family household in Rome. Valerius (the younger) acted as Agrippina's protector. She was later raped and killed in front of Val by his brothers.

Agrippina was afraid of the dark as a child, and Val made her a promise that she would never have to sleep in darkness. Val kept a statue of Agrippina at his house in New Orleans in her honor, accompanied by an eternal flame.

Alexander, Grace   Grace works as a sex therapist at her practice in New Orleans. Her parents died when she was twenty-four.

Grace loves books, pizza, cheesy movies, and her handsome, hunky god of a husband Julian, whom she rescued out of a cursed book in 2002.

HEIGHT: five foot two
HAIR/EYES: brown/light gray
FEATURED NOVEL: *Fantasy Lover*

Alexander, Niklos James   Son of Grace and Julian Alexander (twin to Vanessa Anne).

Alexander, Vanessa Anne   Daughter of Grace and Julian Alexander (twin to Niklos James).

Alkis   Kyrian Hunter's wealthy father. Alkis disowned him when Kyrian married Theone, telling his son that women only loved men like him for their money. When he received word that Kyrian was dead, Alkis went insane and jumped out a window. He died calling Kyrian's name.

Althea   Kyrian's quiet and bashful youngest sister who stuttered when nervous. Althea cut off all her hair when her beloved brother was killed.

Althea   Onboard physician of Megeara Kafieri's salvage vessel in search of Atlantis.

Aristophanes   Ancient Greek comedic playwright circa 450–388 B.C. Aristophanes was the author of *The Birds*, *The Frogs*, *The Clouds*, *The Knights*, *The Wasps*, and many more.

Arnhild   A blue-eyed, white-haired girl that Wulf Tryggvason had a yen for in his past life, only he didn't want to stay on his father's farm and marry her.

Avery, Michelle   One of Cassandra Peters's friends from college.

Bellioi, Gentile   An artist whom Velkan Danesti spirited away from Venice to paint Esperetta's portrait before their wedding.

Berwick, Elise Lenora   Maggie Tigarian's best friend since grade school. Tall, blonde, rich, and augmented. Elise was the founder of their study group.

Brenda   Friend of Cassandra Peters.

Brian   The financial backer of Megeara Kafieri's salvage company. Brian is tall, independently wealthy, and calmer than most humans have a right to be.

Carmichael, Rodney   Obsessive patient who stalked Grace Alexander. Rodney was killed by police when he attempted to shoot Julian. Believe me, the world is a better place without him.

Ceara   Talon/Speirr's little sister, sacrificed in front of him only days before her sixteenth birthday. For two thousand years Ceara refused to cross over, haunting her brother, warning him of danger when it came, but unable to tell him the exact future. After Talon found happiness with Sunshine Runningwolf, Ceara finally chose to leave her brother and let her soul be reborn into the world of man.

Chartier, Menyara   An African-American voodoo high priestess, Menyara watched over Cherise Gautier's grave after Nick turned Dark-Hunter and disappeared for a while. Nick calls her "Aunt Mennie". She was the tenant in the room next to Nick and his mother all the while when he was growing up. She was also the woman who delivered Nick as a baby, since his mother hadn't been able to afford a hospital stay.

HEIGHT: four foot ten
POWERS: clairvoyance

Chatelaine, Todd Middleton   Member of Maggie Tigarian's study group.

Christof   Captain of Megeara Kafieri's salvage boat.

Cobb, Tristan   A regular patron of Sanctuary and part-time bookie. Tristan takes bets only when Mama and Papa Peltier aren't around to catch him.

Cody, Tom   The good-looking guy to whom Cassandra Peters introduced her friend Michelle at a bar.

Corvinus, Mathhias   Ancient member of the Order of the Dragon who lost his wife to a Daimon. He reestablished the order to purge the world of the undead . . . including Were-Hunters and Dark-Hunters. The Corvinuses and the Danestis have a *looooong* history of bad blood.

Corwin, Stephen   Real name: Stefan. Investment banker in Chicago who tried to woo Esperetta Danesti to no avail. Stephen is a descendent of Mathhias Corvinus, and a member of the Order of the Dragon. He and his cohorts kidnapped Retta in order to snare her husband Prince Velkan.

HAIR/EYES: blond/blue

Crenshaw, Richard   Waiter at Mike Anderson's Seafood.

Crystal   A woman in Sin's casino who was pulled from a gallu demon's clutches by Sin himself. Of course, the memories of the event were immediately erased from her mind.

Cynthia   Nickname: Thia. Megeara and Tory's cousin, daughter of the sister of Theron and Eneas who owns a deli in New York. Named after Artemis, Cynthia looks a bit like her, too. Cynthia hates Greece, hunting for Atlantis, and pretty much everything that isn't related to shopping or members of the opposite sex.

BORN: 1978
HEIGHT: six foot two
HAIR: red

Daniels, Leslie The bank president of Wachovia, whom Vane Kattalakis calls when Bride's movers need to verify a money transfer.

Darius Brother of Ias of Groesia/Alexion. Died a year before Ias.

Davis, Matt A college student and bartender, Matt sometimes doubles as a bouncer at Sanctuary.

Dere One of Talon's sisters before Ceara, and only one year Talon's junior. Dere died at the age of four when—while searching for the fey folk Talon told her lived on the edge of the cliff—she slipped on the rocks and fell.

Devereaux, Amanda (See Amanda Hunter.)

Devereaux, Ekaterina Nickname: Trina. Fourth of the Devereaux sisters. Trina is a very good friend of Sunshine Running-wolf.

HAIR: black

Devereaux, Esmerelda Nickname: Essie. Eldest of the Devereaux sisters, Esmerelda works as a midwife.

HAIR: black

Devereaux, Karma Fifth of the Devereaux sisters.

Devereaux, Petra Third of the Devereaux sisters.

Devereaux, Selena (See Selena Laurens.)

Devereaux, Tabitha Lane Nickname: Tabby. Named after the daughter on *Bewitched,* Tabitha is the eighth of the Devereaux sisters and twin to Amanda—identical except for the scar running down her cheek, a memento left by the Daimon Desiderius. She has a master's degree in Ancient Civilizations.

A self-proclaimed vampire slayer, Tabitha has a bizarre fondness for a "strength potion" that consists of curdled milk,

Tabasco sauce, egg yolks, and tea leaves. She owns Pandora's Box, an adult shop on Bourbon Street.

Tabitha is the wife of the Dark-Hunter Valerius Magnus (not to be confused with the Valerius who tortured and killed Kyrian. That was Valerius's *grandfather*. I really can't stress this enough). She was made immortal by Acheron, so that she might walk beside her equally immortal sister Amanda for all eternity.

HEIGHT: five foot ten
HAIR/EYES: auburn/blue
POWERS: clairsentience, psychometry
FEATURED NOVEL: *Seize the Night*

Devereaux, Tiyana   (deceased) Nickname: Tia. Sixth of the Devereaux sisters, Tia was a voodoo priestess. Tabitha used to refer to Tia affectionately as "Gladys", after the nosy neighbor from *Bewitched*.

Tia was killed by the Dark-Hunter Ulric, when he was possessed by the Daimon Desiderius.

HAIR/EYES: jet-black/blue

Devereaux, Yasmina   Nickname: Mina. Second of the Devereaux sisters.

HAIR: brown

Diana   Kyrian's sister, older than him by two years. Diana had a shrewish temperament. She named her first son Kyrian.

Dierdre   The Gaulish-Celt woman Talon/Speirr was supposed to marry.

Dieter   An older man, member of the Order of the Dragon and cohort of Stephen Corwin.

Dimitri   A friend of Kyrian's while in the army.

Diokles of Sparta   (aka Diokles the Butcher) A Spartan stratgoi (top general) with a scar that ran down the length of his left cheek. Diokles was the father of Julian Alexander—he slept with Aphrodite after saving one of her temples. Diokles died in 167 B.C.

Divine, Marla/Marlon   The stylish and outgoing drag queen friend of Tabitha Devereaux. Marla has a fetish for men's coats.

Duvall, Ethan   Recently out of juvenile detention, Ethan is trying to put his life back together. His probation officer got him a job bussing tables for Mama Peltier at Sanctuary. That probation officer's got nothing on Mama. Just ask Ethan.

Eala   The mean-spirited smith's daughter in Talon/Speirr and Nynia's clan.

Father Anthony   Dangereuse St. Richard's priest in Paris.

Feara of the Morrigantes   Mother of Talon/Speirr and Ceara. Once the queen of her clan, Feara seduced their Druid High Priest and then ran away with him, leaving the clan without leadership. She died in sickness, orphaning her young children and forcing them to return to the clan from whence they came.

Fia   One of Talon's sisters before Ceara. Fia died before she was a year old.

Flora   Maternal grandmother of the Devereaux sisters and seer of the family.

POWERS: clairvoyance

Frank   The sleazeball guy who ran the general store in Fairbanks, Alaska, and charged Zarek entirely too much for all his supplies.

Gagne, Terry   Sunshine's ex-husband, whom she met in art school. Their marriage lasted exactly two years, four months, and twenty-two days.

Gagne, Ty Bald, tattoo-covered African-American man who checks IDs at Club Abyss.

Gallagher, Rosalie Daughter of Portuguese immigrants and wife of Jamie Gallagher (they were married June 17, 1925). Rosalie died of old age (Jamie broke the Code of Conduct and visited her in the hospital).

Gallagher, Rose Great-granddaughter of the Dark-Hunter Jamie Gallagher. Rose owns the locket containing the photographs of Jamie and Rosalie. Rose met Jamie in the hospital while visiting her friend Jenna, but she never knew it was really her long-departed relative.

HEIGHT: five foot ten
HAIR/EYES: jet-black/deep blue

Gambieri, Bradley One of the docents who leads vampire tours around the French Quarter in New Orleans.

Gautier, Cherise Nick Gautier's mother (she gave birth when she was fifteen). A former Bourbon Street exotic dancer and Miss Louisiana, Cherise later went to college on a full scholarship. Her parents were wealthy folks who lived in Kenner, but they disowned her when they discovered she was pregnant with Nick.

Nick bought her a house for her birthday when he was twenty with his earnings as Kyrian's Squire, but he never told his mother what he was involved in. She was convinced her son was dealing drugs.

Cherise was a cook and bartender at Sanctuary, and was always trying to get Ash to eat something. She loved romance novels.

Cherise was killed in her house by the Dark-Hunter Ulric, when he was possessed by the spirit of the Daimon Desiderius. It was her death that prompted Nick to commit suicide so that Artemis might make him a Dark-Hunter.

She is entombed in the Gautier family mausoleum at the St. Louis cemetery on Basin Street. Ash sends her flowers every day, and visits whenever he is in town.

HAIR: blonde

Gavrilopolous, Spiro   The official who denied Megeara Kafieri a permit to look for Atlantis. A callous little weasel, Spiro laughed at her for even suggesting such a thing.

George   A tall, gaunt man with a gold-capped tooth, George is a member of the Order of the Dragon and cohort of Stephen Corwin.

George   The Skotos Solin's personal chauffeur in Greece.

Gilbert   Trusted servant and British butler of Valerius Magnus since he was fifteen years old (Lord knows how he managed it). The Squire Council refused to make Gilbert a Squire, due to the close nature of his relationship to Val. He was best man at Valerius and Tabitha's wedding.

Grant, Aloysius   Operated Tigarian Tech after the alleged death of Aristotle Tigarian.

Hector   A Trojan prince, and a key player in the Trojan War. Hector was killed by Achilles.

Heilig, Paul   The Seattle Chief of Police who married an Apollite-turned-Daimon that Ravyn later killed. Paul was working alongside Stryker and the Daimons.

Hesiod   Wrote the *Theogony* (with help from Clio).

Homer   Author of the *Odyssey* and the *Iliad*. He once wrote a record of the birth of the Dark-Hunters called the *Kynigostaia*. It did not survive.

Hunter, Amanda   (née Devereaux) Nickname: Mandy (just don't get caught calling her that if you're not Tabitha). Ninth of the Devereaux sisters and twin to Tabitha. Amanda was killed by the Dark-Hunter Ulric when he was possessed by the Daimon Desiderius, but she was later revived and made immortal by Acheron.

Amanda met her husband Kyrian by waking up handcuffed to him after being attacked at her twin's house. A black belt in aikido and a powerful human sorceress, Amanda is the mother of Marissa Hunter.

HEIGHT: five foot ten
HAIR/EYES: auburn/blue
POWERS: clairvoyance, telepathy, clairsentience
FEATURED NOVEL: *Night Pleasures*

Hunter, Marissa   The daughter of Amanda and Kyrian Hunter who possesses some potentially awesome powers. Marissa is a favorite with Simi and her godfather Acheron.

She has been referred to as "The Final Fate". Whoever possesses her possesses the key to control the most primal, ancient power of all time. Whatever that is. Must be something important, though, because Apollymi believes that by killing her, she can resurrect her son Apostolos.

POWERS: telekinesis, animal telepathy

Iason   Iason met Julian in the Spartan barracks. He was the leader of his group. When Julian took a beating for Iason, they became inseparable. When Julian became jealous of Iason's love for Penelope (and hers for him), Julian shot Iason's heart with Eros's lead arrow to kill his love. When forced by Priapus to drink water from the Pool of Memory, Iason challenged Julian. He was accidentally killed in the duel.

Icarion   King of the ancient Greek island of Didymos. Icarion is the husband of Aara, mother of Acheron and Styxx.

Idiag   Talon/Speirr's uncle and clan chief, who begrudgingly let Talon and Ceara back into the clan after they were orphaned. Idiag was the one who personally gave Talon his tattoo. He died in Talon's arms on the battlefield, causing Talon to seek vengeance on the Gaulish clan he thought to be Idiag's murderers.

Jenna   Neighbor of Susan Kontis.

Jenna   Young woman whom Jamie Gallagher saved from a Daimon attack. A petite brunette with large green eyes, Jenna is the friend of Rose Gallagher, Jamie's great-granddaughter.

Joanie   A writer for the *Daily Inquisitor* in Seattle and official paranoid nutcase. She wears tinfoil in her bra. (Okay . . . maybe that's a rumor. Hopefully it's a rumor.)

John   Erin McDaniels's grumpy, highly caffeinated boss, who also works as an Oracle for the Greek gods.

Justina   Megeara Kafieri's second-in-command on her scientific team.

Kafieri, Athena   (deceased) The wife of Theron and mother of Tory.

Kafieri, Eneas   Megeara's father who died an alcoholic in 1990. Eneas carried out the family tradition in his lifelong pursuit of Atlantis. He was laughed out of both the publishing industry and the academic profession for his wild hypotheses. He died just after discovering artifacts that could have proven the island's existence.

Kafieri, Jason   Megeara's artist brother who died when his diving line tangled and his tank ran out of oxygen while searching for Atlantis.

Kafieri, Megeara   (See Megeara Saatskakis.)

Kafieri, Theo   Megeara's sage grandfather who was blinded by a raiding Nazi party on his ninth birthday and left for dead while the rest of his family was slaughtered. A mysterious man (his "Saving Angel") saved him and shipped him off to America.

Kafieri, Theron (deceased) Megeara's uncle; Eneas's brother. Theron also died in pursuit of the elusive Atlantis. The father of Tory, Theron drowned in the Aegean in 1980 in a diving accident.

Kafieri, Tory Daughter of Theron and Athena; Megeara's cousin. She was five years old when her parents died. Tory is a precocious certified genius who loves nothing more than the obsession of hunting for Atlantis with her cousin. She communicates with Geary in their own secret language, a mix between ancient Greek and Latin. She has a teddy bear named Mr. Cuddles, and a tendency to spout obscure—and correct—statistics at random. Tory is fond of junk food: Moon Pies, Hostess cupcakes, and Pop-Tarts especially. She wears extremely thick glasses, and is not exactly graceful.

BORN: 1981
HAIR: brown

Kichka Tory Kafieri's cat, a Bengal, who liked Megeara so much she adopted her.

Kish Sin's non-Squire, Kish was originally a runaway slave. A liar and a thief, he bargained his soul with a demon in exchange for immortality and wealth. Kish met Sin when he was sent to kill him—which, to be fair, is how most people meet Sin. Kish asked Sin to kill him instead, so that he might be freed from his horrible life of pain. Sin could not ignore the humanity of that plea, so he bartered Kish away from his demon pact.

HEIGHT: five foot eleven
HAIR: black

Landry, Blaine Hunter Member of Maggie Tigarian's study group. Blaine is a conceited, arrogant jerk who hated Nick.

Laroux, Charlie   One of the doormen at the Belle Queen strip club. A friend of Tabitha Devereaux and Nick Gautier.

Laurens, Bill (William)   Married to Selena Laurens, Bill is the son of State Senator Laurens. He is a lawyer who does work for the Were-Hunters (and sometimes the Dark-Hunters). He makes sure they stay "law-abiding", and comes to the aid of Weres who might run afoul of the law. Bill broke his arm once playing basketball.

HAIR: brown

Laurens, Selena   (née Devereaux) Nickname: Lane or Lanie. The seventh Devereaux sister, Selena is a seventh daughter of a seventh daughter. A gypsy by birth, Selena owned a tarot card and palm reading stand under the name Madame Selene, Moon Mistress. After a law was passed that no more psychics could work in the Square and Selena protested, Acheron bought her a building.

   Selena roomed with Grace Alexander her first year at Tulane. Despite her love of New Agey woo-woo, Selena has a Ph.D. in Ancient History and Physics with a specialty in Bronze Age Greece.

Leonard   Friend of the Squire Celena. Leonard specializes in fireproofing houses, underground bunkers for Dark-Hunters, sprinkler systems . . . you name it. If you happen to be in the Mississippi area, give him a call.

Liora   Wife of Ias of Groesia/Alexion and secret lover of Lycantes. Liora did not love Ias as much as he thought, and so dropped the medallion when attempting the out clause after he had become a Dark-Hunter. Instead of freeing Ias, she doomed him to Shadedom, and a life as Acheron's Alexion. As punishment, Ash turned her to stone. Personally, I think she could have suffered a little bit more.

Lisa   Grace Alexander's secretary.

Lycantes   Had an affair with Liora, wife of Ias of Groesia/Alexion. Lycantes later killed Ias, who came back as a Dark-Hunter.

Magnus, Aesculus   Brother of Valerius Magnus; half-brother of Zarek of Moesia.

Magnus, Gaius   Roman senator; father of Aesculus; Lucius; Marcus; Marius; Valerius; and Zarek (whom he sired on one of his Greek slaves). Gaius used slaves to train his sons for cruelty. He killed his wife for smiling at another man. Not exactly a sunshine and puppies sort of guy.

Magnus, Lucius   Brother of Valerius Magnus; half-brother of Zarek of Moesia.

Magnus, Marcus   Brother of Valerius Magnus; half-brother of Zarek of Moesia.

Magnus, Marius   Brother of Valerius Magnus; half-brother of Zarek of Moesia.

Magnus, Valerius   The elder, non-Dark-Hunter. This Valerius captured pre-Dark-Hunter Kyrian in battle, tortured him, and took his wife as his mistress. This Valerius is the *grandfather,* and spitting image, of Valerius Magnus the Dark-Hunter. It would behoove you to remember this very important piece of information. It's not something anyone likes to talk about, and when the subject is brought up in conversation it's a sure bet that someone in the room's temper is well past its breaking point. A wrong word could be your last.

McDaniels, Erin   A creative woman racked by nightmares and hunted by Skoti. Erin fell in love with V'Aidan, a Skotos dragon. She is currently a bestselling novelist.

FEATURED STORY: "Phantom Lover"

McTierney, Deirdre   Bride Kattalakis's sister who lives in Atlanta. Deirdre is divorced (her lousy husband left her).

McTierney, Joyce   Bride's mother. Joyce is a veterinarian like her husband Paul.

McTierney, Patrick   Bride's brother. Patrick works for a firm in the New Orleans business district. His wife's name is Maggie.

McTierney, Paul   Bride's father. Paul is a veterinarian in Slidell. He is the foremost expert in Louisiana on dog cases, and a strong advocate of "If you love your pet, neuter or spay". Paul did in fact know about the Were-world before his daughter brought home an Arcadian Lykos for a boyfriend.

Michael   The slimeball husband of Dangereuse St. Richard. Michael betrayed Danger's family during the French Revolution in order to obtain Danger's father's house.

Min-Quan   A fisherman who purportedly sold the best zong zi ever made. Min-Quan once told Acheron, "He who lets fear rule him, has fear for a master".

Morganette   Danger St. Richard's insane aunt. Morganette thought her cat was her dead husband Etienne, so she would dress him up like a man.

Murrdyd   Talon/Speirr's bastard cousin.

Neely, Margie   Assistant on-site nurse to Dr. Carson Whitethunder at Sanctuary in New Orleans. This petite, red-headed ex-waitress is currently attending veterinary school.

Ryssa   A Greek princess who was one of Apollo's favorite mistresses. She bore him a son, which made the Apollite queen so mad she sent a team of Apollites to kill them both . . . the act that ultimately led Apollo to curse the Apollites. She was also, notably, the sister of Acheron.

Ningal   Sin's unfaithful Sumerian wife, who publicly announced her affairs to shame her husband. (For example, she wore an Atlantean sun on her chest to advertise her relationship with Archon.) In revenge, Sin's twin brother Zakar made her dream of snakes and Gorgons while she slept.

Nynia   Ancient Celt, fisherman's daughter, and Talon/Speirr's true love. Nynia was married to Speirr for five years. She died giving birth to Speirr's stillborn child. (See Sunshine Runningwolf.)

Ora   Talon/Speirr's aunt who was murdered by Camulus's illegitimate son.

Parker, Sharon   Ex-waitress in Alaska whom Zarek saved (along with her baby) from freezing and starving to death. In return, Sharon gave Zarek her friendship and ran errands for him during the days of twenty-four-hour sun.

Parker, Trixie   Sharon's daughter.

Penelope   Born circa 178 B.C., Penelope was promised to Iason before the jealous Julian shot her with Eros's golden arrow. Years later, when Priapus forced her to drink water from the Pool of Memory, she went insane with the knowledge, killing her two children (Atolycus and Callista) and then herself.

Peters, Jefferson T.   Father of Cassandra and Phoebe Peters. Jefferson is the wealthy owner and founder of Peters, Briggs, and Smith Pharmaceuticals, one of the world's largest drug research and development companies.

Phaedra   Kyrian's sister, younger by one year. Phaedra had the voice of an angel.

Plato   Born Aristocles, Plato was an ancient Greek philosopher and student of Socrates. He founded one of the earliest known schools, and is known for his *Dialogues*. He also wrote extensively about the existence of Atlantis and its origins.

BORN: 427 B.C.
BIRTHPLACE: Athens

Rosa   Kyrian's thin, elderly, Hispanic housekeeper and cook. Rosa had a heart attack when she was possessed by Desiderius and tried to kill Kyrian. Thankfully, she survived. She has a son, Miguel.

Runningwolf, Daniel   Sunshine's father. Daniel is a Native American with shamanic powers (and can therefore never touch a Dark-Hunter). He is the owner of Club Runningwolf's on Canal Street in New Orleans.

Runningwolf, Rain   Sunshine's older brother; the middle child.

Runningwolf, Starla   Sunshine's mother; a daughter of the Morrigán. Starla can see auras; a power she passed on to her daughter Sunshine.

POWERS: aura perception

Runningwolf, Storm   Sunshine's oldest brother. Storm is a bad housekeeper who snores. (Well, he does!)

Runningwolf, Sunshine   A very talented artist with a very short attention span. Sunshine is the wife of the Dark-Hunter Talon, and immortal granddaughter of the Morrigán. Sunshine is extremely fond of the colors pink and purple and is constantly losing things . . . including herself. She has a tattoo on her inner left ankle of a stylized Celtic sun and the symbol for creativity.

HAIR: black
POWERS: aura perception
FEATURED NOVEL: *Night Embrace*

Saatsakis, Megeara   Nickname: Geary. Born Megeara Kafieri, named after the Fury of Greek mythology. Geary changed her name and sued for emancipation from her father at age sixteen in order to get into college. She has a Ph.D. in Anthropology from Yale University.

Trained as a lifeguard, Geary is a certified diving instructor and underwater recovery expert. She wears an Atlantean coin (Apollymi's gold medallion) around her neck that her father gave her when he died.

With pure Atlantean blood in her ancestry, Geary is a lucid dreamer who is sensitive to the voices of the gods, especially Apollymi. She is married to the former Dream-Hunter Arikos.

BORN: 1968
BIRTHPLACE: Santorini, Greece
HEIGHT: six feet
HAIR/EYES: blonde/deep blue
FEATURED NOVEL: *The Dream-Hunter*

Santana, Wayne   Convicted and imprisoned for involuntary manslaughter at the age of sixteen, he served twelve years in jail. Wayne lucked out when Sunshine Runningwolf hired him to work in her father's club despite his record. The Runningwolf family lucked out too, in gaining a faithful friend and a good lookout for the absentminded Sunshine.

Schliemann, Heinrich   German treasure hunter obsessed with Homer's works and the discovery of Troy. In his haste and enthusiasm, Heinrich dug too deeply too quickly, possibly destroying important historical evidence of the Trojan War.

BORN: January 6, 1822
BIRTHPLACE: Mecklenburg-Schwerin, Germany

Scipio   According to current history books, Scipio was the assassin of Julian and his family. But who believes the history books?

Scott, Cameron   Once commissioned a painting from Sunshine Runningwolf.

Scott   A fixation of Cynthia's who joined her in Greece to hunt for Atlantis the summer that Megeara Kafieri met the Dream-Hunter Arikos.

Sisyphus   Former king of Corinth, Sisyphus was doomed to Tartarus for his trickery. For all eternity he must push a boulder up a hill. Once he has almost reached the top, it slips and rolls down to the bottom again. Every single time. Forever. That's hell for you.

Stefan   The man who, thanks to the Skotos Solin, ultimately signed the permit for Geary so that she could legally look for Atlantis.

St. Michel, Rudy   A human ex-con who works at Sanctuary, Rudy is responsible for the bar's arcade games and poker tournaments. When needed, he is also a bouncer and all-around rule enforcer. He has lots of colorful tattoos. Ask him about them sometime.

HAIR: black

St. Richard, Edmonde   Brother of Dangereuse St. Richard. Edmonde died when the family was betrayed by Danger's husband. He was only four years old.

St. Richard, Esmée   Maman Esmée, Dangereuse St. Richard's stepmother. Esmée had a weakness for hats.

St. Richard, Jacqueline   Sister of Dangereuse St. Richard. Jacqueline died when the family was betrayed by Danger's husband. She was less than a year old.

Tammy   A friend of Maggie Tigarian. Tammy is a Goth ex-art major.

Teddy   A colleague of Megeara's, Teddy is more like a father to her. With short brown hair and dimples, he is a puckish sort of fellow. My favorite kind.

Tepeş, Vlad   (aka Dracula or Vlad the Impaler) Heir to the throne of Wallachia, and member of the Order of the Dragon. Vlad was the father of Esperetta Danesti. (See Esperetta Danesti, Velkan Danesti.) Vlad was widely known for his cruelty, his elaborate torture, and his tendency toward inflicting death by impaling.

Legend has it that he placed a golden cup in the middle of the square of Tirgoviste to tempt thieves. They were so scared of him that no one touched it for the entirety of Vlad's reign. It is also said that he invited the sick and poor to dine in a great hall in Tirgoviste . . . then he boarded it up and set it on fire.

Nice guy, really.

After Vlad's death, his head was sent to Constantinople and displayed on a stake for all to see.

BORN: A.D. 1431
BIRTHPLACE: Sighişoara, Transylvania
REIGN: A.D. 1456–62

Theone   The daughter of a prostitute, a courtesan herself, and pretty much as evil as evil comes. Kyrian broke his engagement to the Macedonian princess in order to marry Theone. As a repayment for his love, she drugged him, betrayed him to the Romans, and became the mistress of Kyrian's torturer (Valerius the older, not Valerius the Dark-Hunter). She deserves to be crowned Queen Bitch of the Universe . . . only last time I checked, Artemis still held that title.

Tina   The skinny, fashionable secretary of Jefferson T. Peters.

Trahan, Whitney Logan   A member of Maggie Tigarian's study group.

Tress   One of Talon/Speirr's sisters before Ceara. Tress died of the same illness that claimed their mother.

Trish   Esperetta Danesti's assistant at her law office in Chicago.

Tsiaris, Cosmo   The Kafieri family attorney in Greece and pseudo-partner in Eneas Kafieri's salvage company.

Twisted Hearts   The favorite local (Minnesota) band of Cassandra Peters and Michelle Avery.

Vargas, Jose   The cook at Sanctuary; Mama Peltier's right-hand man and assistant.

Vieux-Doo Dogs   A local New Orleans biker gang that frequents Sanctuary.

Warren, Angie   (deceased) Childhood best friend of Susan Kontis. Susan introduced Angie to her husband Jimmy. Angie was the vegan veterinarian who freed Ravyn Kontis in his cat form from the pound by having Susan adopt him . . . right before the Spathi Daimons killed her and her husband.

Warren, James   (deceased) Nickname: Jimmy. A detective and best friend of Susan Kontis. Jimmy was killed by Spathi Daimons alongside his wife Angie.

Winston, Cara   A waitress and short-order cook at Sanctuary. She's quick with a comeback and loves to pick on both Alain and Kyle Peltier.

Woodard, Tony   Sanctuary office assistant and entertainment coordinator. Tony also handles publicity and does the Web site updates.

Xanthippe   An infamous ancient Greek shrew. (Technically she wasn't ancient when she was infamous . . . but she was always a shrew. What can I say? You've got to watch out for those Greek women.)

Xenobia   The Devereaux girls' gypsy aunt who specializes in curses.

Yves   The best friend of Marla Divine.

Zetes   Kyrian's uncle. Zetes bargained with Valerius the older for Kyrian's life.

Yes, Virginia, It Is a Language

Conversational Atlantean for the World Traveler

Never underestimate an Atlantean.
We're not your average pantheon.
—Katra Agrotera

The World According to Plato

But afterwards there occurred violent earthquakes and floods,
and in a single day and night of misfortune all your warlike
men in a body sank into the earth, and the island of Atlantis
in a like manner disappeared into the depths of the sea.
—from Plato's Timaeus, 360 B.C.

Plato was one of the first to mention the fabled city of Atlantis in
two of his works: *Timaeus* and *Critias*. (Believe you me, they're
pretty dry reading.)

Plato covered all the facts and figures. The city was composed
of concentric circles of land and sea; there was the inner island,
a middle ring, and an outer ring. The island was surrounded by
a wall of *orichalcum* (which was supposedly a metal more precious
than anything except gold), the middle ring a wall of tin, and
the outer ring a wall of brass. There was a large, very fertile plain

outside the city that ran from the sea to the mountains, and from it the Atlanteans grew anything their little hearts desired. Their kings were rich, the military was unmatched, the temples were works of art. Everyone was beautiful and sober. There were lots of animals. Even elephants. And then eleven thousand years ago, it was destroyed.

(*Yawn.*)

The annoying part is that just when *Critias* starts getting good and Zeus is about to smite down the whole city for becoming a bunch of vain and ungrateful louts, it ends. The work has been lost to history, just as Atlantis was lost to the world.

There has been much speculation about what happened to the text and what it was that Zeus really said.

Want to know my theory?

(Too bad, you're gonna get it anyway.)

My theory is that Plato's girlfriend, upon reading the stone tablet manuscript, beat him over the head with it, yelling, "You're such a *man*. Who cares about what color the stones were that they dug out of the ground? Who cares about the size of the army, or how many square feet the island was? Were there *any* women in this city? What did they eat? Where did they live? How did they love?" . . . and then she promptly broke up with him.

The World According to the Rest of Us

Plato wrote of a parable about a nation that was destroyed long before his ancestors had been born. He knew nothing of the truth. Anyone who'd ever gotten close to learning about Atlantis didn't live long enough to tell anyone else.
—*Arikos*

Most of what Plato wrote about Atlantis is true. But what about the rest? There are powers so deep and dark buried with this lost continent that they make a mockery of all the pantheons that have come before or after it.

Got your popcorn? Sit back, and I shall enlighten you.

You already know some of it . . . but let me start at the beginning.

Atlantis is named after Atlantia, goddess and eldest sister of the ancient god Archon. With the help of Ydori (god of the Ocean) and Eda (goddess of the Earth), Archon created Atlantis as a gift for his wife Apollymi. Apollymi was so overcome by the gift that she wept, flooding the land and creating the rings of water.

You've learned by now the gods' penchant for the overdramatic.

Since Apollymi was barren, Archon, Ydor, and Eda created a race of people to live in Apollymi's gift: the Atlanteans. They were peaceful, despite their great army, and they were scholars. They were also psychic, and highly skilled in the uses of magic. They were beautiful and wealthy and perfect, and Apollymi probably flooded someplace else with her tears after their birth.

Who wouldn't be jealous?

Well, Zeus for one. Poseidon for two. Apollo for the charm. When Zeus cast out his son's too-perfect Apollites, the Atlanteans welcomed them, securing a place in Apollo's heart forever. They intermarried with the royal family, and future Atlanteans became his children as well.

You always hurt the ones you love.

As you know from chapter 6 (if you've been skipping around, shame on you. Go back and brush up on your Daimon lore), the Atlantean queen became jealous when Apollo fathered a son on the Greek princess Ryssa, so she ordered the son and mother killed. For this, Apollo destroyed Atlantis, and cursed all the Apollites.

Words have power. Actions speak louder than words. Vengeance is not to be treated lightly . . . and neither are the gods.

Here endeth the lesson.

The Library of Atlantis

The entire history of mankind is written by people wanting something they can't have.
—Katra Agrotera

What little we know today of the Atlanteans' sociology comes from legends. In addition to the warriors and the miners and the priests and the farmers, there were scholars and teachers. They were engineers who built a city more technologically advanced than any civilization alive at the time had a right to be. They were philosophers who attained complete peace in their hearts, minds, and souls. They were writers who compiled a library with the knowledge of the ages, a library housing books that contained the secrets of the world.

My favorite tale is of Soteria, the librarian of Atlantis. She intimidated men with her beauty and intelligence (instead of a severe bun and glasses). The books were her whole world; she ate, slept, and breathed the written word. She would always be found reading in the courtyard, telling patrons that it was her goal to read every book in the library. Despite the fact that there were more volumes there than could be read in a lifetime, Soteria was still determined to try.

When Atlantis was destroyed, Soteria refused to leave the library. Upon her death, she vowed to protect the books until the end of time.

Legend has it that somewhere beneath the waves the library of Atlantis still exists, protected by the ghost of the librarian. It is said that if you somehow come across one of the original texts from the Atlantean library (one of the ones that was checked out at the time, perhaps?), you can summon Soteria's ghost and she will lead you to the rest of the books. Until that day I imagine her spirit there, in the ruins under the water, happily reading her way from A to Z.

Abadonna	(ah-ba-DON-na)	Term of honor. Means "the heart of the destroyer".
Aekyra	(AY-kee-ra)	The question "Are you . . . ?" As in: "Are you Bob?"
akra	(ahh-KRA)	lady and mistress
akri	(ahh-KRI)	lord and master
Alexion	(ah-LEX-ee-on)	Title of office. Means "defender" or "protector".
anekico	(ah-neh-KEE-ko)	victory
aracnia	(ah-RAC-nee-ah)	spider
asterosum	(ah-ste-RO-sum)	Ancient drug that completely paralyzes your body, but leaves you able to see, hear, and feel.
Atlantia	(at-LAN-tee-a)	graceful beauty
edera	(eh-DEAR-a)	precious baby (endearment)
efto	(eff-TOE)	this is
eta	(eh-TA)	it is
Eycharitisi	(eh-ka-ris-TEE-zee)	Pleasure. Also the name of a potent aphrodisiac that was the drug du jour in Atlantis. One dose can last up to three days.

(continued)

foremasta	(for-MAS-ta)	long, dusterlike robe
imora	(EE-mo-rah)	love
katoteros	(ka-to-TER-os)	heaven
kolasi	(ko-LA-si)	hell
kyriay ypochrosi	(ki-ri-YAY yip-o-KRO-si)	noble obligation
kyrios	(KEE-ree-os)	lord (respectful)
laminas	(LA-mee-nas)	haven
ma komatia	(ma ko-ma-TEE-a)	precious (endearment) (Ash calls Marissa this.)
metera/matisera	(me-TER-a)/ (mat-tear-SER-ah)	mother
m'gios	(ma-gee-OS)	my son
mibreiara	(mee-bray-AH-rah)	mistress
naiea	(nea)	yes
ochia	(OH-kee-ya)	no
Olygaia	(oh-lee-GUY-ah)	Olympian
Peradomatio	(per-a-do-MA-ti-o)	Hall of the Past
ypnsi	(yip-(n)-si)	sacred sleep that Orasia once dispensed from Katoteros

(AND THE VERY LOOSE TRANSLATIONS OF)

Anekico ler aracnia.   Victory to the spider. (Meaning: Patience wins the day.)

Efto ler kariti u topyra.   This is not the time or place.

Ki mi ypomonitikosi teloson semerie.   And today my patience ends.

Protula akri gonatizum vlaza!   Bow down before your lord and master, slimeball! (This is the Charonte language.)

Chronia apostraph, anthrice mi achi.   Time moves on; people do not.

Imora thea mi savur.   God save me from love.

Apollymi Magosa Fonia Kataastreifa   Apollymi of wisdom, death, and destruction

Apollymi Akrakataastreifa   Apollymi the Great Destroyer (or Lady Destroyer)

ACHERON PARTHENOPAEUS

The Hidden Chapter

*Have you ever noticed that salvation, much
like your car keys, is usually found where and
when you least expect it?*

—*Acheron*

He was the first thing you saw when you awoke to this unlife. He
held your hand and guided you through your personal hell. He
helped. He understood. He told you the truth. He didn't make it
less painful . . . but he made you stronger.

Unfortunately, the understanding in Ash's case does not flow
in the reverse. He may know you down to your heart and nerve
and sinew, but you will never know the real Acheron
Parthenopaeus. To call him friend is easy; to find out anything
personal about him is impossible. He's like a phantom wind that
whispers through the soul. Untouchable. Unreachable. Evocative.
Time has no meaning to him and he is power absolute. He is
intensity. He is also compassion. He is the great conundrum. He
is a puzzle that is not yet meant to be solved. Oh, it will be solved
eventually—all the best puzzles are.

But not by you.

As long as you can accept that, you will be able to trust him
unequivocally. And you need to trust Ash; he is the one thing in
your new life you can always count on. If you let it bother you it
will become a sore that will fester inside you, slowly eating away
at you little by little until you envy even the Shades' existence.

That way lies madness, my friend.

I know.

I've touched it.

Acheron is a god. He is known as the Cursed God, or Cursed
One. His namesake is the Underworld river Acheron, the river of
woe. The river Acheron branches off from the Styx, the river
across which Charon ferries the departed into Hades. It is said

that if any part of your body touches the river Acheron, its woes will seep into your soul and ruin you with their grief.

In the Atlantean pantheon he is known as Apostolos, dreaded son of Apollymi who will bring about the end of the world.

By releasing the Dimme, he almost did.

Ash has the power to erase memories, thoughts, events, even time from your mind. From everyone's mind. No doubt he'll erase this chapter too once he finds it. Again. Again and again. That's why there's no need to number it, or list it in the contents. I keep putting it in, and he keeps erasing it from existence.

It is a game we play, like chess.

Gods are very fond of games.

One day . . . one day the world will remember what Acheron was. They will learn what Acheron has become. One day we will all tremble and fall to our knees, and our tears will be tears of exquisite joy and exquisite sorrow at the revelation. One day these words will stay, and I will not be sorry to have written them.

So I will continue to write them for as long as he continues to erase them.

Again.

And again.

The Inner Ash

I swear, you're even thinner than
the last time I saw you.
—Cherise Gautier

Ash entered this world as a human baby, and died brutally as a human man. He was born a prince, son of King Icarion and Queen Aara of the Greek islands Didymos and Lygos. But even though he was born out of the human, he was never a human. He is a god who had been cursed to be born as a man. His mark is that of a sun with three lightning bolts piercing the center of it.

He was the first of twins. Second-born was Styxx (after the other river, you see). Styxx was the human twin. Unlike Styxx, Acheron was born with the silver eyes that mark him god-blessed—it's why the king refused him. He said the baby was no son of his. He said it was a monster.

The king wasn't wrong, as Ash's real mother is Apollymi.

At Ash's birth a wise woman said of Acheron: *"He will be a destroyer, this child. His touch will bring death to many. Not even the gods themselves will be safe from his wrath."* Not exactly the prophecy you want to bring home to mama.

It was certainly not one that the gods particularly warmed to themselves.

The first death was Acheron's beautiful sister Ryssa. And we all remember the infamous Ryssa and the curse of the Apollites. The details are not unimportant . . . but I will spare you the image that Ash is forced to live with every day of his never-ending life. Just know that he does.

That is enough.

Acheron Parthenopaeus is a god, and a god-killer. He can read thoughts and feel the presence of others. He can lift people up with his mind. He can disintegrate into nothing, and bend the physics of time and matter. The laws of science, you will have learned by now, are not the laws of the gods. Acheron can toss lightning bolts with the flick of a wrist.

Ash lives in Katoteros, the Atlantean term for "heaven", and the place where all Daimons and Apollites dream their souls will one day again rest. With him in Katoteros are Simi (naturally), the pterygsauri, Alexion, and his companion, the former Dark-Huntress Dangereuse St. Richard. Also in Katoteros is a humon-gous television that, thanks to Simi, pretty much permanently stays on QVC.

He's like a lion in the wild, beautiful to behold, but one that can never be touched or tamed. He is scarred by his past and trapped by his future. You'll have noticed the handprint scar on Acheron's neck—it comes and goes, just like the accent and random body piercings. His hair constantly changes colors because he hates the inescapable blond stamp of his Atlantean heritage. He doesn't eat real food, so don't offer it, or encourage your mother to fatten him up.

Cherise Gautier was doing that all the time, bless her heart.

In addition to the scar, which is said to visibly run from throat to navel while he is in residence in Katoteros, Acheron's true skin color is iridescent blue, streaked and marbled. His silver eyes have been caught before burning with a blood-red flame. And according to Simi, Ash has black lips and horns . . . but if we saw them we'd certainly be dead soon after.

I'm going to give Simi the benefit of the doubt on that one.

Acheron will always stand at the back of the room, with the crowd in front of him—he never allows anyone the opportunity to have him at a disadvantage. Some call it paranoia, some call it protection.

Mostly, Ash doesn't care what anyone else thinks.

Not that he's got much to be paranoid about—one of the only substances ever known to incapacitate Ash is *Aima*, a poison available only from the Destroyer herself. Stryker was the clever one that dreamed that up. My guess is, his plan won't work again anytime soon.

Ash is the total embodiment of perfect male beauty. At the height of his sexual prowess and attractiveness, he possesses a raw, unearthly magnetism. Omnipotent and omniscient, he is dangerous and lightning-fast, but at the same time he holds timeless wisdom and can be playful and caring. He protects those he loves and spoils the people who are close to his heart. He is the godfather (literally) of Marissa Hunter, and calls Simi his daughter. He will protect them with his life, and has done some pretty rough things to anyone who might endanger his girls. (Nick Gautier was the first to spring to your mind too, huh?)

Unfortunately, while he does have that pesky prophetic vision that's so impossible to rid oneself of, Acheron is blind to the destinies of those he holds near and dear. Distance may not make hearts grow fonder, but in this case it does make visions clearer.

Ash and Artie

Unlike a normal woman, you're cranky
for twenty-eight days out of the month.
—Acheron

Many a Dark-Hunter has tried to get to the bottom of what secrets lie between Acheron and the goddess Artemis, and each has inevitably failed.

Twisted doesn't even begin to describe this relationship. Yin and yang: They hate each other as much as they need each other. Without Artemis to feed on, Ash would become a soulless killer with no compassion. Without Acheron, Artemis would have no conscience. Beneficial for the fate of the world, perhaps, but . . . honestly . . . I worry about them.

It started with infatuation and a kiss, the way most wonderful stories end.

This is not a wonderful story.

Acheron kissed Artemis hoping for death, for freedom from his wretched life. He was not hoping she would fall for him.

At the age of twenty, Acheron was ordered beaten by his human father until Artemis showed herself . . . which she did, but not to the humans. She thought Ash deserved the beating for betraying her and publicizing their relationship. He hung for three days in her temple, naked and bleeding. The humans shaved his head and branded the back of his skull with Artemis's symbol.

But he hadn't betrayed her. He hadn't told anyone about her and their relationship. Even to this day, he doesn't mention it.

He was sterilized and could not father children, until his twenty-first birthday, when Simi's mother came to him and unlocked his Atlantean god-powers.

Hello, Katra.

Acheron died at the hands of Apollo and was brought back by Artemis who couldn't live without him (literally). Ash is Artemis's dirty little secret. She hides him up there, you know, in her temple on Olympus whenever she forces him to visit. So he is forbidden to act out against her or use any magic there—the gods will notice. They always do. I'm sure Zeus wouldn't be too pleased to know that daddy's little girl is letting the riffraff in the back door.

Acheron and Artemis are blood-bonded, so to destroy Artemis would be to destroy himself. For Ash, there is no out clause. He wears his shackles with dignity and spends his life trying to help those who need it. Only the Fates know if he will ever be free of the goddess who possesses him, and they speak even less clearly than he does.

Hearsay

I know exactly who and what he is. I know
exactly what he can do. And more to the point
I know what he cannot do. Or what he dare not do.
—Menyara Chartier

There are many rumors spread about Acheron, by Daimons, Rogue Dark-Hunters, and plain-old stupid ignorant folk alike.

According to bitter, betrayed, confused, and complicated ex-Squire Nick Gautier, the aftermath of Hurricane Katrina is all Acheron's fault. He believes that Ash could have prevented

Katrina altogether. And if not, he could have at least used his incredible powers to help clean up the city in its aftermath.

Perhaps some of this is true, but you do have to keep in mind how tenuous a line is drawn between Acheron and the Fates. They are the final law when it comes to what happens when in the tapestry of life, and they don't like it at all when someone tampers with their weaving. Which is to say, none of them harbors any small love for Acheron, who is the god of Final Fate.

As far as Katrina is concerned, I believe Acheron's hands were tied. I base that hypothesis on the fact that Ash remained in New Orleans, saving the lives of as many people as he could. But he knows firsthand what happens when someone tries to circumvent fate. As Ash so often says, just because you can doesn't mean you should.

Ultimately, what you decide to believe is up to you. But, as Menyara says, "Don't judge him by one bad act when he has done so many good ones."

The Daimons view Ash as the Grim Reaper, the soulless bringer of death. (Note to self: Buy Ash a Holocaust cloak next Christmas. That ought to pay him back for that time he got me a . . . but I digress.)

The Reaper analogy is a valid one, since few Daimons have fought Acheron and lived to tell about it (and those who did didn't exactly go around bragging, if you know what I mean). But the Daimons also say that Ash can control their thoughts and make them kill *each other*. True or not, that is very, very interesting indeed.

The rumor often perpetuated by Rogue Dark-Hunters is that Ash works in conjunction with Apollymi to essentially run a soul racket. They will say that Artemis is long dead, and that Ash uses some other woman to make your deal for vengeance in her name.

They say when you trade your soul, Ash actually eats it . . . and those devoured souls inside him are why he can walk safely through cemeteries and hallowed ground no sane Dark-Hunter would dare to tread.

They say that Apollymi keeps the souls in Kalosis, and when Ash wants one, he just breaks in and gets it. If you partake of the out clause, the soul that is returned to you is not necessarily the soul you traded for. It is *a* soul, but not *your* soul.

They say Acheron is a Daimon, with powers so strong that he can mask his presence from Dark-Hunters, which is why you will feel no draining of your powers around him.

Yeah. That's what they say, anyway.

You buying any of this?

Me neither.

And if you ever do?

Well, you better start running now then. Just like many of his all-powerful brethren, Acheron does not suffer fools to live.

Habits

What can I say? This is one of the few places
I can take Simi where she doesn't stand out.
Hell, she actually looks normal here.
—*Acheron*

Acheron (always with Simi in tow) can often be found at a local hospital. He visits one every few months, and sometimes more often around Christmas. (Simi in Christmas gear is truly a sight to behold.) While he is there, patients' blood pressures drop, no one needs painkillers, and everyone sleeps soundly the night after he leaves. Cancer patients often go into remission after his visits.

Needless to say, the hospital staff encourages his presence.

While you may be able to reach him over the holidays, do yourself a favor and don't try to get in touch with Ash over Labor Day weekend, because his phone will be turned off. That is the weekend of Dragon*Con, my friend, one of the biggest science fiction-fantasy conventions in the world. Thirty thousand or so people come from all over the globe to steep in book, comic, film, and television geekdom for four exquisitely sleepless days of revelry. If you can dream it, someone will come dressed as it.

It's a family reunion of the oddest kind, and some of the most fun you'll ever have.

Check out Dragon*Con on the Web: www.dragoncon.org.

All Greek to You

Insight into Being and Speaking Greek

*We're Greek. Family is family no matter what
and we always take care of our own.*
—Solin

It's all about family, food, and bearing gifts.

The funny part is, I'm not kidding about any of that. Especially the food.

The importance of family is foisted upon a Greek child at birth. Even today, the name of the child is traditionally taken from the names of his or her immediate family—parents and grandparents. It's why many Greek names such as John (Yannis), George (Yorgos), and Gus (Costa) are so incredibly common. Don't believe me? Next time you're at a Greek festival, yell "Hey, John!" and watch as half of the men there turn around.

Regardless of whether or not the Greek family decides to follow this tradition, their children must be named after saints. If they choose against this, then their child will have a different baptismal name from their birth name. That is the name under which the church will legally recognize them.

Most saints are associated with a day, and that day becomes the child's name day. Greek name days are almost as important as birthdays, and sometimes more so. If a child is not given a saint's name at birth, or their saint does not have a name day for any reason, the child will celebrate his or her name day on November first: All Saints' Day.

Babies are baptized into the Greek Orthodox religion when they are only a few months old. Be prepared for a screaming baby and a big tub of water—but it's a beautiful and solemn event attended by more people than you see at most weddings. The godparent assists the priest in the anointing of the child, thus taking on a very important role in the child's life. The christening is a momentous occasion, with a gorgeous ceremony followed by a large celebration with lots of food.

And that's just the beginning.

At a Greek table, food isn't just meant to be eaten. It is meant to be *experienced*. Sharing this experience brings the people at the table closer together. Food is not just sustenance; it is a way of life.

Both at home and in restaurants, dinners are served "family style", as opposed to individual meals for each person. (Greeks never eat alone.) A great deal of the meal is meant to be consumed with the hands as opposed to a knife and fork. (It's all part of the *experience*. How can you truly experience something if you don't touch it?) So if your instinct is telling you to dig in, indulge yourself. No one will be offended. In fact, they'll be thrilled that you feel comfortable enough at their table to take such an interest in sating yourself with wild abandon.

There is *always* too much food at a Greek table. We never want anyone to leave our home hungry. A host will want to show off his bounty and prove his generosity and genuine care for his guest. Finishing your meal, however, is a double-edged sword. If you don't clean your plate, the host will assume that there was something wrong with the food, or that you did not like it. If you do clean your plate, your host will assume you have not had enough, and urge you to take more.

I have found the best way to avoid this is to take as small a portion as you can get away with . . . and then push away from the table after three helpings and pat your belly happily. There will always be some left over. You need to find a way to deal with it.

Paying for the bill among Greeks should have been an Olympic sport. The check is rarely—if ever—split, and great arguments are held at restaurants over who will be picking up the check for the table. Some have often resorted to piratical tactics, such as slipping the waitress a wad of cash before the meal has even started, or sneaking to the restroom and paying the bill on the way back so that the bill never arrives at the table. The latter ruse is one of the best ways to cause fewer arguments, as no one is aware who paid the bill. The party only knows it's been "taken care of".

Everyone's heard of the famous plate-smashing, of course, which in modern times is usually only done for tourists, or special ceremonies. Some say that plates and glasses were thrown at the feet of dancing girls to proclaim their beauty, and at men for their virility. Others say that the plates were smashed in order to honor the cook of a fine meal: To use the plates again would be blasphemous—any meal served on that plate hereafter would never be as good as the meal just served, so it is deemed useless. Perhaps it is a melding of both traditions . . . coupled with the tradition of loud, drunk, rowdy Greeks who like the sound of breaking glass.

Many of you have heard the saying "Beware of Greeks bearing gifts" because of the ill-famed Trojan Horse. However, it has always been—and still is—the custom of Greeks to bring a host gift with them whenever they have been invited to the home of a friend or relative. Flowers, alcohol, chocolates—these gifts are always welcome.

If you happen to be visiting a person on their name day, they will undoubtedly be hosting an enormous party for their friends with the requisite ton of food—like an open house, they will expect people to drop by all day long.

You are welcome to bring a present (you will not be expected to do anything special; it would just be the present you would be bringing to this friend's house anyway), but know that your gift will not be opened in front of you. It is custom at any gathering to open gifts after the guests have left, so as to avoid any uncomfortable situations (the recipient is disappointed with the gift, two people accidentally give the same gift, and so on).

The demarcation is exceptionally fuzzy between Greek traditions, religious beliefs, and superstitions. The Orthodox Church split from the Roman Catholic religion in 1054 because of differences in theological, political, and cultural beliefs. Many Greeks today call themselves devout, but most of the traditions that they follow hearken back to customs, symbols, and rituals of pagan origins. As do many of their sayings and superstitions. Over the years, the Orthodox Church has integrated these beliefs into a rather unique religious dogma.

Superstitions

We will always be known by our actions.
Let them always be good ones.
—*Theo Kafieri*

COFFEE

Coffee is very important to the Greeks, as is the drinking of Greek coffee. Proper Greek coffee is made on the stove in a *briki*, a small, hammered copper pot. Coffee grounds (usually a strong Turkish blend) are added to the water and sugar. The *briki* is then brought to a boil three times (three is a number of power, remember). The potent coffee is served in demitasse cups, and sipped slowly.

If you are in the company of someone who reads coffee

grounds (like reading tea leaves), and they are in the mood to indulge, they might offer to read your cup for you. (You would never put upon the person by asking, of course.) There are many different ways to do this—your reader will instruct you.

When you have sipped down to the "mud" in the bottom of the cup, you place your saucer on top of the cup. Keeping the cup right-side up, spin it in the air three times, then flip it upside down. The grounds will slide down the sides of the cup and dry there. Some readers have you tip the cup and roll it around before the spinning, to ensure that the mud makes lots of pictures along the sides of the cup.

After the mud has had time to dry, the reader will turn the cup over. Some readers may make the sign of the cross over the cup before they read it, to bless it and ask that only good news be found inside. Shapes in the cup will form pictures in the reader's mind, and they will tell you stories about the events they see.

The time line is loosely based on the distance of the image in the cup from the handle, and how close to the lip of the cup it is. As with many other psychics, things a reader tells you may have already come to pass, may eventually come to pass, or may never happen at all. But it is always good to write them down anyway, just in case.

EASTER EGGS

Easter is the most important Greek holiday, surpassing even Christmas. Many of the traditions celebrated on this day date back to long before the advent of Christianity. Even the day that Orthodox Easter falls on is calculated using an equation that involves the vernal equinox, the phase of the moon, and the Julian (as opposed to the Gregorian) calendar. Rarely do Catholic Easter and Orthodox Easter ever fall on the same day.

Easter not only honors Christ's sacrifice and rebirth, but it also represents the rituals of spring and the never-ending circle of life: the eternal Passover from life to death and then back to life again as the world itself is reborn.

Lamb as Easter dinner represents the ancient lamb sacrificed in honor of Christ's sacrifice on the cross. Easter eggs are not rainbow shades of pastels; they are only colored blood-red, for the blood of Christ. Sometimes the eggs are cooked into a sweet bread called *tsoureki* (yeasty bread also "rises again", you see).

On Easter Sunday, a game is played by young and old alike, where people rap their eggs against their friends' eggs. The owner of the last egg uncracked on one or both sides is considered lucky.

EVIL EYES (MATI)

In Greece and Turkey, many shops sell *mati*, or Evil Eyes. The eyes themselves are not evil; on the contrary, the eye is worn (usually on a necklace or bracelet) as protection *against* someone putting a hex on you. When an Evil Eye breaks, that means that it has done its job and protected the wearer.

Most Evil Eyes are blue, but they can come in a variety of colors. The blue originates from the rare occurrence of that color ever appearing throughout the dark Greek heritage—people with blue eyes were considered evil, powerful, cursed, or just really good at hexing others. On Crete, it is not an eye but a light blue bead that is used for protection.

It is important to note that an Evil Eye is more powerful, its warding strength more potent, when it is given as a gift.

The Orthodox Church recognizes the Evil Eye as something terrible, but it does not support the efforts of men and women who say they can remove it. These common people are considered charlatans. According to the Church, only the priest has the power to remove the effects of the Evil Eye.

The Church also does not recognize the Evil Eyes sold by street vendors as actual talismans of protection. Only a priest has the ability to make a proper *filokto*, a religious article that protects you from evil. It can be made from anything, but it is usually something like a locket containing blessed items such as cotton soaked in holy water, tears from a crying icon, or scrapings from a candle from a holy monastery.

NEW YEAR'S BREAD

In honor of the New Year, Greeks celebrate with *loukoumathes* (fried dough covered in honey and powdered sugar), and *vasilopita,* or New Year's Bread, seasoned with almonds and Metaxa brandy. A coin (washed and wrapped in foil or plastic wrap) is baked into the bread. Each member of the family gets a slice, a slice is cut for the house, and a slice is cut for Jesus. Whoever receives the coin will have a fortunate year with lots of good luck and good news. If the house gets the coin, the whole family will have good news together. If the coin falls to Jesus, then there will be health and happiness for everyone all year long.

All the bread must be eaten, of course—bread is a gift from God and must never go to waste. Feed it to the birds, if you must, but never throw it away.

KNIVES

Knives are very symbolic. A knife handed to someone else means that there will soon be a quarrel between the giver and the recipient. If you have to pass someone a knife at the table, you put it down onto the table and let them pick it up.

Knives are never given as a gift. A knife as a gift is symbolic of the severing of the relationship. If someone does give you a knife for a gift, you must pay them for it, even if it is only a penny. Then it is not a gift; it is a purchase.

WORRY BEADS (KOMBOLOI)

Komboloi, or "worry beads", are a string of beads like a small rosary that one puts in their pocket to fiddle with (usually men). Most *komboloi* have an odd number of beads or groups of odd numbers of beads, as odd numbers are lucky. Playing with *komboloi* is a meditation, a contemplation, as the beads click together. It is said that the *komboloi* represent infinity, the beginning and end of all things in endless cycle.

MONEY

Money attracts money. Never leave your wallet, purse, or pocket empty. If you ever give a wallet or purse as a gift, put some money inside it. If you see a penny, pick it up, because leaving money lying on the ground is just silly.

PALM

If your palm itches, you will soon be coming into some money.

RED

When two people say something at the same time, some Greek people say "Touch red"—like a combination of "Jinx" and "Knock on wood". It is thought that two people speaking at once is prophetic, and may foretell of a dispute between the two speakers. Touching something red (usually accompanied by some spitting for good measure), thwarts this possibility.

SNEEZING

If you sneeze, it is because someone is talking about you. Where one would say, "Bless you", the Greeks say, "Ya'sou".

SPITTING

Words have power. Spitting is what people do to try and dilute that power.

If someone says something nice about you, they spit (or make the sound *"Ptou, ptou"* while mimicking spitting), so as not to tempt Fate or call down an unwanted Evil Eye. There is nothing worse than to call a baby or a bride beautiful and then have them turn ugly because of your careless words. By doing so, you can inadvertently put the Evil Eye on someone.

Also, if there is bad news, someone will spit so as to ward off any *more* bad news. So, good news or bad news, it's important to stay hydrated.

Sometimes, a person will spit three times, in honor of the Holy Trinity—yet another example of the gray area between Christian and pagan beliefs.

THIRTEEN

Thirteen is a lucky number for the Greek people, as thirteen was the number of all the apostles plus Jesus. The only time thirteen is unlucky is on Tuesday.

TUESDAY

Tuesday is considered unlucky by the Greeks because it was on this day that Constantinople, the capital of the Ottoman Empire, fell. An American's Friday the thirteenth is a Greek's Tuesday the thirteenth.

Pearls of Wisdom

You're baked bread.

—Artemis

If you've ever heard Artemis try and conquer colloquial slang, you've possibly winced so hard you pulled something. Why is it, you wonder, that this beautiful, all-knowing, all-powerful goddess must murder the language the way she does?

You know she's not doing it on purpose. And no, it's not because she's really a blonde (don't you ever let Aphrodite hear you say that). The reason she just can't seem to make that cultural leap is because the Greeks have a long, lovely tradition of sayings even weirder than anything we might dream up in our wildest imaginings.

"The best thing since sliced bread" or "You're toast" have nothing on these fabulous truths the Greeks have been spouting for centuries. Here are a few for you—literally translated, of course, for the highest humor quotient—and explained for your enjoyment and further confusion.

Go on, try one on Artemis next time you see her. She might be impressed. (She might also squash you like a bug . . . but that's Artie for you.)

YOU SHOULD ALWAYS BUY SHOES WITH YOUR EYES SHUT.

There it is in black and white, folks: proof that women and their addiction to shoes is an honored, worldwide tradition dating back centuries. The root of this one, however, highlights the importance of function over beauty. Believe it or not, the best shoes for your feet are not necessarily the best-looking. Just like the most reliable car is not always the flashiest or most expensive. Just like the most wonderful guy is not always the sexy god with the tawny skin and the washboard abs and the haunting eyes and the . . .

On second thought, I might have to contemplate that one for a while.

THE MORE YOU STIR, THE WORSE IT SMELLS.

The more Daimons you hunt, the more you scare up. The more you poke at a sore, the more it bleeds. The deeper you dig into a scandal, the more dirt-covered skeletons you tend to uncover. The more you learn about the gods in order to use that knowledge against them, the more creatively they will find ways to curse you (so sayeth the Oneroi). The more you fight, the more your opponent resists. Out of the frying pan, into the fire. It can only go from bad to worse.

And all that.

WHERE YOU HEAR THERE ARE A LOT OF CHERRIES, BRING A SMALL BASKET.

This is actually sound advice from an economic point of view. Say Tabitha Devereaux's store just got overshipped a pallet of fabulously sexy and irresistible lace undies in all sizes, and she's selling them all at 75 percent off. Well, you just heard this from Sunshine Runningwolf, who, bless her pink-lovin' little heart, can't keep a secret if her life depended on it . . . and there are more than a few streets between the one on which you're currently standing and Tabitha's sultry shop. Who knows how many people already know about this fabulous offer?

Chances are, they all do. And they're all your (or your girlfriend's) size.

This saying doesn't advise you to not head down to the store—a Greek would never pass up a bargain!—but don't expect to leave the shop carrying a bag overflowing with a thousand-and-one wicked little surprises for your lucky partner. *You'll* be lucky if you get one decent, unblemished pair out of the insanity. And you'll be extra-lucky if they don't chafe or ride up into unmentionable places. Not that actually wearing them is the point, of course . . .

WHERE YOU ARE, I WAS AND WHERE I AM, YOU WILL BE.

This phrase is often said by the all-knowing-and-powerful world-weary gods who like to remind the rest of us immortal whippersnappers from time to time that we did not in fact invent treachery, betrayal, tricksters, curses, or sex. Especially sex.

LOOK WITH FOUR EYES.

No, it doesn't mean put your glasses on—though that would certainly be helpful to people who *do* need glasses to see anything. What this phrase means is look once, and then look again. Look carefully. Look with your mother's eyes. Examine things, and don't let the smallest detail escape your attention. Take everything in, and make a note of it. If you're looking for something, you will find it. If you're witnessing something important, there are always useful blackmail implications later on.

YOU MADE IT LOOK LIKE YOUR FACE.

This one is a *serious* insult, and should never be used lightly. The first thing it assumes right off the bat is that the person you are insulting is dog-ugly (no offense to any Weres who might be reading this). The second thing it implies is that this person did such a shoddy job on whatever it was he just finished, that the result is no better than the previous aforementioned dogface. He'd be better off getting a job at a freak show and running away with the circus. Or he could . . .

GO BE A VILLAGE POLICEMAN!

The village cop is, I am to understand, one of the least-desired and most thankless jobs in the world. You don't have to pass a test or be a rocket scientist (at least, you didn't used to)—pretty much all you have to do is fit the uniform. If someone you know is *so* incredibly worthless that being a village policeman would be a step up for him . . . well, I wouldn't be asking him to look after your cat while you're out of town, if I were you. He's one beer short of a six-pack, if you catch my drift.

SHE MADE HIM A HAMALI.

A *hamali* is the Turkish word for stevedore, a dock worker, a position considered the lowest class of laborer. (I'm not sure which is worse, a stevedore or a village policeman, but I'm not sure it matters much. I'm just glad I'm neither.) Contrary to the village policeman comment, however, this saying is not insulting the man in the relationship. This saying implies that the woman in question did not support her husband enough, and as a result he has not lived up to his full potential. In Greek custom, it is very important that a wife supports her husband above all. If she does not believe in him and stand behind him, then she is not a good wife.

IF THE CROW IS BAD HIS SON WILL BE, TOO.

An ancient Greek saying that essentially means "Like father, like son" or "The apple doesn't fall far from the tree". If you've got bad blood in your family, it will be automatically assumed that you're cut from the same cloth. People will be on their guard. They will lock their doors and spit at your feet. They will judge you before you can even open your mouth to utter a greeting or kind word.

Now do you understand why Valerius the Younger had so much trouble getting folks to warm up to him?

THE PRIEST'S CHILDREN ARE THE DEVIL'S GRANDCHILDREN.

Following on families and bad seeds … everyone knows what they say about the son of a preacher man. Well, they say it in Greece, too. Of course, it also implies that the priest is the son of a devil … or that the priest's wife is … a sentiment that might not go over too well with your new neighbors.

ON A DEAF MAN'S DOOR YOU CAN KNOCK ALL DAY.

I like using this one when trying to explain to someone what reasoning with a god is like. You can present evidence and bring witnesses and signed documents and other gods and talk until your tongue bleeds and *still* they will go do whatever they want to do. It's like talking to a brick wall, that deaf man's door. You may as well quit knocking; you're just going to skin your knuckles.

ONLY THE MOUNTAINTOPS NEVER MEET.

This phrase is one of my all-time favorites. It reminds us that in this very small world, there is no such thing as coincidence. Be careful who you talk about and what you say, because you never know who might be listening. You never know whom you will run into just around the corner. Also, it could be considered a beacon of hope for the perpetual bachelor or bachelorette—there is someone out there for everyone and, sooner or later, you will find each other.

IN THEIR VILLAGE IT MUST NOT BE THE CUSTOM TO SAY "THANK YOU".

As mentioned before, giving gifts is very important in Greek society. With that comes the importance of saying "Thank you", upon the receipt of said gift. It's amazing and unfortunate how infrequently you hear those words nowadays. But those Greeks, I tell you, they never fail to step up and give credit where credit is due when the opportunity presents itself. I even heard someone once thank a god for cursing them. I did, I swear . . . but I also swore that I would never reveal who it was.

This phrase, you can imagine, is said with a razor-thin layer of professional, thinly veiled sarcasm. The Greeks are so exceptionally biting with their sarcasm they have all but raised it to an art form. Perhaps I should recommend a tenth Muse?

FROM TIME TO TIME EVEN GOD NEEDS TO REST.

Ah, yes, ever the saying of the Oneroi, for they alone have the ability to wreak havoc in the dreams of gods. Of course, they got their shiny heineys cursed for doing that, too, so it's a subject around which everyone treads lightly. But they never forget it.

Neither do the gods.

To the mortal Greeks, this saying is a completely legal justification anytime a wife happens upon her husband in repose while she's slaving her tail off in the kitchen. It doesn't necessarily get him off the hook, but mentioning a god or two might save him from being smacked with a broom.

DAY LOOKS UPON NIGHT'S WORK AND LAUGHS.

The idea behind this one is that if you work all day long on a project, chances are that you'll be so tired at night, you'll screw up everything you were doing and have to redo it over again in the morning. So why bother? Save yourself the extra work and stop when you're supposed to stop. (The Greeks know how to appreciate a well-deserved break time.)

While this saying is possibly true for most mortals, I feel the need to point out that it isn't an expression often used by Dark-Hunters, Dream-Hunters, Daimons, or night-owl authors.

ONLY PEASANTS EAT STANDING UP.

I remember hearing this one from my esteemed noble grandmother. I'm not sure where it originated, but she, of all people, would certainly know the truth. She very well could have picked it up from Valerius Magnus. It's certainly the type of thing I can hear him saying as he drinks his Chablis in his impeccable Armani suit. You'll have to ask Tabitha next time you see her; if he's pulled that old gem out on anybody, it will have been her.

I WANT TO BE A SAINT, BUT THE DEVIL WON'T LET ME.

As much as I would love to go on at length about this saying, it really doesn't require explanation. I need it on a bumper sticker or a T-shirt. Or both.

IT IS CONSIDERED EXTREMELY BAD MANNERS TO BE INVITED TO DINNER AND BRING JUST YOUR APPETITE.

Remember how I said eating is a Greek way of life? This is only one of about a million Greek sayings associated with food. Here, the underlying universal wisdom is to always consider your motivations. It also touches on the gift-giving aspect of visiting a friend or neighbor: You never come empty-handed as a guest to someone's house. Only a very selfish and unworthy person would come bearing only their appetite. Very much like Daimons, actually. No one likes a selfish person. No one likes Daimons either. See?

WHEN YOU WATER THE PLANT, THE POT ALSO GETS WATER.

This saying is more about the big picture. It reminds us to consider the impact of our actions on the world around us, especially the selfless ones. The more we give, the more we get back—it's a basic pagan tenet dating back centuries. When someone cooks a wonderful meal for their guests, that person reaps the benefit of partaking of it as well. Every time you kill a Daimon, think of all the souls you will be saving.

We concentrate on the promotion of selfless acts because it would not (or should not) occur to a Greek person to be selfish or vengeful. They have learned from eons of history that you get back what you give, the good as well as the bad. When Artie granted you your Act of Vengeance, your payback—a dispensation from a goddess—was a special exemption. Don't go thinking you can just be vengeful all the time without serious repercussions. The bank of the Fates has interest rates that would make credit card companies blush.

DO A GOOD DEED AND CAST IT TO THE SEA.

Not only should you do that selfless act, but you should not dwell upon it. Don't spend too much time patting yourself on the back for it, or hint that others should do the same. At some point, it stops being selfless and starts being self-congratulatory. Do your wonderful thing, cast it out into the world, and then go off and do another.

There is a school of thought that seems to think Poseidon came up with this tidbit, and he wasn't exactly being selfless when he said it. Which I would totally believe.

BLESS YOUR HANDS. (YA'STA HERIASOU.)

This saying is often said to a cook to congratulate them on a fabulous meal. It can be said to people who have made anything with their hands, but—like most Greek sayings—it is usually only used in conjunction with food.

I'M SAVING THAT TO DO WHEN I'M OLD.

The epitome of procrastination. And more so than Scarlett O'Hara; she only put things off until tomorrow. Everyone knows Greek people don't ever get old. It's almost taboo.

Immortals such as yourself love using this phrase. They think it's a laugh riot. And rightly so.

YOU'VE EATEN ALMOST AN ENTIRE DONKEY. DON'T STOP JUST BECAUSE YOU'VE REACHED THE TAIL.

"In for a penny, in for a pound" is the essence of this one, but the fact that the person in question is *eating a donkey* just smacks of hilarity. Some Greeks—heck, some men in general—have a hard time finishing a task once it's started. I think the donkey might represent a huge task that someone decided to take on and boasted about it, and now that it's nose-to-the-grindstone time, less and less gets done as the days go by. It's too late to turn back now; like it or not, you're going to have to polish off that donkey—tail and all.

And you're not getting dessert until that plate is clean, mister.

THEY ARE LIKE ASS TO UNDERWEAR.

Similar to the expression "like white on rice", or one that pops to mind regarding odor and fecal matter that I won't mention here. It, of course, refers to two people who are so physically close you think that maybe you're going to have to get a crowbar to pry them apart . . . or you hope at the very least that one of them has considered contraception.

This phrase was also once used by Dark-Hunters to intimidate Daimons who thought they were cleverly going to get away from their foe. I think now it's been largely replaced by the rice analogy. Or the other, less tasteful one. Most likely the latter.

FROM YOUR MOUTH TO GOD'S EAR.

And here I thought this was strictly a Southern American expression. Imagine my complete surprise to find it wasn't! (Then again, I thought "Bless your heart" was, too, until I realized that the British have been saying "Bless" to mean the same thing for hundreds of years.)

This phrase is an automatic selfless response to someone who pays you a compliment. It may be used in lieu of—or addition to— spitting to scare away evil spirits and avoid tempting the Fates. With this phrase you are piously saying, "Why, yes, I do hope that lovely thing you have said about me does come true," and you are hoping that the proper gods are listening and bearing witness to your humility so they might grant you your desire.

The truth behind this sage saying, however, is that it works for bad things said as well as complimentary things. A good rule of thumb is to just watch what you say at all times. Don't say anything about someone you wouldn't say to their face. Or just don't say anything bad. Ever.

THE POT ROLLED AROUND UNTIL IT FOUND THE LID.

A reference of sorts to the number of fish in the sea . . . but associated, like most Greek sayings, to cooking. Each pot has a lid that will fit it perfectly, just as every soul has its mate.

The part I find amusing is that the pot has to do quite a bit of rolling around to find this lid. What kind of rolling can a pot do? It can't walk, obviously, but doesn't that handle get in the way? And how come the lids aren't searching for the pots? Why has it always got to be the pot that has to do all the work? Huh? Tell me that!

WINE AND CHILDREN SPEAK THE TRUTH.

Three guesses which god came up with this one ... and the first two don't count. Yes, Dionysus, the baby of Olympus and god of Wine and Spirits was having an exceptionally good day when he came up with this universal truth. He also mentioned something about secrets and children both being hidden at the bottom of that prophetic bottle of wine.

MEND YOUR OWN FAULTS, THEN LOOK AT MINE.

Oh, yes, this is a good one, too. I like to remind Artemis of this one from time to time and knock her down off her pedestal. (Her marble, carved, and gilded pedestal. She actually has one, you know, in her gold and white temple among the clouds on Olympus. And she's up there quite a bit more than is healthy.)

All gods need to be reminded every so often that each of them has enough skeletons in their closets to populate a Third World country. After all the curses ... and the affairs ... and the murders ... and the curses, who are they to pass judgment on any of our tiny, insignificant sins?

Oh, right. They're gods. Now I remember.

Dark-Hunters like to throw a version of this one at Daimons who try to insult them. No matter how many different colors a Dark-Hunter's past has been shaded, it's nothing compared to what a soul-sucking Daimon has done to become what he is.

And, if you start getting testy around your employer, Ash will never hesitate to use this one on you. You know your faults, but you have no idea what Ash has been through . . . so it very much applies.

Again, it all comes back to thinking before you speak.

EXTEND YOUR LEGS ONLY AS FAR AS YOUR COVERLET REACHES.

Dark-Hunters don't have to worry about this one too much, since Artemis showers them in riches for all the work that they do, but the rest of the mortal world does need to consider it: Live within your means. Extravagance and gluttony will only lead to ruin, and after you die the gods will laugh and say they told you so.

DO YOU HAVE TO ADD THE ACCENT?

I *love* this expression. To understand it you need to have heard some of the Greek language, listened to its rolling cadence. You will notice that a great many of the words are heavily accented on the last syllable, and very often those entire words will work to punctuate the end of the sentence. I say *this*. And you say *that*. And I say *this*. And the conversations goes like *so*. Only I get the last *word*.

That's what it means about adding the accent—it's a commentary on someone having to get that last word in all the time, every time.

Every time.

Because I *said*.

BLOOD CANNOT BECOME WATER.

The essence of this saying is "blood is thicker than water", but it's a bit more than that. It is true; the bonds of family—both the one you are born into and the one you make along the way—are stronger than water. But these bonds, once forged, can also never *become* water. You cannot turn your back against them and pretend they don't exist. You are obligated to stand beside your blood no matter what. Which is really hard, when your blood is a bit of an ass. Just ask Zarek . . . if he stops throwing thunderbolts at his brother long enough for you to ask.

This saying also applies to the Apollites, and the curse that has followed every single one with even a drop of Apollo's blood down through the centuries. They will never escape, unfortunately, and they are doomed to live with their fate. It almost makes you empathize with Daimons, doesn't it?

I did say *almost* . . .

TOGETHER WE SPEAK, BUT APART WE UNDERSTAND.

I feel this way around Acheron sometimes. And Julian, or any of the Oracles for that matter. You ask them a question, and they tell you an answer that may as well have been found in a fortune cookie, or written in the dust on the back of someone's car. The words are there, and you feel like they should make sense, but they just don't.

Then, later on, while you're watching a movie . . . or when you wake up in the middle of the night (or the middle of the day, rather) . . . or when you've done the difficult thing you never thought you'd be able to do, it *comes* to you, and the pieces all fit together, and it makes so much sense that you have no idea why you didn't see it in the first place.

That's what that saying means.

TAKE A SHOE FROM YOUR OWN COUNTRY (OR TOWN) EVEN IF IT IS PATCHED.

And we're back again to women and their shoes. (I know, the saying doesn't really specify that it's a woman, but can you name me a man in the history of men who has ever been that concerned about their footwear?) It's an odd way to get the point across, but in essence, the devil you know is better than the devil you don't. You never know how shoes from another country will pinch your toes, or rub your heels raw, or trip you and make you break your ankle on those stilettos. Your old, comfortable shoes look just fine; just color over that scuff with a Sharpie and no one will ever notice.

TELL ME WHO IS YOUR FRIEND, AND I SHALL TELL YOU WHO YOU ARE.

It's as true as it is unavoidable—people will always judge you by the company you keep. Decent people usually end up with decent people, and miscreants usually end up running with miscreants. In fact, this is one saying that Alexion lives by if he is ever sent by Acheron to pass judgment on a Rogue Dark-Hunter. Those who side with the Rogue Hunter will share his fate, so be sure to make it very clear which party you're with when you enter the restaurant.

WHEN YOU GET INTO THE DANCE, YOU MUST DANCE.

This phrase is essentially the same as the donkey phrase earlier, with a much less negative connotation about the project in which you've immersed yourself. Plus, it reminds me of cheesy '80s movies.

Nobody puts Baby in a corner.

A FINE DAY FROM DAWN SHOWS ITSELF.

Like Mary Poppins says, well begun is half done. If you start out doing the best job you can do on a project, it will show, and only get better as the work progresses. If you start out slipshod and looking for every shortcut you can find, then no matter how hard you work the finished project will never be as good as it could have been. Worse, your enthusiasm for it will dwindle, and you will inevitably find yourself dancing around the donkey's tail that bears a striking resemblance to your face.

Interesting, isn't it, how many of these old sayings revolve around motivating a person to finish what they've started? It makes a body think no Greek ever finishes anythi—

NUMBERS		
1	ena	(EHN-na)
2	theo	(THEE-oh)
3	tria	(TREE-ah)
4	tessera	(TESS-er-rah)
5	pende	(PEN-deh)
6	eksi	(ek-SEE)
7	efta	(ef-TAH)
8	okto	(ok-TO)
9	enea	(eh-NEH-ah)
10	theka	(THEH-ka)

Greek Dictionary

Not only is the Greek language difficult to translate based on all the ancient customs woven into its vernacular, but it is virtually impossible to spell in English. There is technically no *c* in the Greek alphabet, nor is there a *d*—the sound is more a *th*. There are three *e*'s (*i*, *e*, and *y*), and several more made from combinations of letters. And how exactly does one spell the guttural *x* (khee)?

Because of this, spellings of translated Greek words and names will very often vary, and depend on the person doing the

A α	alpha	(al-fah)
B β	beta	(vee-tah)
Γ γ	gamma	(gah-mah)
Δ δ	delta	(thel-tah)
E ε	epsilon	(eh-psi-lon)
Z ζ	zeta	(zee-tah)
H η	eta	(ee-tah)
Θ θ	theta	(thee-tah)
I ι	iota	(yo-tah)
K κ	kappa	(kah-pah)
Λ λ	lambda	(lahm-dah)
M μ	mi	(mee)
N ν	ni	(nee)
Ξ ξ	xi	(ksee)
O o	omicron	(oh-mee-kron)
Π π	pi	(pee)
P ρ	rho	(row)
Σ σ´	sigma	(seeg-mah)
T τ	tau	(taf)
Υ υ	upsilon	(ee-psi-lon)
Φ φ	phi	(fee)
X χ	chi	(khee, guttural)
Ψ ψ	psi	(psee)
Ω ω	omega	(oh-meh-gah)

translation. The best rule of thumb when presented with a Greek word that has been translated is to *pronounce every letter*. Chances are, the approximation of the Greek word will look very much like the word would sound phonetically.

One last thing about Greek names—pay close attention when a Greek person tells you his or her name. That really is how they pronounce it. Don't tell them that they are wrong...chances are, they have "Americanized" the pronunciation for you. If they give you a nickname to use, take advantage of that. No matter what their descent, there is little any person hates worse than having their name mispronounced. (And believe me, if you want to see me angry, call me Althea.)

Here are some conversational Greek words that you might find useful.

Adelphos   (ah-DEL-fos)   brother

Alethia   (ah-lee-THEE-ah)   truth

Alithos anesti   (ah-lee-THOS ah-NEH-sti)   truly risen
(response to the traditional Easter greeting of "Christos anesti")

Anexi   (ah-NEX-ee)   spring (the season)

Baba   (ba-BA)   daddy

Bira   (be-ra)   beer

Christos anesti   (krees-TOS ah-NEH-sti)   Christ has risen (traditional Easter greeting)

Efharisto   (ef-CHA-ri-sto)   thank you (the "cha" is guttural)

Ella   (EL-la)   come

Ella etho   (EL-la THO)   come here

Ellas   (eh-LAHSS)   Greece

Endaksi   (en-DA-ksee)   okeydoke (okay)

Ftenoporo   (ften-OH-po-rho)   autumn

Gataki   (gah-TAH-kee)   kitten

Helios   (ee-lee-OS)   sun

Kako   (ka-KO)   bad

Kalimera   (ka-lee-MER-a)   good morning

Kalinikta   (ka-lee-NEEK-ta)   good night

Kalispera   (ka-lee-SPE-ra)   good evening

Kalo   (ka-LO)   good

Komboloi   (ko-bo-LOY)   worry beads

Krasi   (kra-SEE)   wine

Krio   (KREE-oh)   cold

Ksoma   (KSO ma)   earth

Levendi   (le-VEN-di)   really good-looking guy

Mikro   (mee-KRO)   small

—mou   (moo)   suffix at the end of a word or name used as an endearment, meaning "my". Example: *pethi* means "child", but *pethimou* means "my child".

Nai   (neh)   yes

Nero   (ne-RO)   water

Nouna   (nou-NA)   godmother

Nouno   (noo-NO)   godfather

Ochi   (O-khee)   no (the "khee" is guttural). Greeks also look up and click their tongue making a *tsk* sound for an emphatic "No".

Oneiro   (OH-nee-ro)   dream

Oneiropulos   (oh-nee-RHO-pu-los)   dreamer

Oreo   (oh-RAY-oh)   nice, beautiful

Pagoto   (pa-go-TO)   ice cream

Pamai   (PA-may)   let's go

Papou   (pa-POO)   grandfather

Parakalo   (pa-ra-ka-LO)   please or you're welcome

Pethi   (peh-THEE)   child

Pethimou   (pe-THEE-moo)   my child

S'agapo   (sa-ga-PO)   I love you

Scoupethia   (skoo-PEE-thia)   trash; junk

Selini   (see-LEE-nee)   moon

Signomi   (sig-NO-mee)   excuse me, sorry

Thea   (THEE-ah)   aunt

Thelo   (THEH-low)   I would like . . .

Theo   (THEE-oh)   uncle

Tikanis?   (ti-KAHN-ees)   How are you?

Tipota   (TEE-po-ta)   nothing

Ti thelis?   (tee-THE-lees)   What do you want?

Trogo   (tro-GO)   I eat

Vlaka   (VLA-ka)   big fat jerk

Ya'sou   (YA-sue)   bless you (also used when giving a toast). A catch-all phrase—sneezing or dancing, blessing people is never a bad thing.

Ya'sta heriasou   (YA-stah HAIR-ee-ah-sue)   bless your hands

Yiayia   (YA-ya)   grandmother

Zesti   (ZE-stee)   it is hot

We have three kinds of family. Those we are born to, those who are born to us, and those who we let into our hearts. I have let you into my heart, so the Simi is your family and she won't give you up.

—Simi

I'm probably going to be kicked out of my family for this . . . but I can't let you go without having a few Greek recipes for you to take with you. Sharing food around a table means that you are family and will forever be treated as such. Sharing recipes, on the other hand, means that you are a traitor and deserve to be killed.

Maybe I should put my Evil Eye on before I write this next part. Hold on . . . okay, got it. I feel better now. Not to mention, knowing some of these recipes can come in handy should Simi ever visit. Word to the wise, the demon lives to eat, so make sure you have lots of things for her to snack on that aren't you and your Squire.

This first one is so incredibly simple you're going to wonder why you've never tried it before. Have it once a week if you like, and be sure to trot it out when company comes. They will think you've slaved all day, and they'll talk about it for years and years to come.

I know from experience.

It's best when served with a warm loaf of crusty bread. You're welcome to add a side salad, if you need something green in your diet other than lots and lots of oregano—the heart of every great Greek dish.

Well, oregano and butter.

GREEK CHICKEN

potatoes

chicken

1 stick butter (roughly)

oregano

optional: salt, pepper, olive oil, lemon juice

Go on, say it. You think I'm making this up as I go along. And you'd be right. The thing about Greek recipes is that they're all kind of nebulous. How much you make depends on how many people you're having. It also depends on your particular taste—the Greeks expect you to monkey around with the recipe and alter it to your own state of "perfection", so they give you the basics and let you run with it.

It's not so much a recipe as it is ... more like guidelines, really.

Ready?

Peel a bunch of potatoes and cut them up. (The bigger the pieces you have the longer this dish takes to cook. I cut them in long wedges, like making homemade French fries.) Dump them into a pan (probably a big one, because you're going to want left-overs). Clean your chicken pieces (I usually use boneless chicken breasts because I like white meat and don't want to bother with fussing with the bones), and dump them in the pan with the potatoes. Put in a bit of olive oil, if you want, and maybe a bit of lemon juice. Cut up the stick of butter into pieces and drop them all over the chicken and potatoes.

Hopefully, you've got a big fat can of oregano. The best kind is grown and dried yourself—the little purple flowers are the best part—but store-bought is absolutely fine. If you have store-bought, go ahead and take that little shaker piece off the top of the can. Shaking is for wimps. Dump a nice handful of oregano into your palm. With help from your other hand, crush the oregano between your palms while sprinkling it over the chicken and potatoes. Be generous. Salt and pepper if you desire. I usually forget.

Place the pan in the oven at 350°F for an hour or so, until the potatoes are done. (Remember, the potatoes take the longest to cook.) And be patient, no matter how good your kitchen smells—underdone potatoes are no good for anyone except maybe Jacob Marley. And it's a good idea to stir the dish once or twice during the baking, just to make sure everything gets covered in butter and oregano.

It looks like a lot of words, but I promise you this will be the best and easiest dish you have ever made.

AVGOLEMONO (CHICKEN AND RICE SOUP)

1 chicken
6 cups chicken broth
1 cup rice
3 eggs, separated
1 lemon, juiced
salt and pepper, to taste

You'll be thrilled to have this staple of the Greek kitchen next time you're feeling miserable and chicken noodle just won't cut it.

Boil the chicken until fully cooked, then let it cool. Tear into pieces for addition to the soup later.

Boil the broth and add rice, adding salt and pepper to taste. When the rice is cooked, lower the heat to simmer.

Beat the three egg whites until stiff, then add the yolks and lemon juice. Add broth from the rice a little at a time, still beating. When most of the broth has been used, return the mixture to the rice.

Stir well; add as much chicken as you desire.

BAKLAVA

1 to 2 sticks melted butter

1 box phyllo sheets

NUT MIXTURE

1 bag (16 oz.) walnuts, crushed

¼ cup sugar

2 tsp. cinnamon

SYRUP

1 cup water

1 cup sugar

1 tbsp. lemon juice

¾ cup honey

Again, quantities are variable in this recipe. A lot of the old recipes call for "a handful" of this or "a saucer" of that, so amounts really are subjective. As long as you've got the items on the list, the interpretation is up to you.

Butter, however, is something you never skimp on. My great-grandmother always said that the difference between a good cook and a great cook was half a pound of butter. Be generous; your guests will thank you for it.

In fact, I should tell you, I've received marriage proposals after making this dish. Take that however you want. Just be prepared. You can't say you weren't warned.

Start with that melted butter and a big glass baking dish—the deeper the dish, the deeper your baklava can be. It's all up to you. Butter the dish with a basting brush, and lay 3 to 5 sheets of phyllo down at the bottom. (Your unused phyllo should be kept in between the plastic and/or some dish towels so that it doesn't dry out while you're working.)

There are two ways to do the layering—you can lay down each sheet and the nut mixture and *then* pour the butter over everything at the end, or you can brush each sheet as you go. I usually tend to brush each sheet—it keeps everything in place a little better. The latter method tends to use more butter—again, you can take that as a good thing or a bad thing.

Between each sheet, sprinkle 2 to 3 tablespoons of the nut mixture. Layer to your heart's content. Layer until you run out of phyllo or walnuts or you're sick of looking at it—whichever comes first. The first few layers are a bit tricky, but take your time. You'll get the hang of it after a while, and then it goes a lot faster.

The top 3 to 5 sheets should be nice and pretty and unbroken, so your baklava looks lovely (stick all the broken sheets in the middle where no one will care).

Cut the baklava before you cook it. This is very important. Squares or triangles . . . however you prefer. It is *so* much easier to do when the phyllo is soft and full of butter and not flaky and crumbly. If you haven't previously covered the baklava in butter, now is the time to do so. It's not officially baklava until the phyllo sheets—and you, and the counter—are all covered in butter.

Bake the baklava at 350°F for about an hour, or until brown.

While you're waiting on that, boil the water and sugar until the sugar is fully dissolved . . . and then a couple of minutes after that, just for good measure. You want a seriously supersaturated mix, and this will ensure it. Take the saucepan off the burner, and then stir in the lemon and honey.

Pour it over the cooked baklava, and then let it sit and think about itself for a while. Sometimes cutting through the pieces again helps everything soak in better. You don't need to refrigerate it; you can leave it on the counter covered in plastic wrap for up to about a week. I've heard from a friend that it survives freezing tolerably well, but baklava in our house has never stuck around for that long.

If you're giving it as a gift or bringing it to a party, it's best to use tinfoil baking cups so that the honey doesn't go all over the place. Just save the paper ones for later, when you want to make muffins.

Nothing goes to waste in a Greek household.

And, if you like to be preemptive, you can include a recipe card with your gift—the recipient will surely be asking you for it.

It ... and possibly your hand in marriage.

VASILOPITA (NEW YEAR'S BREAD)

10 eggs, separated

2½ cups sugar

2 tsp. vanilla

½ lb. butter, melted and cooled

5 oz. cognac (or Metaxa if you've got it)

juice from 8 to 10 oranges

1 tsp. baking soda

1 tsp. baking powder

2½ lbs. flour

grated rind from 1 orange

egg yolk (optional)

½ cup slivered almonds (optional)

2 tbsp. sesame seeds (optional)

powdered sugar (optional)

coin (vital)

(makes two large or three small breads)

Beat egg yolks; add sugar a little at a time until dissolved. Add vanilla and the melted and cooled butter. Beat until smooth.

In a separate container, mix the cognac, orange juice, baking soda, and baking powder.

Beat the egg whites until stiff, but not dry.

Into the egg yolk mixture, slowly add the flour and the cognac-orange juice mixture. Finally, fold in the egg whites.

Pour batter into a greased (or buttered and floured) baking pan.

The lucky coin needs to go into the batter before you bake it—

it's best to wrap it in a bit of plastic wrap or aluminum foil. (It's always safer, of course, to find the coin in the bread before you go sinking your teeth into it.) Hide it well—and then forget where you hid it. If you can't forget, then let everyone else choose their slices before you to be fair.

If you wish, you can decorate the top of your bread using egg yolk (for a nice brown crust), almonds (it's always fun to spell out the year with them), and sesame seeds. If you use egg yolk do that first—don't brush the almonds with yolk.

Bake at 350°F until done (the bread will start pulling away from the sides of the pan).

Feel free to decorate further by sprinkling powdered sugar on top before serving.

Eat with caution, and good luck!

GREEK COFFEE

water
sugar
Turkish or Greek coffee

Now, if you can't get Turkish or Greek coffee locally, don't fret. You can use any kind of coffee really—the stronger and bolder the blend, the better, of course. If you grind it yourself, you'll note that at the store (or on your grinder), there is actually a setting for Turkish. It means that the beans will be as finely ground as humanly possible. That's what you're going for.

Three is the number of power, remember; this recipe is so simple it's deceptive. For each cup of coffee you want, add one demitasse cup full of water, one teaspoon sugar, and one heaping teaspoon of coffee to your copper *briki*. (If you don't have a *briki* you can use a small saucepan, but it's harder to get the coffee into the demitasse cups—the *briki* actually has a specially designed lip that facilitates pouring from the side.)

Beat or stir the coffee vigorously over heat until it comes to a boil, then remove from heat and wait until the foam goes down. Replace over heat—this procedure must be done three times.

Fill the demitasse cups each a little at a time, to ensure equal consistency. There should be mud in the bottom of each cup, and each should have a light foamy froth. Do not stir, or add cream.

Serve with lots and lots of pastries.

Drink slowly.

TZATZIKI SAUCE

3½ cups not-thick yogurt
1 tsp. salt
1 cup cucumber, finely chopped
1 clove garlic, crushed
2 tsp. olive oil
1 tbsp. fresh dill, mint, and parsley
1 tbsp. lemon juice

The guys at the gyro place never give you enough of this fabulous sauce—it's like the Greek version of crack. Personally, I think it's the garlic that makes us keep coming back for more.

To thicken the yogurt, place 3½ cups yogurt mixed with 1 tsp. salt in cheesecloth or a towel. Hang over a bowl until the dripping stops (about 2 hours). This should give you roughly 2 cups of very thick yogurt.

Sprinkle a little salt over the cucumber. Let stand for 15 minutes, then press dry. (Watery cucumber only gives you watery sauce.)

Combine all remaining ingredients and enjoy, enjoy, enjoy!

The Big Easy

A Brief Tour of New Orleans
and Cajun Culture

*How many times can a person get lost in a city where she's
lived her whole life?*
—Sunshine Runningwolf

New Orleans (pronounced New-AW-lenz or New-OR-lenz). The Big
Easy. Home of Mardi Gras, beignets, and Louis Armstrong. Haven
of voodoo, Daimons, and vampire lore. Colorful and glamorous,
slow and seductive, New Orleans has a history wrapped in blood,
beauty, and mystery that will live forever.

Nouvelle-Orléans was founded by the French in 1718 and named
after Philippe II, Duke of Orléans and Regent of France. Many
fought for control of this prosperous Mississippi River port over
the next century. The Spanish took it from the French; the
British took it from the Spanish. American forces later defeated
the British in 1815, at the Battle of New Orleans. Due to the constant mercantile traffic—including slaves—by the 1840s, New
Orleans was the wealthiest city in the nation.

Hurricane Katrina hit the city of New Orleans in August 2005,
flooding 80 percent of the city. The residents had been evacu-
ated or moved to shelters, but still more than 1,500 people died.
Due to extensive damage, many did not return. The city's current

population is roughly half of what it was. Many efforts have been made since that time toward a revival of the city, a rebirth to a new glory.

Much like the Dark-Hunters themselves.

It is for this reason that Sherri began holding the annual K-Con (Kenyon/Kinley Convention) there. It brings much-needed business to the city and she always holds charity events to donate funds to the library. Many Dark-Hunter fans even come in early to volunteer with Habitat for Humanity. And in Ash's book, there is a scene with his Goth Chicness working with Habitat for Humanity.

Points of Interest

> *By the way, I want hazard pay for this.*
> *I seriously hate the mall.*
> —Nick Gautier

New Orleans is central to the Dark-Hunter mythos and, like many settings, is herself one of the most important characters in the series. I've put together only a few highlights of New Orleans to show you here special points of interest as they relate to the Dark-Hunters. The best way to fully appreciate the scope of New Orleans is to visit her yourself.

Information can be found on the official New Orleans tourism Web site: www.neworleansonline.com.

ACME OYSTER HOUSE
724 Iberville Street
(504) 522-5973 or (877) 815-6412
www.acmeoyster.com

Located just off Bourbon Street, Acme Oyster House is the favorite restaurant of self-proclaimed vampire slayer Tabitha

Devereaux. According to Tabitha, Acme has the best oysters in the world. Acme is famous among the locals for its casual dining and plastic tablecloths, the staple of all great seafood restaurants. You might also find Vane and Bride Kattalakis or Kyrian and Amanda Hunter here, as they like to frequent the oyster bar.

ANTOINE'S

713 St. Louis Street

(504) 581-4422

www.antoines.com

Closed Sundays

Reservations recommended

This exquisite French restaurant was established in 1840 by the young Frenchman Antoine Alciator, and has been operated by the same family for more than 160 years. (His son Jules, who became chef after his father's death, was the inventor of the famed Oysters Rockefeller.) The menu is written in French—but not to worry, the lovely waitstaff will be happy to *aidez vous*.

At Antoine's you can dine in one of the many historic rooms. There are rooms named after the Antoine's Mardi Gras krewes: Hermes, Proteus, Rex, and the Twelfth Night Revelers. There is the Japanese Room, whose unique Oriental splendor was closed to the public for more than forty years after the bombing of Pearl Harbor. The Mystery Room celebrates the era of Prohibition, a time when the floors were covered with sawdust to soak up any illegal alcohol on the premises in the event of a raid. Antoine's also features a massive and exquisitely well-stocked wine cellar.

Antoine's is definitely a treat for any special occasion. Nick Gautier once brought his mother, Cherise, here for her birthday to celebrate . . . one of the last birthdays they were able to share together before her untimely death.

BRENNAN'S RESTAURANT
417 Royal Street
(504) 525-9711
www.brennansneworleans.com
Reservations recommended

Established in 1946, Brennan's is famous for the legendary breakfast and infamous for the Bananas Foster. In the evenings you can experience a lovely French Quarter dinner in one of twelve beautiful dining rooms, or the romantic gaslit courtyard patio. This romantic atmosphere at Brennan's was taken advantage of by Vane Kattalakis, who met Bride McTierney here for their first date. There is always a table reserved for them once a year, on their anniversary.

CABILDO
701 Chartres Street
(504) 568-6968 or (800) 568-6968
http://lsm.crt.state.la.us

The Cabildo is the flagship building of the Louisiana State Museum, and the site of the famous 1803 Louisiana Purchase transfer. It was constructed at the end of the eighteenth century, and was the seat of the Spanish municipal government in New Orleans. The building takes its name from the "Illustrious Cabildo", or city council, who met there.

CAFÉ DU MONDE
800 Decatur Street
(504) 587-0833 or (800) 772-2927
www.cafedumonde.com
Open twenty-four hours daily

A trip to New Orleans is not complete without a stop at the world-famous Café Du Monde, where Dark-Hunters everywhere are sure to stop in for a chicory coffee (sometimes au lait) and beignets. The original coffee stand was established in the French Market in 1862. Café Du Monde is located directly across from where Selena Laurens had her tarot card stand, before Ash bought her the building where Madame Selene currently runs her operations.

CAFÉ PONTALBA
546 St. Peter Street
(504) 522-1180

Located in the historic Pontalba building, Café Pontalba features traditional Cajun and Creole food. (Be sure to try the jambalaya fries!) Café Pontalba's casual atmosphere is frequented by both tourists and locals alike. It is open daily for lunch and dinner, and features breakfast on Saturdays and Sundays.

COMMANDER'S PALACE
1403 Washington Avenue
(504) 899-8221
www.commanderspalace.com

Established in 1880, Commander's Palace is known for its upscale, gourmet dining and historic antebellum rooms. The restaurant was redesigned in 1974, under the management of the Brennan family, to enhance the beauty of the building and embrace the outdoor atmosphere of the Garden District. Commander's Palace is still overseen by the Brennans, who we hope by now have forgiven Tabitha for eating that centerpiece.

DREAM DOLLS AND ACCESSORIES
Royal Street

A trip to New Orleans is not complete for any Dark-Hunter if it does not include a visit to Liza's little shop. Get those girly thoughts out of your head—the former Squire is certainly not all sugar and spice and everything nice. If she invites you into the back room, consider yourself fortunate (unless Ash happens to be there playing with his goddaughter). A treasure trove of wonders awaits you there . . . an armory the likes of which you have never seen before and, I daresay, never will again.

YE OLDE DUNGEON
738 Toulouse Street
(504) 523-5530
www.originaldungeon.com
Must be at least twenty-one to enter

One of the New Orleans nightspots frequented by Acheron and Simi, the Dungeon has its own history of vengeance and retribution. It is broken up into three main areas: the Main Chamber Bar, the Dance Floor and Sound Bar, and the Venus Bar. Indulge yourself in drinks such as Witch's Brew or Dragon's Blood, or participate in the tattoo contest. There is never any live music, only DJs, and it's never Top 40s. House rules. (House rocks, technically.) This is a fave spot of Acheron's whenever he's in town.

French Quarter

Also called *Vieux Carré*, or "old square". One of the favorite tourist scenes in New Orleans, the French Quarter is designated as the area bordered by Rampart Street, Canal Street, Esplanade

Avenue, and the Mississippi River. Bourbon Street, Jackson Square, the St. Louis Cathedral, and the French Market are all located in the French Quarter.

FROSTBYTE CAFÉ
1100 Royal Street
(504) 555-3223
www.geocities.com/frostbytecafe

Indulge your sweet tooth without leaving the Internet. Frostbyte Café is your one-stop shop for ice cream, baked goods, and e-mail. Located in the French Quarter, this cybercafé features an intimate courtyard, fun holiday specials (Halloween is a treat!), and occasional live entertainment by local talents.

HARD ROCK CAFE
418 N. Peters Street
(504) 529-5617
www.hardrock.com

There's one in every corner of the globe, and there's one in the French Quarter, too. Drop by for fun American food, rock 'n' roll memorabilia, and your very own Hard Rock Cafe New Orleans T-shirt.

Jackson Square

Located in the French Quarter, Jackson Square was named after General (and later President) Andrew Jackson, victor over the British at the Battle of New Orleans. Artists have been displaying their work along the wrought-iron gates encircling Jackson

Square for more than fifty years. In the 1970s, the city of New Orleans decided to close the streets to vehicular traffic and make the area surrounding Jackson Square a pedestrian mall.

JACKSON BREWERY
600 Decatur Street
(504) 566-7245
Open daily from 10 A.M. to 6 P.M.
www.jacksonbrewery.com

Jackson Brewery, or The Shops at Jax Brewery, is a historical landmark situated in the heart of the French Quarter, along the Mississippi River. It really was a brewhouse, built in 1891 by Dietrich Einsiedek. The Jax Brewery was once the largest independent brewery in the southern United States. It is now home to a variety of upscale stores, restaurants, and attractions—including the Jax Collection, a historical retrospective of the Jax beer legacy.

The Jax Brewery is where Grace and Julian went shopping to buy Julian clothes after she and Selena found a way to get him out of that cursed book. Also, while you're in the brewery, keep an eye out for anyone selling those pralines Selena's so immensely fond of. I hear that the futures of the folks who bring pralines to Madame Selene are always lucky and bright.

LILAC & LACE BOUTIQUE
Iberville Street

Owned by Bride McTierney (now Kattalakis), this one-of-a-kind vintage clothing store caters to women of all shapes and sizes in search of something unique to their tastes. Looking for the perfect gift? Be sure to check out Lilac and Lace's fantastic array of custom and costume jewelry, shoes, and accessories.

LOYOLA UNIVERSITY
6363 St. Charles Avenue
(504) 865-2011
www.loyno.edu
Campus tours Monday through Friday at 11:30 A.M. and 3:30 P.M.

Loyola University is located fifteen minutes from downtown New Orleans and the French Quarter. This university, and its sister universities of the same name around the United States, were named after Saint Ignatius of Loyola, the founder of the Roman Catholic Church. Loyola University New Orleans was founded by the Jesuits in 1804, and remains the largest Catholic university in the southern United States.

Dr. Julian Alexander teaches an Ancient Civilizations class here, and also at Tulane University. He's a fantastic speaker and easy on the eyes, but boy, is he tough. Don't think you're getting off easy by taking his class.

MAGNOLIA CAFÉ
200 Chartres Street
(504) 524-4478

Indulge in more casual New Orleans cuisine at the Magnolia Café. They've got the basics, from seafood to red beans and rice, but their specialties are their omelettes.

MIKE ANDERSON'S SEAFOOD
215 Bourbon Street

Another favorite of Tabitha Devereaux's, a woman in search of the perfect oyster. Originally established in Baton Rouge, Louisiana, Mike Anderson's expanded into the French Quarter in 1985. A location was also opened up in Riverwalk Mall, but both restaurants have been closed since Hurricane Katrina.

OLD ABSINTHE HOUSE
240 Bourbon Street
(504) 523-3181
www.ruebourbon.com

Built in 1807, the Old Absinthe House was originally an importing firm, then a corner grocery, and then a coffeehouse. It was in this coffeehouse in 1874 that Cayetano Ferrer mixed the Old Absinthe House Frappé, from which the current famous Bourbon Street bar gets its name. The Old Absinthe House still has the decorative marble fountains that were used to drip cool water over sugar cubes into glasses of absinthe. The House is also known for its calling-card-adorned walls; no visit is complete without leaving your own among the many. Their motto is "Everyone you have known or ever will know, eventually ends up at the Old Absinthe House".

OLD URSULINE CONVENT
1100 Chartres Street
(504) 529-3040
NATIONAL SHRINE OF OUR LADY OF PROMPT SUCCOR
2701 State Street

Built in 1752, the Ursuline Convent is the oldest building in the Mississippi River Valley. When the Americans fought the British at the Battle of New Orleans in 1815, the Mother Superior at the Ursuline Convent vowed that if General Andrew Jackson's army was victorious, there would be a Mass of thanksgiving sung every year to commemorate the occasion. True to her word, every year on January 8, a Mass of thanksgiving has been offered in the National Shrine of Our Lady of Prompt Succor.

PANDORA'S BOX
Bourbon Street

Spice up your life with a visit to Tabitha Devereaux's famous adult shop in the French Quarter. Come with an open mind—just like Tabitha, some things in her shop are not for the faint of heart.

PIRATE ALLEY

This alley is one block long, extending from Chartres Street at Jackson Square to Royal Street. Originally Orleans Alley, the city changed its name in the 1960s to Pirate Alley. (That's what the locals always called it, and the tourists kept getting confused.) Legend has it that it was frequented by pirates in days past. That may or may not be true, considering its proximity to the old Spanish Dungeon. The Faulkner House is on Pirate Alley, and is where William Faulkner reportedly wrote his first novel.

PRESBYTERE BUILDING
751 Chartres Street
(504) 568-6968 or (800) 568-6968
http://lsm.crt.state.la.us

The famous Presbytere building was designed in 1791 to match the Cabildo (Town Hall) on the other side of the St. Louis Cathedral, but the building was not finished until 1813. It was originally used as commercial property and later a courthouse; it has been part of the Louisiana State Museum for almost a century. It closed after Hurricane Katrina, reopening its doors less than a year later on April 28, 2006.

RUNNINGWOLF'S
Canal Street

This happening club is run by the Runningwolf family, and frequented by the locals. Daimons are very much not welcome here.

ST. LOUIS CATHEDRAL
615 Pere Antoine Alley
(504) 525-9585
www.stlouiscathedral.org

This picturesque Catholic Church, named after Saint Louis, king of France, and situated between the Cabildo and Presbytere buildings, overlooks Jackson Square. It is one of the most photographed landmarks in New Orleans. The first church opened on this site in 1727, but was later destroyed by the Great Fire of 1788. Over the centuries, the church has been restored and rebuilt, weathering hurricanes, fires, and even a bomb that was once set off in the cathedral in 1909.

SANCTUARY
688 Ursulines Avenue

The famed biker bar where the Peltier clan hangs out. There's more information on this in chapter 3, "Were-Hunters".

TEMPTATIONS
327 Bourbon Street
(504) 525-4470

A gentlemen's club in an upscale, restored antebellum mansion, Temptations was frequented—and much appreciated—by the infamous former Squire Nick Gautier. Imported wines, fine cigars, beautiful women . . . yes, I'm sure he was only there for the ambiance.

TIPITINA'S
233 N. Peters Street
(504) 566-7095
www.tipitinas.com

Tip's was established in 1977 by a group of young music fans who called themselves the "Fabulous Fo'teen". It was named for a song by Henry Roeland Byrd (aka Professor Longhair), one of the most revered rhythm and blues musicians in the legacy of New Orleans. That neighborhood juke joint later grew into the enormous music venue it is today, hosting a variety of well-known artists. Tipitina's continues to support its musical roots with a Walk of Fame honoring New Orleans music legends past and present, a recording studio, and its own recording label.

TULANE UNIVERSITY
6823 St. Charles Avenue
(504) 865-5000
www.tulane.edu

The "Harvard of the South", Tulane University was founded in 1834 as the Medical College of Louisiana (its name was changed in 1884 to Tulane, after wealthy benefactor Paul Tulane). Its campus sprawls over more than 110 acres, and it has more than 10,000 students enrolled. Their motto is *Non Sibi Sed Suis,* translated as "Not for one's self, but for one's own".

Tulane is living up to its reputation as one of the foremost independent national research universities in the United States by concentrating its research efforts on Hurricane Katrina, and the impact of its aftermath.

Dr. Julian Alexander teaches an Ancient Civilizations class here, as well as at Loyola University.

Fun Facts

Remember that time you attacked the Anne Rice-Lestat reenactment group in the cemetery?
—Amanda Hunter

CEMETERIES

It's all about the water table. Like when you're at the beach, digging a moat for your sand castle: You dig about a foot down, and your moat's already magically got water. That's what all of New Orleans is like. The French Quarter itself is only about ten feet above sea level . . . and that's high ground.

Burying the dead in New Orleans was a serious business. Weighing down the caskets with stones and sandbags didn't work, nor did drilling holes in them. Eventually, people gave up trying to bury anything at all. Graves were created aboveground, in the form of tombs, crypts, and vaults. Cemeteries are literally called the "Cities of the Dead" because of their massive acreage. There are rules as to how many family members can be put inside a vault, and how long a time period must pass before a new family member can be put on top of, or in place of another.

The cemeteries of New Orleans are beautiful and haunting . . . and dangerous. It is wise not to travel through them alone, and I'm not saying that just because of the Daimons—Nick Gautier's infamous father once ran with a gang who used to rob tourists who were stupid enough to enter cemeteries alone.

There are more than forty cemeteries in New Orleans, and most of them offer guided tours.

In every cemetery you visit, always remember to respect the monuments to the departed. There are groups who help try and protect New Orleans' historic cemeteries from the ravages of time, neglect, vandalism, theft, and that pesky little hurricane named Katrina. Yes, there are people who are actually trained in the art of tomb restoration. Nifty, huh?

Find out more about the preservation of New Orleans cemeteries at www.saveourcemeteries.org.

MULES

Romantic couples visiting New Orleans will certainly want to take a carriage ride around the French Quarter. Those who do will notice that a large percentage of the carriages are drawn not by horses, but by mules. It's survival of the fittest—mules are apparently much heartier animals than their equine cousins. Although for a time, horses were used, mules have since replaced them. They can withstand the humidity and much higher temperatures of the New Orleans climate. Like you've seen so many times in movies, horses will continue to work for their owners until they drop dead. Mules, on the other hand, will simply stop as soon as they become tired.

There are, of course, rules that all carriage operators must follow. Mules can only work if the outside temperature is at or less than ninety degrees. They are not allowed to pull more than nine people, including the driver of the carriage. They are required to have a fifteen-minute rest between each ride. In the summer, that break increases to thirty minutes, and mules are not permitted to work more than six hours a day.

For more information, contact the Louisiana Society for the Prevention of Cruelty to Animals (www.la-spca.org).

ROMEO SPIKES

No, they're not named after Romeo Pontis (but it is funny to watch his face when you mention it . . . right before he kicks your butt). These are the wrought-iron or steel spikes you will see decorating balconies and their supporting pillars all over the French Quarter. The Romeo moniker came into use when the story got around about how their existence was due to well-to-do fathers who wanted to keep their daughters safe from unworthy male callers.

They look lethal because they are—the spikes have claimed the lives of various suitors over the years. Many a not-so-surefooted Romeo has met his maker after a tryst with his beloved. The clever trick to conquering the spikes was to throw a horse blanket over them and use them as support to aid the climb. The more difficult task was getting down again, especially if the blanket had fallen away or been stolen. The standard joke is that a young man would ascend a Romeo, but come back down a Juliet.

Cajun Dictionary

Boy, I'm backwoods Cajun, I ain't ever got no class, cher.
—Nick Gautier

It's not quite French, it's not quite English, and most of it has to do with food. More so than most cities, New Orleans has a vernacular all its own.

Don't fret, boo; here's a quick reference guide to help you out with all the li'l things, so you can relax and have your café au lait in peace.

Andouille   (ahn-DO-wee)   A spicy pork sausage used in most gumbos and jambalaya dishes.

Bayou   (BI-yoo)   The streams and swampy regions across Louisiana.

Beignet   **(ben-YAY)**   A square of deep-fried dough served with a generous helping of powdered sugar. Essentially, a French doughnut.

Boo   A term of endearment.

Boudin   (boo-DAN)   Spicy pork, rice, onions, and spices stuffed in a sausage casing. It's fantabulous, and you must try it.

Bourre   (BOO-ray)   A Cajun card game.

Café au lait   (kah-fay-oh-LAY)   A drink consisting of half chicory coffee and half steamed milk. Goes great with a beignet.

Cajun   (KAY-jun)   Refers to the Acadians, French-speaking people who migrated to South Louisiana from Nova Scotia in the eighteenth century.

Cher   (sha)   From the French, meaning "dear", a term of endearment.

Chew   (choo)   From the French, slang meaning "rear end", this is often used to refer to an undesirable person. Especially when you're speaking directly to them.

Chock a block   Packed full.

Couche couche   (koosh koosh)   Fried cornmeal topped with milk and/or cane syrup. Served at breakfast.

Creole   (KREE-ole)   This term originally described those of mixed Spanish and French blood who were born in southeast

Louisiana. Creole is now used to describe both cuisine and architecture.

Crescent City Another nickname for New Orleans, because it is located in a crescent-shaped bend of the Mississippi.

Envie (ahn-VEE) Your heart's desire.

Fais do do (fay-do-do) A traditional southern Louisiana dance party. Fais do do literally means "to make sleep".

Filé (FEE-lay) Ground sassafras leaves used to season gumbo (and other dishes).

Garry (GE-ree) Porch.

Gris gris (gree gree) A voodoo spell.

King Cake Traditional Mardi Gras ring-shaped cake decorated in green, gold, and purple, with a small plastic baby baked inside it. Traditions vary, but it is most often said that whoever gets the baby has to buy next year's King Cake. Others think the recipient will have a year's worth of luck, or will become pregnant by year's end.

Lagniappe (LAN-yap) A little something extra. The residents of New Orleans always do all they can to add that small bonus that makes their guests feel special.

Levee (leh-VEE) An embankment constructed to keep a river from flooding the surrounding area.

Moodee (moo-DEE) Cursed.

Muffuletta This sandwich is named after the bread used to make it, of course, and is well known in New Orleans. It was invented in 1906 at the Italian-American-owned Central Grocery on Decatur Street in the French Quarter. Other than the bread, the sandwich consists of an olive salad, capicola, salami, provolone, mortadella (a pork sausage), and Emmentaler (a cheese).

Nonc (nonk) Uncle. Much shortened from the French "*mon oncle*" meaning "my uncle".

Ovadaddy   Over there.

Pain Perdu   (pan pair-DUE)   French toast; literally "lost bread".

Parish   (PEAR-ish)   Louisiana state district or county.

Po'Boy   (POE boy)   Once five-cent meals for the poor boys, a po'boy is any sandwich served on French bread and often "dressed" with lettuce, tomato, and mayonnaise. A fried oyster po'boy is definitely a treat to be experienced. A fried oyster po'boy with Tabitha Devereaux *is* an experience.

Praline   (PRAW-leen)   New Orleans candy made with pecans, brown sugar, and cream. According to Selena Laurens, eating pralines is like putting a little piece of heaven in your mouth.

Remoulade   (REM-oo-lad)   A spicy sauce served on or with most seafood.

Roux   (roo)   A roux is undoubtedly the hardest thing to properly make in Cajun cuisine. Unfortunately, étouffées, gumbos, *everything* starts with a roux, so it's something you just have to master. It's just a mixture of flour and oil . . . but if you're anything like me, you'll burn it at least the first five times you try to make it.

T   Used in front of any name, T means "petite" or "little".

Tasso   (TAH-so)   Cajun pepperoni; smoked strips of spiced pork or beef used to flavor dishes.

Trinity   Cooking slang that refers to celery, onions, and bell pepper: the staples of Cajun cuisine.

Turducken   It is as bizarre as it sounds. In fact, probably more so. Invented in Louisiana, a turducken is a turkey stuffed with a duck, and that duck is in turn stuffed with a small chicken. (All are deboned.) In every other possible place, even in between the meats, there is a breadcrumb and/or sausage stuffing. After it's slowly roasted, and all the juices have mingled, then you get to stuff yourself with it. (That's a lot of stuffing.) I hear there's even a vegetarian version made with tofu. I'm going to let you figure out the spelling of that one on your own.

Zydeco   (ZIE-de-ko)   Cajun country music; a combination of traditional Cajun music and Afro-Caribbean blues. The name comes from the Cajun pronunciation of *les haricots* (snap beans), a phrase used in one of the earliest songs of this genre.

Lagniappe

Coffee . . . Daimons . . . Coffee . . . Daimons . . .
—Talon Runningwolf

In true New Orleans fashion, I couldn't let you go without my own little something extra.

Like every rich, history-steeped culture, New Orleans is famous for its food. Unique because of its blend of French, Spanish, and African roots, spicy, flavorful Cajun cuisine has that certain . . . *je ne sais quoi.*

No, wait, I do know what: *yum.* That's the word I'm looking for.

BEIGNETS

1 envelope active dry yeast
¾ cups hot water
¼ cup sugar
½ teaspoon salt
1 egg, beaten
½ cup evaporated milk
3½ to 4 cups all-purpose flour, divided
⅛ cup shortening, softened
oil for frying
lots and lots of powdered sugar
   (use a sifter if you've got one)

In a large bowl, dissolve the yeast in the water and let stand for about 5 minutes (until bubbling). Add sugar, salt, the beaten egg, and evaporated milk. Add half the flour, then shortening, then gradually blend in the remaining flour until the dough is soft, but not sticky. It may be easier to finish the mixing with your hands.

I'm not going to lie, it makes a mess. And you haven't even come to the frying part yet. Or the sugar part.

Let the batter chill overnight in a nonstick or oiled bowl. The next morning, it will have risen to about twice its original size. Roll out the dough and cut into squares. (The dough can also be precut at this time and frozen for later use.) Let separate beignets rise again for about half an hour (at room temperature this time, or in a warm oven). Deep fry for 2 to 3 minutes until lightly browned on both sides. Drain on paper towels and sprinkle *generously* with the powdered sugar.

Be sure to have made your café au lait first, because you're going to want to eat these puppies hot. Oh, and it's a good idea not to eat beignets while wearing your favorite black leather pants. Trust me.

CHERISE GAUTIER'S GUMBO

1 onion, chopped
2 chili peppers, chopped
4 green bell peppers, chopped
½ cup celery, chopped
10 cups water or chicken broth
1 lb. okra
gumbo filé powder, sage, thyme, pepper, cayenne,
and oregano to taste
1 chicken, cut into pieces
2 lbs. andouille sausage
3 lbs. shrimp, peeled and deveined
1 lb. crawfish tails, peeled
green onions and fresh parsley

ROUX

½ cup flour

1 cup vegetable oil

OPTIONAL

rice

crackers

hot sauce

First, you make a roux. (See? Told you so.) Good luck. Combine the flour and oil, stirring constantly over the heat until the mixture is dark brown, *not* burnt. If you burn it, toss it out and start over again. Don't fret—sixth time's the charm. You need patience to cook this one anyway. Best start learning it right up front.

Add the onion, peppers, and celery. Cook until vegetables are soft.

Add the water (or chicken broth), okra, and spices. Add the chicken to the water and simmer for about 1 hour.

Add the andouille sausage and simmer for 1 hour.

Add shrimp and crawfish and simmer for another 15 minutes.

(You might want to leave the house, or seriously distract yourself so the fabulous smell doesn't drive you wild.) Also, after all this time, you're going to want to check your spices again. Add to taste.

Add the green onions and parsley right before serving (over rice, or with crackers).

Don't worry if you make too much—gumbo is even better the next day, and freezes very well.

Note: For those of you who might not know, gumbo filé powder is simply powdered sassafras leaves. Along with its unique taste, filé powder also works as a thickener for the gumbo.

PAPA PELTIER'S BAYOU SAUCE

mayonnaise
ketchup
mustard
hot sauce

A not-so-secret Sanctuary favorite, this fabulous sauce is the perfect complement to your shrimp or crab boil, as well as a yummy topping for a fried oyster po'boy.

Amounts vary to your taste—start with the mayonnaise as a base, using the other ingredients to "spice" it up. For the hot sauce I like chili or garlic sauce, but the choice is ultimately yours. Use as much or as little as you wish.

Just be sure to make lots. You'll need it.

The Author Goddess

Interview with Sherrilyn Kenyon

What do you do whenever Mom leaves you alone like this?
—Katra

New York Times bestselling author Sherrilyn Kenyon lives a life of extraordinary danger ... as does any woman with three sons, a husband, a menagerie of pets, and a collection of swords that all of the above have a major fixation with. But when not running interference (or dashing off to the emergency room), she's found chained to her computer, where she likes to play with all her imaginary friends. With more than ten million copies of her books in print in thirty countries, she certainly has a lot of friends to play with, too.

Writing as both Kinley MacGregor and Sherrilyn Kenyon, she is the author of several series including, The Dark-Hunters, Brotherhood of the Sword, Lords of Avalon, Nevermore, and BAD. With an international cult following, her books have appeared on the top five of the *New York Times*, *Publisher's Weekly*, and *USA Today* bestseller lists.

A versatile, award-winning writer, Sherri has carved out multiple bestselling series in numerous genres and subgenres (science fiction; romance; fantasy; horror; contemporary; historical;

romantic suspense; futuristic; urban fantasy; high fantasy; and time travel).

Along with her work in fiction, Sherri is an accomplished nonfiction author who has contributed to such works as *The Character-Naming Sourcebook*, *Everyday Life in the Middle Ages*, *The Writer's Complete Fantasy Reference*, and essays in *Seven Seasons of Buffy* and *Five Seasons of Angel*. Her articles and short stories have appeared in hundreds of large and small journals and magazines worldwide. She's also written for television, radio, and was once a copywriter and science fiction/fantasy editor.

Like a literary Willy Wonka, whatever you want, whatever your dream, Sherri can provide it. And despite the wide range of genres, the differences in time periods, settings, and dialects, certain elements remain consistent. There will always be adventure. There will always be some aspect of the fantastic grown from a seed of the mundane world that the average reader can relate to. And there will always be strong heroines and heroes— real people of all shapes, sizes, and backgrounds. Be they schoolteachers, artists, musicians, gods or goddesses, they still have relationship problems, familial obligations, and skeletons in the closet.

That's the great escape—Sherri's amazing talent of tapping into the Peter Pan psyche in all people. She lets the reader still believe in magic and pay the bills, work out, car pool, and do the laundry. No matter how fantastic things get, if you believe hard enough it *might* just happen . . . and it might just happen to you.

How did you get started writing?

I've always been a writer. I came out of the womb, literally, wanting to do this. In my Brownie manual, it has scrawled, "When I grow up, I want to be—" and I wrote, "A writer and a mother." I wrote my very first novel when I was seven and I published my first piece when I was in third grade. I made my first professional sell at age fourteen. I've written for every paper at every school I ever attended. A writer is who and what I am and it is what I will always be.

The first story I ever published was a horror short story called "The Neighbors". I went on to publish many, many more short stories in science fiction, fantasy, horror, and mystery. I started writing nonfiction articles for magazines such as *Brides*, *Seventeen*, and dozens of others because they paid significantly more. Ironically, I ended up selling a nonfiction book first. But it was always my dream to publish a novel.

You and your husband both work full time, you have three kids, and you still manage to put out anywhere from four to eight books a year. How do you do it? What's your writing regimen like?

Because I've always wanted this, I'm basically a workaholic who spends anywhere from thirteen to twenty hours a day writing. It's what I live for. Writing is my full-time job and I treat it as such. I've never understood writers who take time off between books or who write when the mood hits them. I have set business hours and I adhere to them unless I'm working overtime.

My "average" (and I laugh uproariously as I say this) day starts around 11 A.M. (my husband gets the children off to school). I answer e-mails, make a few business calls. Around noon, I eat lunch, then return to the office to make more calls if I need to, tend to administrative matters and mail. My children come home at three thirty and I spend the next few hours with them. We have dinner between five and six. I kiss the little ones, read to them, and return to my office around seven. Then the phone goes off and I spend the rest of the night writing until I'm too tired to go any longer (usually around four in the morning).

I prefer to work at night because there are no distractions. My friends are in bed, my editors and agent can't call, and the children are asleep and safe. There's nothing on my mind except the story. But that being said, those stories have a nasty tendency to wake me up anywhere from 5 A.M. and on. I am a slave to my muse. But I wouldn't have it any other way.

What drove this particular obsession with the paranormal? Did you like scary movies as a kid?

Oh, yeah. My mother was a true horror fan. She lived for it. I grew up with her reading Barker, King, and Straub at the breakfast table. I honestly can't remember the first time I saw a horror movie; I was most likely in diapers. But I grew up seeing everything from *Amityville Horror* to *The Exorcist* with my mom. We'd be watching late-night *Creature Feature* and she'd be sitting in her chair one minute, and in the next she'd get this glazed look in her eyes and start drooling. "Brains, brains," she'd chant. "I want brains . . ." Then she'd chase us through the house. She scarred me for life, but that's what I loved most about her. She was the best and she gave me a lifetime love of all things that go bump in the night.

How are the Dark-Hunter books different from everything else out there?

These aren't your mama's vampires. Born from my imagination and years of research, the Dark-Hunters are unique. I've never been the kind of person who treads the well-worn path of others. I'd much rather find my own way. So with machete in hand, I reexamined the folklore and myths of the vampire and created my own take on how they came into being.

Whereas traditional vampires are innately evil, mine can be, but their vampirism doesn't come from an evil source per se. It comes from the deep desires of a race that just wants to live a little longer. Fighters and warriors who don't want to lie down and die because some ancient god cursed them for something their ancestors did. I took the vampire world and reworked it with a new set of rules and laws. I wanted something that would be uniquely mine, something that would surprise the reader in every book so that the story and characters would never grow stale in the retelling.

How did you first think of the Dark-Hunters?

I started the series back in the mid-1980s when I "met" Acheron and based several short stories on him and the vampire hunters he ran with. From there, the Hunters, as they were then called, stayed with me, and I worked on them in between other projects. They are a culmination of my lifetime of interest in vampires and history. The very first Hunter stories were written while I was attending Georgia College, in Milledgeville, Georgia. I wrote the very first Acheron short in Room 222 of Wells Hall.

Most all of your books are part of a series. Have you written any stand-alone books? Would you prefer that over series?

Ironically, I have one book that was published as a stand-alone, but that wasn't my fault. (Laughs.) The publisher refused the second book. I don't think I could do a stand-alone if I tried. I spend so much time with the people and places in the book, and they are so real to me that I always want to go back and revisit them for more. It's like coming home again.

Most writers focus on only one or two series at a time. Yet you have many more. Is there a reason for that?

The reason why I write more than one series is simple. I love spaghetti. It's without a doubt my favorite food on the planet. I can eat it for days, but you know, around about that third or fourth day, I do get a little tired of it. By the fifth or sixth day, I'm honestly sick of it. By the seventh I never want to see it again. Writing is the same way—the variety of the different series is what helps to keep it fresh.

I love each and every series I write. They are like my children and I have no favorite. However, I, like all authors, do need a little time-out after I've spent months working on a book. If I wrote nothing but Dark-Hunter or Nevermore or the Lords of Avalon, I would burn out on it. I think that may be why most authors who write a single series take a while between each book. You have to freshen the well and give new ideas time to grow.

By writing entirely different series in entirely different genres, I get to continually renew my creative well. It allows me the variety I need to stay healthy and happy.

Your heroes come from a bewildering array of times and cultures. How much research do you do and how do you keep track of them all? Has history always been your passion?

I always laugh whenever someone asks me how I keep track of them. How do you keep track of your family and friends? The Dark-Hunters are as real to me as my family is. I live with them constantly and those details are stored in the same place in my brain as my sons' shoe sizes, clothing sizes, and eating preferences. My best friend often calls me the idiot savant of all things Dark-Hunter. I think that's why I can't remember where my car keys or shoes are on any given day. My brain is too cluttered with Dark-Hunter facts.

As for the research, most of the Dark-Hunters come from the time periods I am intimate with: ancient Rome and Greece, the Middle Ages, and such. The other Dark-Hunters are from areas that I researched a lot in college or I have friends from that background who can help me with details. The easiest thing to say is that I spent ten years of my life prostrate to the goddess Clio.

I was lucky to have been born with a tremendous curiosity. Plus, I've kept up with a lot of friends who are now teaching various topics. If there's something I can't find, I ring them up and ask.

Why did you choose Artemis to be the goddess of the Dark-Hunters?

Artemis was a minor deity in Greece, but a major goddess in

other areas. Ancient writers wrote many, many stories about her. And while some portray her as a virgin (some claim that she asked Zeus for eternal virginity when she was three years old), others portray her quite differently. Her cult followers were never required to stay virgins. It was a common ceremony that whenever a cult member wanted to leave, all they had to do was go to Artemis's temple and place a lock of hair with their toys and other objects of their childhood on her altar and then they were free to go marry (which Artemis didn't object to).

She was a natural to lead the Dark-Hunters since she is goddess of the Hunt and is associated with Selene, who was the goddess of the Moon. Not to mention her twin brother, Apollo, is the god of the Sun and of Plagues. If you're building a world about a race of people who have been banished from daylight, who better than Apollo to pick on? It was only natural, after he cursed his race to prey on mankind, that his twin, who was goddess of the Hunt, would be the one to set up another race to control and kill those who were hurting humans.

But more than that, there are hundreds of different legends and stories written by the ancient Greeks and Romans that often contradict one another. Each ancient writer took a god or goddess and a story and made it their own. Artemis and Apollo were gods of many facets and faces. All the gods were. Apollo is both the god of Healing and the god of Plagues. Artemis is the goddess of Childbirth and is said to have shot her arrows into the bellies of mothers who were laboring, to kill both mother and child. These writers portrayed their gods as being very human with all human foibles.

I have always loved the complexity of the ancient plays. Take Ares, for example: the all-powerful god of War, and yet you often find him in myths where he is being bested by mortals and at times he's even shown as a crybaby. Ancient writers didn't shirk from making their pantheon real. We see ourselves in the gods. It's why I love Artemis so much. She was and has always been portrayed as a goddess of extreme contradictions. She's complex and highly unpredictable. I never know what she's going to do.

Where did you find your inspiration for the Atlantean pantheon and their stories?

Since Atlantis is a mythological place that has yet to be proven to exist, I took quite a lot of liberties with it. I love Hesiod and I have always admired his *Theogony*. I spent hours as a child reading and rereading it. I found the origin stories of the Greek gods fascinating and I wanted to create something every bit as complex and gripping. I wanted to build my own world.

The story of the Atlantean pantheon is totally my own. I started with the premise, what if Atlantis was real? Who would have been their gods if not the Greeks? What stories would they have told? What caused their empire to crumble? If I were an ancient writer, how would I have explained their origins and death? And I built my world from there.

One day I want to write my own *Theogony* for the Atlanteans.

Bad boys are a recurring element in your novels. Where do you get your knowledge of bad boys and the crazy things they do?

That has to come from the lunatics I was raised with (sorry, guys). I love the guys in my family, but they are definitely a different breed. You know, they think duct tape really is a bandage and a cure for, oh, everything—ironically enough, modern medicine has proven that it will cure warts. (See, Buddy, you were right and I admit it.) So they may be vindicated yet. Every time I turned around, one of them was doing something remarkably weird and foolish.

As a child, my official job was to call for the ambulance whenever they got hurt—which was often. They are the kind of guys who hook jumper cables to power lines just to see what will happen (I really wish I were making that up). Or who set fire to themselves while having a blue flame contest (again, I wish I were that imaginative).

Case in point, a brother called recently complaining about one of the guys who was in his garage where he keeps his race car and racing fuel (this is the most flammable fluid on the planet). He looks up and the guy is actually smoking while working on the car.

They have never recognized danger.

You also have strong female Dark-Hunters. How much do you identify with them?

They are their own unique people. I'm not sure if I "identify" with any per se. I guess because I was around so many guys, I've always been a take-charge kind of person and I respect that in all people, male or female.

Your Web site is amazing. Where do you get the energy to keep it up-to-date, and do you do it all yourself?

I think the Web site has been a real godsend in that it has brought people closer to the books and characters. It's a wonderful place where friends can meet and chat. Readers have said repeatedly that it's like a real Sanctuary where they can sit for a bit with old friends and relax.

I have a couple of helpers who tweak it for me, but I play on the site every day, and much like a museum, you only see a percentage of what's there. We have many more pages that are under development at all times.

The Dark-Hunter presence in the chats and on the bulletin board is one of my favorite aspects of the Web site. How does that work?

The "live" Dark-Hunters are friends and family who have graciously volunteered their time to role-play. The only thing they have in common with the characters are their names, and maybe a few of the more annoying personality traits. They know basic Dark-Hunter information, but not all details of their characters have been revealed to them.

Is Sanctuary a real place?

Oh, how I wish. Believe me, if Sanctuary were real, I'd be parked on a bar stool ogling Dev and the guys in New Orleans and not in my little room writing the books.

The only place Sanctuary exists is in my mind. And no, it's not based on any real bar in New Orleans. Sorry. If you look up the address 688 Ursulines, you'll find a convent there. That address was chosen for two reasons. One, it pays tribute to my favorite punk bar in the 1980s: 688, which was on Spring Street in Atlanta. And two, I wanted an address that didn't exist so that people wouldn't show up at someone's house in the French Quarter looking for the Peltiers.

The Dungeon, however, is real and on Toulouse Street (and if you're over twenty-five, wear ear plugs—it's really loud there).

If you had one piece of advice for aspiring writers, what would it be?

Never give up, never surrender. This is a hard business, but it's so worthwhile. There's nothing better than doing what you love. So don't ever let anyone tell you that you don't deserve your dream. You do. You just have to make sure that you don't give up too soon.

If you could be any superhero, who would it be?

Super Peanut. It's the superhero my son created for his own comic strip. I love Super Peanut. He has the power to clone himself at will (boy, what I wouldn't pay for that ability!). He's always taking down the evil Robot Monsters to save the world and he hangs with the coolest friends, Super Egg and his sidekick the Amazing Yolk.

The best part about being Super Peanut is I would then get to spend all my time making my son laugh. He has a beautiful laugh.

How did the term "Author Goddess" originate?

Author Goddess, or AG for short, came from the original members who played on the Dark-Hunter site. Hellion, aka Helly, was the one who coined both that and "Kenyon Minion". Thank you, Helly. You've always been the best. And thank you to the original members who helped make the Dark-Hunter message boards a true fan sanctuary. To everyone, past and present, who come and play, thank you from the bottom of my heart.

Goody-Goody Gumdrops

Bonus Material

An Interview with Acheron

If you could shrug off all your duties and responsibilities for one evening and break out your guitar, who would you, Acheron Parthenopaeus, jam with?

That's hard to say. I have extremely eclectic tastes, but it would probably be a toss-up between Bo Diddley, Black Eyed Peas, or Papa Roach. The where wouldn't matter really. It's all about the music. It really does soothe the savage beast within.

Ash, what's the one thing you want most out of life?

Peace. It's strange how the simplest of things is often the most difficult to obtain. I guess that's why it's so valuable.

What effects do microgravity and high g-forces have on the physiology of Dark-Hunters, Arcadians, Katagaria, Apollites, Daimons, Charontes, and you?

Hard to say on the Dark-Hunters, Daimons, and Apollites, since they've never been exposed. The Were-Hunters who fly deal with it constantly, so no real effect there, but the Charontes have a game where they see how fast they can reach escape velocity. They love the rush of it. But once they are in microgravity, it's a bit tricky to get back—oh, the fun with Simi here. The first time she did it and realized that she couldn't belch fire in space was not fun. She pouted for a month. As for myself, I like cruising space. It's entertaining.

You have lived longer than any human on the planet, seen more, heard more, than anyone else can ever dream of. In all those years and all the knowledge that you've learned, what does it mean to be human?

It means letting the sun shine on your skin. Braving the possibility of bad to have the good. But most of all, it means seizing the moment because it may never come this way again. By the way, that's something I once read on a Bazooka bubble gum wrapper. The true answer is I have no freaking clue since I'm not now, nor have I ever really been, human.

What was your favorite pastime before you became a Dark-Hunter?

Going to the theater. It was particularly entertaining in the past when men played the parts of women. And one time in Rome, the stage fell apart. They fed the stage director to the lions afterward. Ancient man wasn't particularly forgiving. Makes you wonder how much more challenging baseball would be if you upped the stakes for errors.

What will you do when Simi finds her mate?

See above about being fed to lions. Or maybe cannibals. Yeah, definitely one of those two things.

So who and/or what is Savitar?

A big pain in my ass.

What is in that backpack you guard so zealously?

Simi snacks. Trust me, a demon without snacks is a scary thing. Global warming takes on a whole new meaning.

While I understand and appreciate the comfort of leather . . . umh . . . doesn't it get kinda hot during the summer? Do you have stock in baby powder?

The beauty of not being human: I don't sweat. But you're right. On some it can get a little gamy.

What is your favorite comic?

Neil Gaiman's "Sandman".

Do you play video games? If so what's your favorite kind?

I certainly do. Dead to Rights or Resident Evil. I also have a strange fixation with Destroy All Humans. Not sure why. But I think you humans should be afraid.

How are you coping with the two new female additions to your household?

I now understand why the Chinese symbol for war is two women under one roof. I don't know how humans suffer this. It's almost enough to make me want to go live with Artemis.

Why do you like Goth so much?

I look good in black. Seriously though, the Goth community is more accepting. They like my fangs and don't think twice about my eyes, height, or Simi's horns. Plus, most of them have read Kierkegaard, Kant, and Sartre. And they love to debate the Hobbesian State of Nature with me.

What's the most annoying, frustrating, or irritating thing that you've come across?

Computers. Are they not the bane of all humanity? And spam. I'd like to feed spammers to Simi.

An Interview with Simi

Simi, what have you learned about Charonte demons since your sister has moved in?

That we don't like to share. Not that the Simi didn't know that before Xirena came in and started hogging my things, but since she's been here . . . let's just say the Simi has set up a lot of boundaries and barriers to keep her from touching my stuff. By the way, it's all *my* stuff. I don't know why she wants to touch it. But I won't let her. It's mine.

When did you first come to Ash?

Whach you mean by that? You mean when was the Simi given to akri or when was the first time he called for me and I obeyed? I don't really remember either one. Probably because I have never willingly done the second one. Well, that's not true. The Simi has come when akri called her to eat, 'cause it's never good to miss a meal—that's how people and demons go hungry. Hunger isn't good. It's bad. Very bad. What was the question again?

What is it like to live with Ash?

Live with or live on 'cause again they are very separate things. Live with is easy 'cause akri does mostly what I say. He's very kind to his Simi that's why the Simi loves her akri. He my daddy, you know? As for on him . . . well that leaves a lot to be desired 'cause akri has a hard body. He just not soft. I remember once, being on this . . . oh never mind. Akri don't like me talking about that. Suffice it to say, he's wonderful, but a little belly pooch wouldn't hurt him any from my perspective. You ever tried to lay down on a hard man? It's just not fun.

Besides BBQ sauce, what else is your favorite food?

Hmmm, the Simi like it all. BBQ isn't really a food, it's an enhancer and it make everything taste better. Even ice cream. Don't believe me? Try it. It good, especially on that coffee flavored ice cream. Oooo the Simi gotta go eat. I be right back.

Is Ash ever going to let you fry the heifer goddess?

(Licking lips) Ummm, no. I keep trying, but akri keep telling me, "No, Simi, no." I don't like no. It's an ugly word. No. See. It don't even roll off your tongue. It just sits there looking all small and . . . ugly. We need to expand akri's vocabulary. "Why yes, Simi, you may eat the heifer. Have some sauce for her." See how much nicer that sounds?

Why does Ash always change his hair color?

Akri does that to match my outfits 'cause the Simi has to match. You don't want your hair to clash with your hornays now, do you?

What happened to Atlantis?

It got eaten. Trust me. I saw it. But the Simi didn't do it.

If given a chocolate Easter bunny would you eat the tail first . . . or the ears?

I'd put my best sauce on it, then eat it whole, 'cause that's how you gots to do it. Trust me, I know.

What is the most amazing thing you've seen or done in all your long years?

That would be watching the old, and I do mean old, heifer goddess choking on a chicken bone. Not that she's ever done it. But the Simi keeps dreaming that maybe one day she will and akri won't be there to save her. Wouldn't that be nice? I told that once to them Santas in the mall and they called security on the Simi. What were they thinking? Can't the Simi have a little dream? The heifer may not like it, but it sure makes my night.

Why?

Well, why not?

Widget Bones's Diary

A Dark-Hunter Parody

Thursday 1 January.
201 lbs. (all muscle); third-degree burns, 2 (good start); blood units, 12 (Acheron'll have my ass); Daimons slain, 1 (died laughing, must work on slaying technique); jokes about being man named Widget, 1000 (mostly Talon).

7:00 P.M. Crawl out of bed. Pull back curtains.

7:01 P.M. Grah!! Sun not down. Bloody hand crispy. New Year off to bad start. Going back to bed and starting over.

11:45 P.M. *"Widget!* Get your ass out of bed and get to work!"

Hate Acheron. So bossy, just because he's the boss. Roll out of bed for second time and look for clothes, though is shame to cover body like this. Will make up for it by posing seductively whenever females nearby.

12:30 A.M. Stupid police think I'm soliciting on Bourbon Street. Why? Why? Attempt to explain that multitude of concealed medieval weaponry is required uniform for Dark-Hunters.

12:32 A.M. Police think am kinky, bondage-dominance slave, or similar.

12:35 A.M. Am wearing leg irons. *Leg irons.* Is insane for police to waste money on capturing me when are dangerous monsters out there to catch instead.

12:37 A.M. Is also insane that am madly powerful creature of the night, yet cannot break out of cell. Note to self: Renew gym membership.

1:15 A.M. Leg irons actually rather sexy. Perhaps being kinky bondage-dominance slave has possibilities.

1:25 A.M. Apparently cellmate agrees. Wish would cross legs or something. Don't need to see that sort of thing. V. disgusting.

4 A.M. Fucking Talon. Keeps me waiting all fucking night before arriving with bail. Do not appreciate his howls of laughter.

4:30 A.M. Finally am back on streets fighting evil as am supposed to be. Actually am chatting up hot bird in Sanctuary, but keeping eye on crowd as do so. Talon not impressed bail was so high (although am v. proud of it personally). Do not know why as is pointlessly rich so doesn't matter anyway.

5:15 A.M. Ooh, new all-night tanning salon on Decatur. Wonder if would look good with tan?

5:17 A.M. Yes, v. good idea. Tan would set off rugged good looks, would become babe magnet.

5:25 A.M. Like salon immensely. Clerk not pretty but with v. good rack—real? Wonder if tanning bed would provoke daylight-exposure type reaction, screams and flames or similar? Doubtful.

5:27 A.M. Yes. Yes, it does. Fire extinguisher needs fragrance additive, as is v. harsh with chemicals. Doubt my cologne survived. Wonder if cologne added to combustibility of skin?

6:45 A.M. Hate this job. Am calling Acheron and Talon to report tanning beds v. safe and pleasant.

Saturday 3 January.
209 lbs. (surely swelling will go down soon); sprained ankles, 2; hair gel used, 1 lb.; Daimons slain, 5 (not by me but heard about slayings, must count for something); jokes about clothing, 10,000 (must kill Talon).

11 P.M. Must get out of bed. Must get out of bed. Oh, gods, must get out of bed.

11:05 P.M. Stupid bloody woman with her stupid bloody heels and her stupid bloody perfect aim! How could ugly cow be so sensitive that must kick family jewels into next year simply because commented on extraordinary size of ginormous ass? Swelling unbelievable.

11:07 P.M. Desperation setting in. Why hasn't combination bed-toilet been invented? Would buy one.

11:08 P.M. Just invented it. Note to self, make more absorbent.

1:25 A.M. Message from Valerius's Squire: "Your presence is requested in the Garden District to assist with the slaying of five evil Daimons. 1:30 sharp. Dress: casual."

1:27 A.M. Shit! Am still in pajamas.

1:28 A.M. Maybe could go in pajamas? Sort of sexy disheveled look?

1:30 A.M. No, pajamas have ducks on them. Better find leather trousers.

1:31 A.M. Leather trousers too tight to accommodate swelling. Screams of agony still echoing. Have black sweats somewhere. Black v. frightening, serious color, no matter what fabric.

1:34 A.M. Fuck! Can only find powder blue. Must have been stoned, drunk, and unconscious when purchased fucking *powder blue* sweats. Wonder if bad-ass trenchcoat long enough to disguise unfortunate color.

1:35 A.M. And anyway, why get Squire to send messages? Can't Mr. I'm Bloody Important 'Cos I Ran An Army Two Thousand Fucking Years Ago write his own texts?

1:40 A.M. Unless is dyslexic. Crap. Feel guilty now.

1:50 A.M. Fuck, really late now, and hair still doing mad peaked horns thing.

1:55 A.M. Fuckety fuck. How is it possible to be three hundred years old and yet still not have mastered hair gel? Is ridiculous. Am immortal being. Hair gel stupid invention.

2:07 A.M. Hair finally under control. Where are shoes?

2:10 A.M. Cannot slay Daimons without shoes. Have killed too many by looking ridiculous. Am dangerous, violent killer. Cannot have fiends laughing at me.

2:16 A.M. *Where* the fuck are my fucking boots? Can only find red stilettos (prank gift from Talon) and refuse to wear them.

2:28 A.M. Stilettos only shoes in house. Shit shit shit!

2:41 A.M. If Talon hears of this, will never live it down.

3 A.M. *Finally* ready to go. Hope slaying hasn't started without me, as need to improve totals.

3:20 A.M. Hard to hurry in stilettos. Who invented stupid ankle-killing shoe anyway? Will just lean against lamppost for moment.

3:55 A.M. Dammitdammitdammit! Running in stilettos to escape vice cop. *Why* do they always assume I'm soliciting???

7:22 A.M. Just checked in box. Seventeen e-mails from Talon, all re: fashion faux pas of red stilettos and powder blue sweats. Also recommendation of motels with hourly rates. Bastard.

Sunday 4 January.
211 lbs. (swelling is evil device of Satan); kicks to manhood, 2 (women are evil devices of Satan); same-day shipping for black sweats, $35 (bargain); time spent plotting Talon's bloody demise, 23 hrs. 45 mins. (better).

9:23 P.M. Don't want to get out of bed. Swelling v. painful. Wonder if covered by insurance?

9:27 P.M. Is anything covered by insurance? Do I even have insurance? Must ask Ash.

9:45 P.M. Called Ash re: insurance. Was v. rude of him to laugh so loudly. Wouldn't be laughing if his bollocks were the size of cabbages.

9:52 P.M. Ooh, online shopping!

9:55 P.M. Express delivery available. Black sweats in minutes. *Click click click.*

10:20 P.M. Express delivery excellent invention.

10:23 P.M. What the hell?!? Positive did *not* order capris with lacy flower-trimmed cuffs!

10:28 P.M. V. comfy despite unfortunate style issues. Will wear with bad-ass trenchcoat. Positive flowers won't be noticed.

10:42 P.M. Daimons dropping like flies when walk by. Finding this method of slaying v. effective and low-impact on joints unlike swordplay or similar. Perhaps should learn to love self for self and stop trying to change for others (Talon, Ash) as advised in *Don't Let Their Derisive Laughter Get You Down.*

10:55 P.M. Yes, feeling better already. Am v. mature and secure individual unaffected by others' childish taunts.

10:56 P.M. Oh gods, there's Talon! Must hide, must hide! Can't be seen in flowered capris!

10:58 P.M. V. smelly in Dumpster. Mystery why vagrants inhabit them so often.

11 P.M. Drunk, rubbish-covered vagrant teasing me. Oh gods, I want to die.

11:05 P.M. Told vagrant am immortal vampire slayer and had better fuck off with teasing. Was not funny enough for him to wet himself. Am sure was just by-product of disgusting vagrantness, not loss of bladder control due to flowered capris.

11:06 P.M. Suggest vagrant invent/purchase combination bed-toilet for incontinence issues.

11:07 P.M. Vagrant laughed until keeled over dead. Must have been Daimon in disguise. Am fearsome warrior of justice. Will wear flowered capris for slaying of Daimons, then wave sword and tell Ash that am genius in manner of Van Helsing, Buffy, or similar.

11:10 P.M. Cell phone ringing. Bet it was fucking Talon who set ringer to play "I'm a Little Teapot".

11:11 P.M. Phone slimed with ooze of indeterminate origin. Dropped phone in garbage. Fuck, fuck, fuck! Now must track down phone before stupid teapot song ends.

11:13 P.M. Find phone, check voice mail.

11:14 P.M. *Fired?!?!* Fucking *fired?!?!* Acheron must have made mistake. Am v. frightening, serious Dark-Hunter, not "stain to reputation of Hunters worldwide" nor "laughingstock of Pantheon" nor "disgrace to human race and entire animal kingdom".

11:15 P.M. He can't really repo my house, can he?

1:25 A.M. V. glad vagrant no longer claiming Dumpster. Home stinky home.

4 A.M. Found copy of *When Life Gives You Lemons, Throw Them at Someone and Make Them Cry* beneath moldy potato peelings. V. inspiring book. Will look at career change as step forward, not step back.

4:12 A.M. Chapter titled "Down In The Dumps?" eerily fitting.

4:25 A.M. "What strengths were underappreciated in your last job? In what areas do you excel? Search your soul and you will find your true calling." V. deep.

5:40 A.M. Soul-searching useless. Forgot I sold that.

Saturday 10 January.
Weight—???; jokes about name, 0 (excellent); flowered capris, 12 (commonly discarded item, strangely); alligators circling, 4 (improving).

"Lemon" book used for toilet tissue. No idea what time is. Watch stolen by large angry drunk, was rendered helpless by his nonexistent sense of humor. Find landfill v. charming once sense of smell damaged beyond repair—adventure, treasures, variety. Am in promising relationship with blind deaf-mute homeless ex-exotic dancer named Polly Wolly. Situation looking up. Polly knows man in patent office, sending bed-toilet proposal tomorrow. Riches and fame certain. Dark-Hunter gig overrated anyway.

Second Chances

A Short Story

"Second Chances" originally appeared in the exclusive Dark-Hunter collectible booklet that was published in 2005 and released alongside Sins of the Night. *Only a handful of these booklets came with each floor display of* Sins of the Night. *Those copies were immediately snatched up and are still coveted by Dark-Hunter fans all over the globe.*

A shiver of déjà vu crawled down Ash's spine as he walked along the eerie, fog-filled hallway he'd hoped to never see again. The nether realm of Tartarus was reserved for those who were being punished in the afterlife for crimes committed in a human lifetime.

The screams of the damned echoed off walls as black as Ash's own soul. He would give Hades credit—the ancient Greek god definitely knew how to make people suffer.

Moments like this, Ash hated being a god. It was unbearable to know he had the power to stop and change things, and the profound responsibility to let nature take its course. Human free will should never be altered. His own damnation was a constant reminder of exactly why.

Still the reality of it ate at him constantly. How he envied Artemis, Hades, and many of the other gods who could shrug off human suffering as par for the course.

But having once been human, he wasn't immune to it. He understood what caused people to make the decisions that they would spend the rest of eternity paying for. And that human part of himself wanted desperately to ease their pain.

It was a bittersweet gift his mother had given him when she had made the decision to hide him in the human world. To this day he wasn't sure if he should thank her or curse her for it.

Today, he wanted to curse her.

"You don't have to do this."

He ignored Artemis's voice in his head. He did have to do this. It was time.

Ash stopped at a doorway that was covered with an iridescent slime. It shimmered like a rainbow oil slick in the dim light. To his surprise, there was no sound coming from inside. No movement. It was as if the occupant was dead.

But unlike the others who lived in Tartarus, this particular person couldn't die.

At least not until Ash did and since he was a god . . .

He used his powers to open the door without touching it.

It was completely black inside the small, dingy room. Horrifying images of his human past slammed into him at the sight. Long-buried emotions ripped at him with daggers of pain that lacerated his heart.

He wanted to run from this place.

He knew he couldn't.

Grinding his teeth, Ash forced himself to take the six steps that separated him from the man who was curled into a ball in one corner. An identical replica of himself, the man had long blond hair that was gnarled from the time he'd spent here and hadn't brushed it.

But then Ash never willingly wore his hair blond. It was a wretched reminder of a time in his past that he wanted his damndest to forget.

The man on the floor wasn't moving. His eyes were clenched shut like a child who thought that if he made no sound, no moves, the nightmare would end.

Ash had lived a long time in just such a state, and like the man before him, he had prayed for death repeatedly. But unlike his prayers that had gone unanswered, Styxx's would be answered.

"Styxx," he said, his low tone echoing off the walls.

Styxx didn't react.

Ash knelt down and did something that had disgusted Styxx when they had been human brothers in Greece. He touched his brother's shoulder.

"Styxx?" he tried again.

Styxx screamed as Ash broke through the brutal memories of horror that Mnimi had given to Styxx as punishment for trying to kill him. It was a punishment Ash had never agreed with. No one needed the memories of his human past. Not even him.

He could hear Styxx's thoughts as they left Ash's past and returned to Styxx's control.

Knowing his brother would be disgusted by him, Ash let go and stepped back.

As humans, he and Styxx had never been close. Styxx had hated him with an unreasoning logic. For his own part, he had aggravated that hatred.

Ash's human rationale had been that if they were going to hate him anyway, then he would give them all good cause for it. He'd gone out of his way to repulse them. Out of his way to antagonize them.

Only their sister had ever given him kindness.

And in the end, Ash had betrayed her. . . .

Styxx struggled to breathe as he became aware of the fact that he wasn't Acheron.

I am Styxx. Greek prince. Heir to . . .

No, he wasn't the rightful heir to anything. Acheron had been. He and his father had stolen that from Acheron.

They had taken everything from him.

Everything.

For the first time in eleven thousand years Styxx understood that reality. In spite of what his father had convinced him, they had greatly wronged Acheron.

The Greek goddess Mnimi had been right. The world as Prince Styxx had seen it had been whitewashed by lies and by hatred.

The world of Acheron had been entirely different. It had been steeped in loneliness and pain, and decorated with terror. It was a world he'd never dreamed existed. Sheltered and protected all his life, Styxx had never known a single insult. Never known hunger or suffering.

But Acheron had. . . .

Styxx's body shook uncontrollably as he looked around the dark, cold room. He had seen such a place in Acheron's memories.

A place they had gleefully left Acheron in to face alone. Only this place was cleaner. Less frightening.

And he was a lot older than Acheron had been.

Styxx covered his eyes and wept as the agony of that tore through him anew. He felt Acheron's emotions. His hopelessness. His despair.

He heard Acheron's screams for death. His silent pleas for mercy—silent because to voice them only made his situation worse.

They echoed and taunted him from the past.

How many times had he hurt him? Guilt gnawed at him, making him sick from it.

"I'll take them away from you."

Styxx flinched at the voice that sounded identical to his own, except for the soft lilting quality that marked Acheron's from the years he had spent in Atlantis.

Years Styxx wished to the gods that he could go back and change. Poor Acheron. No one deserved what had been handed to him.

"No," Styxx said quietly, his voice shaking as he gathered himself together. "I don't want you to."

He glanced up to see the surprise on Acheron's face.

It was something Acheron hid quickly behind a mask of stoicism. "There's no reason for you to know all that about me. My memories have never served good to anyone."

That wasn't true and Styxx knew it. "If you take them from me, I will hate you again."

"I don't mind."

No doubt. Acheron was used to being hated.

Styxx met that eerie swirling gaze of his levelly. "I do."

Ash couldn't breathe from the raw emotions he felt as he watched Styxx push himself to his feet.

They were so much alike physically and yet polar extremes when it came to their past and their present.

All they really had in common was that they were both longed-for heirs. Styxx was to inherit his father's kingdom while Acheron had been conceived to destroy the world.

It was a destiny neither of them had ever fulfilled.

To protect him from the wrath of the Atlantean gods who wanted him dead, Ash's true mother had forced him into the womb of Styxx's mother and then tied their life forces together to protect Ash. Ash had been born human against his will and against the will of his human surrogate family who had somehow sensed he wasn't really one of them.

And they had hated him for it.

"How long have I been here?" Styxx asked, looking around his dark prison.

"Three years."

Styxx laughed bitterly. "It seemed like forever."

It probably had. Ash didn't envy Styxx having to suffer the

memories of Ash's human past. Then again, he envied himself even less for having lived them.

He cleared his throat. "I can return you to the Vanishing Isle again, or you can stay here in the Underworld. I can't take you into the Elysian Fields, but there are other areas here that are almost as peaceful."

"What did you have to bargain with Artemis and Hades for that?"

Ash looked away, not wanting to think about it. "It doesn't matter."

Styxx took a step toward him, then stopped. "It does matter. I know what it costs you now . . . what it cost you then."

"Then you know it doesn't matter to me."

Styxx scoffed. "I know you're lying, Acheron. I'm the only one who does."

Ash flinched at the truth. But it changed nothing. "Make your decision, Styxx. I don't have any more time to waste here."

He took another step forward. He stood so close now that Ash could see his reflection in Styxx's blue eyes. Those eyes pierced him with sincerity. "I want to go to Katoteros."

Ash frowned at him. "Why?"

"I want to know my brother."

Ash scoffed at that. "You don't have a brother," he reminded him. It was something Styxx had proclaimed loud and clear throughout the centuries. "We only shared a womb for a very short time."

Styxx did something he had never done before. He reached out and touched Ash's shoulder. That touch seared him as it reminded him of the boy he'd been who had wanted nothing more than the love of his human family.

A boy they had spat on and denied.

"You told me once, long ago," Styxx said in a ragged tone, "to look into a mirror and see your face. I refused to then. But now Mnimi has forced me to look at my own reflection. I've seen it through my eyes and I've seen it through yours. I wish to the gods that I could change what happened between us. If I could go back, I would never deny you. But I can't. We both know that. Now I just want the chance to know you as I should have known you all those centuries ago."

Angered at his noble speech and at a past that no mere handful of words could ease, Ash used his powers to pin him back to the wall, away from him. Styxx hovered spread-eagle, above the floor, his face pale as Ash showed him his powers. He could tell by Styxx's thoughts that he was aware of exactly what he could do to him. Even though they were linked together, Ash could kill him with a single thought. He could shred him into pieces.

Part of him wanted to. It was the part of him they had turned vicious. The part of him that belonged to his real mother, the Destroyer.

"I am not a god of forgiveness."

Styxx met his gaze without flinching. "And I'm not a man used to apologizing. We are linked. You know it and I know it."

"How could I ever trust you?"

Styxx wanted to weep at that question. Acheron was right. How could he trust him? He'd done nothing but hurt his brother.

He'd even tried to kill him.

"You can't. But I have lived inside your memories for the last three years. I know the pain you hide. I know the pain I caused. If I stay here, I will go mad from the screams. If I return to the Vanishing Isle, I'll languish there alone and in time I will probably learn to hate you all over again."

Styxx paused as grief swept through him at the truth. "I don't want to hate you anymore, Acheron. You are a god who can control human fate. Is it not possible that there was a reason why we were joined together? Surely the Fates meant for us to be brothers."

Ash looked away as those words echoed in his head. It was a divine cruelness that he could see the fate of everyone around him except for those who were important to him, or those whose fates were intertwined with his own. He held the fate of the entire world in his hand and yet he couldn't see his own future.

How screwed up was that?

How unfair?

He looked at his "brother". Styxx was more likely to skewer him than he was to speak to him.

And yet he sensed something different about him.

Forget it. Erase his memory of you and leave him here to rot.

It was kinder than anything Styxx had ever done to him. But deep inside, down in a place that Ash hated, was that little boy who had reached out for his brother. That little boy who had cried out repeatedly for his family, only to find himself alone.

What should he do?

He set Styxx back on the ground.

Ash didn't move as memories and the emotions they reawakened assailed him. He could sense Styxx was approaching. He tensed out of habit. Every time Styxx had ever drawn near, he had hurt him.

"I can't undo the past," Styxx whispered. "But in the future, I will gladly lay my life down for you, brother."

Before he realized what Styxx was doing, Styxx pulled him close.

Still Ash didn't move as he felt Styxx's arms around him. He'd dreamed of this moment as a child. He'd ached for it.

The angry god inside him wanted to shatter Styxx into pieces for daring to touch him now, but that innocent part of him . . . that human heart, shattered. It was the part that he listened to.

Ash wrapped his arms around his brother and held him for the first time in their lives.

"I'm so sorry," Styxx said in a ragged tone.

Ash nodded as he pulled away. "To err is human, to forgive divine."

Styxx shook his head at the quote. "I don't ask for your forgiveness. I don't deserve it. I only ask for a chance to show you now that I'm not the fool I was once."

Ash only hoped he could believe it. The odds were against them both. Every time Styxx had been given an opportunity to assuage their past, he had used it to hurt him more.

Closing his eyes, Ash teleported them out of Tartarus and into Katoteros, the realm that had once been home to the Atlantean gods.

Styxx pulled back to gape at the opulent foyer where they stood. Everything was white and crisp, almost sterile. "So this is where you live," he breathed, awed by the beauty.

"No," Acheron said, as he folded his arms over his chest and indicated the tall, gilded windows that looked out over the tranquil water that stretched toward the horizon. "I live across the River Athlia, on the other side of the Lypi Shores. There is no Charon to ferry you across the river to my home, so don't bother looking."

He was completely confused by that. "I don't understand."

Acheron took a step back from him and Styxx was puzzled by the suspicion he saw in his brother's silver eyes. "I will see to it that you have servants and all you could ever desire here."

"But I thought we were going to be together."

Acheron shook his head. "You made your choice and you wanted to come here. So here you are."

But this wasn't what he wanted. He'd thought . . .

Styxx tried to approach him, only to find his pathway cut off by an invisible wall. "I thought you said, 'To err is human, to forgive divine'."

Those swirling silver eyes burned him. "I'm a god, Styxx, not a saint. I do forgive you, but trusting you is another matter. As you said, you shall have to prove yourself to me. Until then, you and I shall take this one step at a time and then we shall see what is to become of us."

And as soon as those words were spoken, Styxx found himself alone.

Synopsis for Saving Grace

This isn't a deleted Dark-Hunter scene, but it is the original synopsis for Fantasy Lover, *originally titled* Saving Grace. *In this synopsis, Julian was going to be a jewelry maker(!). Needless to say, the story that became* Fantasy Lover *radically changed. So enjoy in good fun!*

(Caveat! Sherri is the first to admit she stinks at writing synopses. It's why she will never teach a class on it.)

Sex therapist Grace Alexander is a devout loner who has long ago given up on the dream of any man ever appealing to her. And most especially given up the dream of some mythic hero coming in out of nowhere and sweeping her off her feet. That is until her best friend, a tarot card–reading pseudo-gypsy, conjures a Greek general out of the past to save Grace from her boring isolation.

In 325 B.C., Julian of Macedon was one of the greatest, most feared generals who served Alexander the Great. His skill in battle was legendary, but even more impressive was the rumor of his skill in bed. It was this rumor that led a consecrated virgin to seek him out. Terrified of being brutally sacrificed, she begged Julian to take her virginity. For the first and only time in his life, Julian felt pity and did as she asked.

When the High Priest learned of their actions, he condemned Julian to an eternity of slavery. From full moon to full moon, he must make love to his summoner, but never can *he* be satisfied by a woman's body.

It is a hell he would gladly give up, but long ago he learned that for him there would never be a reprieve. Besides, his mortal past is filled with crimes that have made this an apt punishment.

Yet from the moment Grace releases him, he senses something different. Something unusual about this incarnation.

To begin with, Grace isn't an easy conquest. For the first time in his life, he must actually struggle to get her into bed—and then she insists on both of them wearing clothes and on going to sleep!

Grace doesn't know what to do. Once unleashed, Julian is hard to control. Always a man of action, he is used to taking what he wants and in this case what he wants is Grace, who isn't sure what to make of this man who loves pizza and keeps begging to make love to her. After all, Grace is a far cry from beautiful and the shy therapist hasn't had much experience with a man chasing after her.

All she knows is that she wants to kill Selena for getting her into this predicament! Not that she's completely ungrateful. Grace is tired of living alone and having no one to share her life with, but a horny Greek love slave isn't the answer to that dilemma.

Still, she can't resist him. The torment in his eyes, the fire in his touch. He is strong when she needs strength and tender when she needs compassion. But for all that, he is also stubborn and chauvinistic. Demanding and unyielding.

In a nutshell, he is everything she has ever wanted and everything she despises!

And worst of all, he will vanish in a few weeks.

Julian wants nothing more than to stay with the woman who makes him laugh and who touches a heart he thought was long ago frozen in ice. But that is impossible. Worse, he knows that this may be the last time he will be summoned. Computers are steadily taking over the world and his little book may be lost forever, damning him to an eternity of being alert and alone. Lost in a lightless void. Unless Grace and Selena can come up with a way to save him.

The three of them put their heads together and review not

only the curse, but the history that surrounds Julian. What they find is that the curse wasn't just for him—the virgin, Alexandria, was also condemned, as well as any woman who summons Julian. What the High Priest didn't tell him was that after he leaves, the woman goes slowly insane while she pines for him.

It is truly the curse from hell.

Now Julian knows he can't go back into the book. He can't condemn Grace to such a fate. But fighting the curse is a terrible thing. The only way he can save her is to not have sex with her until the last night of his cycle.

Talk about a problem! All he can think about is her. And all Grace wants is him. What good is it to break the curse if they're both going to be insane from deprivation?

Still, Grace believes that where there's a will, there's always a way and she refuses to lose Julian so easily. After all, she is his only hope—as the curse began so shall it end. It started with Alexandria and it can only end with a woman who shares her name—Grace Alexander—a woman who is more to Julian than just a piece of ready meat. Grace truly is his last hope.

But the curse is strong, and so is their attraction. So strong that the last few days of the curse, she is forced to tie him down to keep him away from her. And she nearly goes broke from the water bill from trying to keep her own hormones neutralized.

On his last night, she unties him and they consecrate their love—but there's still one more catch. If he leaves her body before morning, then he will return to the book. They must make love all night long. No easy task, but hey, where there's a will, there's a way.

In the morning, Julian is free. With his freedom comes more terrifying complications. One, Julian can now pursue any woman he wants and Grace isn't really so sure he won't do that. And two, Julian doesn't really belong in this world. Of course, he does offer to be a sex surrogate for Grace's clients—a proposal she doesn't find particularly funny.

In the end, Julian convinces Grace that she is the only woman in the world, in any time period, that he will ever love. And he reveals to her a talent for metalwork, which he uses to make jewelry for tourists—replicas of Greek jewelry that quickly become very sought after.

Julian is no longer haunted by his past actions and Grace is no longer terrified by her fears. She has learned to depend on someone again, to trust that not everyone leaves. And together, they make a perfect whole.

Deleted Scene #1 from Night Embrace

This is one of the fight scenes that was removed from Night Embrace.

Vane sat off to the side of camp in human form while he listened to the idle conversations around him. Half the pack was in human form while the others were wolves.

Many of the men were restless. There was a disturbing scent in the air. One that denoted trouble, but no one could get a handle on it. Not even he was sure what was causing it.

But he was just as edgy as the rest of them. One wrong word or action and he was just as likely to take a life as a Daimon. More so, in fact.

Fang walked up to him and offered him a cold beer. "You want to go patrolling and see if we can find out what's going on?"

Vane popped the lid and tilted his head so that he could see around Fang's body where Stefan and the others were gathering. He shook his head.

If he went out with Stefan in the mood he was in, one of them would end up dead. "Whatever it is, it's coming this way. I think we should hang close to the women."

Fang laughed at that. "I love the way you think, *adelphos*. Hanging close to women is what I do best."

He laughed at Fang's words.

"Vane!"

Vane choked on the beer as he heard his sister's frantic, scared voice in his head.

"What?" he sent back silently.

"The pups are coming. I need you."

His beer forgotten, Vane shot to his feet and ran for her. He found her to the side of the camp, near a small outlet of water.

"I've got you, babe," he said gently as he knelt down by her side to help her.

She licked his chin, then whined as more labor pain hit her.

Fang joined them a few minutes later with blankets. "You want me to get Dad?"

"No," Vane said. "We can handle it."

As he reached to pet Anya, his cell phone rang. Pissed at the timing, he answered it to find Acheron on the other end.

"I'm busy, Dark-Hunter. This isn't a good—"

"I know, but there's a massive number of Daimons converging around Miller's Well. They're coming for your pack, Vane."

Vane went cold at the news. "Are you sure?"

"I'm positive. Looks like they want a supercharge before tomorrow night's festivities, so you guys have got to get out of there."

How he wished it were that simple. "Anya is in labor. We can't move her. But I'll make sure the others get out."

"All right," Ash said. "Sit tight and I'll have some reinforcements to you ASAP."

The implication tore through Vane and insulted every animal part of him. "I don't need your help, Dark-Hunter. We can take care of our own."

"Yeah, just the same, we'll be there shortly."

The phone went dead.

Snarling, Vane returned the phone to his pocket and told Fang what was going on. "Get the others mobilized."

Fang nodded, then ran off to spread the word.

Ash cursed as he hung up the phone and walked quickly down Bourbon Street toward Canal. Where the hell was Talon?

The Celt was supposed to be in his swamp and instead there was no sign of him.

Closing his eyes, Ash sensed the Celt was fine. But he didn't have time to fetch him away from Sunshine. The Daimons were moving fast and he didn't have long before they'd reach Vane and his family.

He flipped his phone open and called Valerius, who was still at home. "Valerius, I'm on Bourbon—"

"I will not venture down that street of crass iniquities and plebeian horror, Acheron. Don't even ask it."

Ash rolled his eyes at the Roman's haughty tone. "I need you in the swamp."

Silence answered him.

"We have a situation, Valerius," he said sternly. "A group of Daimons are after a Katagaria pack and they have a woman in labor—"

"Where do you need me?"

Ash smiled. The Roman had his moments. Good and bad. Luckily, this was a good one.

"I'll be right there." Ash hung up the phone. He dashed into a nearby doorway where no one could see him and flashed to Val's side.

Valerius did a double take at seeing Ash in his living room before the Roman could even return his cordless phone to its pedestal.

The only hint of shock Valerius showed was a slight arching of his right brow.

"We don't have time for conventional means of transportation," Ash explained.

Before Val could ask him what he meant, Acheron grabbed him and they materialized close to the Katagaria den.

Val scowled at him. "How did you do that? Are you some odd Were-Hunter hybrid like Ravyn?"

Ash gave a dark half-laugh. "Long story. The pertinent part is that I can't use my powers around the Katagaria without forcing them to change shapes. If the pregnant wolf is forced into human form by my powers, it'll kill her and her babies instantly. So, I'm fighting strictly hands-on as a human. Your powers aren't ionically charged, so you should be safe to fight as always."

Val nodded in understanding.

Acheron manifested his warrior's staff, then led Val toward the den.

The camp was in total chaos as the men, most in human form, tried to gather up the pups, and move them without using their magic.

Vane and Fang stood over a pregnant wolf in labor while another male who bore a striking resemblance to Vane knelt by her side and held her. The man was quite a bit older than the brothers.

Ash remembered him well. The ruthless Katagari ruler hated everyone outside the pack.

Then again, he amended as he looked at Vane and Fang, their father hated many who were in the pack as well.

"I hate to leave you, little one," their father said. "But know I will raise your pups in love."

The she-wolf whined.

Their father stood up and raked a sneer over Vane and Fang. "This is your fault. I curse the day I ever had werewolf sons."

Vane growled at the insult and started for his father, but Fang caught him.

His father curled his lips. "You better protect her young. God help you both if something happens to them." He stalked off toward the others.

Acheron and Val headed to the brothers.

"What are you doing here?" Vane demanded as soon as he saw them. "I told you we can handle this."

Acheron planted the end of his staff in the ground and eyed him with impatience. "Don't play hero, Vane. The last thing you need is to fight Daimons off your back while Anya labors."

Vane narrowed his eyes at them. "Do you know anything about delivering a baby?"

"I do," Ash said. "I've helped deliver more than my fair share of them over the last eleven thousand years."

In spite of his earlier words, Vane appeared relieved by Ash's answer.

Vane looked at Val. "What about you?"

Val's answer was as out of character for him as his presence here. "I don't know nothing about birthing puppies, Miss Scarlett, but I can cleave the head off a Daimon without breaking a sweat."

"All right, you can both stay." Vane crouched down beside his sister and nuzzled her snout with his face while the she-wolf panted and whined. "Hang in there, Anya. I'm not going to leave you."

Ash sat down by her side and held his hand out for her to sniff him. "I'm a friend, Anya," he said gently. "I know you're in pain, but we're going to stay with you and help you."

She looked up at Vane who made wolf noises back to her.

A loud curse sounded. "Vane!" Fang shouted. "We got gators moving in all over the place."

"It's okay," Ash said. "They're with me. They won't attack you unless you hit them."

"You sure?" Fang asked skeptically.

"Positive."

The last of the Katagaria pack moved out, leaving Val, Anya, the brothers, and Ash alone with the gators. The quiet stillness of the swamp was broken only by Anya's pants and whines.

As they waited, Ash felt for the grief in Vane's eyes.

"She'll be fine," Val assured him as he noticed it as well. "We'll get her through this."

"No," Vane said, shaking his head. "All we can hope for is to save her puppies. As soon as the last one leaves her body, she'll die."

Val frowned at him. "Don't be so fatalistic."

"I'm not, Dark-Hunter. She was claimed by her mate. They bonded their life forces. Had she not been pregnant and carrying new life when he died, she would have died with him. As soon as the puppies are born, she will be off to join him on the other side."

Ash's stomach drew tight in sympathetic grief as he heard the pain in Vane's voice. He knew how much Anya meant to both of her brothers. He also knew what was about to happen and though he wanted to change it, he also knew he couldn't. "I'm sorry, Vane."

"Thanks." Vane brushed his hand through his sister's white coat.

Suddenly, out of nowhere, a horde of Daimons attacked.

Vane shot to his feet to confront them. "I don't know how to birth the puppies," he told Ash. "You stay with her and I'll fight."

Ash nodded and stayed crouched by Anya as she snapped and whined.

Fang transformed into a wolf, his stronger form, to fight, but Vane remained human.

Ash heard the Daimons scream as they found the alligators lying in wait for them.

Anya began thrashing as the fight broke out. Ash kept his attention focused on the she-wolf and only looked up to make sure the Daimons weren't making their way any closer to Anya.

Fang was doing a remarkable job keeping them off in wolf form while Valerius and Vane fought them with knife and sword. The bad thing though was that the brothers couldn't use their magic any more than Ash could. Any random shot of their energy could accidently hit Anya and her pups and kill them instantly.

"Vane!"

Ash started at the human noise from the she-wolf. He looked up to see a Daimon about to attack Vane's back. Forewarned, the Katagari saw the Daimon and whirled around in time to stab the Daimon through the heart and kill him.

Anya lay back.

Ash held her still as the first of her puppies crested. "That's it," he said to her in a calm, soothing voice. "We're almost there."

A Daimon came up through the hedges beside them. Ash sprang to his feet and whirled to defend Anya as Vane caught the Daimon and knocked him away from them.

"Take care of my sister," Vane said between clenched teeth.

Ash quickly returned to Anya.

With the Daimons so close now, he was having to watch the baby, Anya, and the Daimons. It wasn't easy.

"Push," he said to Anya. "Just a little bit more."

The next few seconds happened rapidly, and yet they seemed to move slowly through time.

Two Daimons rose up from their fight with Fang. One of them shot Fang with a Taser gun, immediately turning him human. Fang let out a howl as his body convulsed uncontrollably back and forth between wolf and human.

Vane went after the second one at the same moment the first one aimed the Taser at Vane, who dove at the ground. The Daimon pressed the button and the Taser blast missed Vane by a fraction of an inch.

It struck Anya instead.

Ash cursed in anger as Anya was transformed from a wolf to a woman and back again. Her screams echoed in the trees and then she fell eerily silent.

Back in her wolf form, she didn't move at all.

Vane ran to her, but it was too late.

She was dead.

Ash let out his battle cry and rushed the Daimon who had killed her. He punched the Daimon hard in the jaw, then used his bare hands to finish him off.

Now that he could use his powers without restriction, Ash made short work of the remaining Daimons.

Fang's transformations had slowed down, but he was still alternating between human and wolf forms as he dragged himself slowly toward his sister's body.

Vane walked stonily toward Anya and sank down beside her. He gathered her wolf's body up into his arms and cradled her as if she were a baby. Tears streamed down his face as he rocked back and forth with her and whispered in wolf to her.

Fang let out a fierce howl and turned into a man. His body bare, he laid his head down on Anya's back and held onto her too.

Ash would never forget the sight of the three of them huddled there in their grief. It would haunt him forever.

All too well, he remembered the past. . . .

Pain like that never fully healed. He knew it for a fact.

His face grim, Ash took a step toward them. "Do you need me to—"

"Get away," Vane snarled, his voice feral and cold. "Just leave us alone."

"There might be more Daimons coming," Val reminded Vane.

"And I will kill them," he growled. "I will kill them all."

There was nothing more to be done to help them and Ash hated that most of all. The brothers needed time to grieve.

Disintegrating his staff he turned toward Val, who watched the brothers with a troubled gaze.

"There was nothing more you could do," Valerius said to Vane. "Don't blame yourself."

Vane let out an inhuman snarl.

Ash pulled Val's arm and led him away from the scene before Vane attacked out of sorrow.

"The innocent should never have to suffer from the battles of others," Val breathed as he followed Ash.

"I know," Ash said, his heart heavy. "But it seems to always be the case."

Val nodded. *"A furore infra, libera nos."*

Ash paused at the Latin quote. Spare us from the fury within. "You know, Valerius, there are times when I think you might actually be human after all."

Valerius scoffed at that. "Trust me, Acheron, whatever human part of me that ever existed was killed a long, long time ago."

Deleted Scene #2 from Night Embrace

This is one of the epilogues pulled from the back of the book.

New Orleans, three hours later
"Did he eat?"

Vane swallowed at Mama Bear Peltier's question and shook his head no. Fang hadn't eaten a bite since the bears had taken them in.

His brother was dying, and just like with Anya, there was nothing Vane could do to save him.

Impotent rage filled him and he wanted blood for what had happened that night. Most of all, he wanted Talon's heart in his fist.

Mama Bear brushed a kind hand over his shoulder. "If you need anything, ask."

Vane forced himself not to growl at her.

What he needed was his brother to be whole again. But the Daimon attack had left Fang without any will to survive. They had taken more than his brother's blood, they had taken his dignity and his heart.

Vane doubted if his brother would ever be normal again.

Mama turned into her bear form and ambled off. Vane was only vaguely aware of Justin padding by outside in his panther form, followed by a tiger and two hawks. All were headed for their rooms where they could spend the day in their true animal bodies, safely locked away from the unsuspecting world.

"It's a zoo, isn't it?"

He looked up at Colt's voice coming from the doorway. Standing six foot four, Colt was one of the members of the Howlers. Like Mama and her clan, Colt was a bear, but unlike them, he was also an Arcadian.

Vane was amazed the bears had tolerated one in their midst. Most Katagaria packs killed any Arcadian on sight.

He would have.

But then, Mama and Papa Bear weren't the usual bunch.

"What do you want?" Vane asked.

Colt shifted uneasily. "I was thinking . . . you know it would be a lot safer for everyone at Sanctuary if there were two Sentinels protecting the Peltiers."

Vane sneered at that. "Since when does a Sentinel protect a Katagaria clan?"

Colt gave him a droll stare. "That from a Sentinel who is stroking a Katagari wolf's fur?"

Rage darkened Vane's sight and if it wasn't for the fact that he needed to stay here for Fang's welfare, he'd be lunging for Colt's throat. "I'm not a Sentinel and I'm not Arcadian."

"You can't hide from me, Vane. Like me, you have chosen to hide your facial markings, but it doesn't change what you are. We *are* Sentinels."

Vane cursed him. "I will never be a Sentinel. I refuse that birthright. I won't hunt and kill my own kind."

"Haven't you already done that?" Colt asked with an arched brow. "How many Sentinels have you slain for your birth pack?"

Vane didn't want to think about that. That had been different. They had threatened Anya and Fang.

"Look," Colt said. "I'm not here to pass judgment on you. I'm just thinking it would be easier to—"

"I'm not staying," Vane said. "Wolves don't mix with others. Once I'm strong enough to protect Fang again, we're out of here."

Colt took a deep breath and shook his head. "Whatever." He turned around and left.

Vane's heart ached as he left the room long enough to take Fang's uneaten food to the kitchen.

If his brother didn't snap back soon, he didn't know what he'd do. They were both under a death sentence.

It wouldn't be long before their father would send scouts back to determine their fate. Once they found out that both of them had survived, assassins would be coming for them. He needed Fang mobile.

He could fight alone, but carting Fang's catatonic ass around with him wasn't going to be easy and it wasn't something he looked forward to doing when all he wanted was to lie down and lick his wounds too.

Damn Fang for being so selfish.

When Vane returned to his room upstairs, he found Wren just inside the door and Aimée Peltier on the bed beside Fang.

In his early thirties, Wren looked much younger. He wore his dark blond hair in dreadlocks and had yet to speak a word to Vane.

Mama Bear had told him that Wren had been left for dead a few years back and brought to Sanctuary. No one knew anything about Wren other than the fact that Mama didn't like or trust him.

Aimée Peltier was a beautiful blonde—that was if a man liked his women extremely skinny and Vane didn't. She was the pride and joy of the Peltier clan and from what he had seen she was one of the few truly kindhearted bears.

Vane frowned as Aimée leaned over and whispered something to Fang.

To his amazement, Fang licked her hand.

Aimée patted Fang's fur, then rose from the bed. She froze as she caught sight of Vane.

"What did you say to him?" Vane asked.

"I told him you were both welcome here. That no one would ever hurt him again."

Vane glanced at his brother, who had returned to his unmoving wolf state.

"We're not staying here," Vane reiterated.

Wren gave him a wry smile. "Funny. That's what I said ten years ago."

Deleted Scene #3 from Night Embrace

This was a scene in which I wanted to show why Talon lived in the swamp. My editor thought it was unnecessary, so it was cut.

Acheron placed a hand on his shoulder. The touch was electrifying, sizzling. It burned without pain and it shot him straight into the past.

Talon couldn't move as he saw himself more than two hundred years ago. He was in his old plantation home that he'd built before he'd gone into the swamp. It had been just after midnight when he and Acheron had returned from hunting to find a small bundle on his doorstep.

At first he had thought it nothing until he heard the soft whine of an infant. The moment he had seen the abandoned baby girl, his emotions had overwhelmed him.

"I will keep this child."

"Talon," Acheron snapped. "Are you mad? Dark-Hunters don't have children. She's a foundling and you need to find her a family."

"Nae, I willna do it, Acheron. She was given to me by the gods to care for. Besides, other Dark-Hunters have children around them."

"But they are the children of their Squires."

"Then send me a Squire to tend her."

Acheron had balked, but in the end, he had given in and found Talon someone to help raise the baby.

Talon's thoughts tumbled with images as he saw his adopted daughter grow in his mind. Sirona as a toddler taking her first steps and laughing as she reached up for him. Sirona as a little girl running in to hug him before bed. Sirona saying her prayers each night before he tucked her in and left her to hunt Daimons.

She'd been the most beautiful girl he'd ever beheld. Her laughing blue eyes and golden hair had reminded him much of Nynia and at times he would imagine that she was their daughter.

He'd protected and cared for her as a father, giving her anything and everything she wanted.

He'd told her that he was her uncle and that her parents had died and left her to his care. No one had ever questioned it. Only his Squire had known the truth.

"How do I look, Uncle?"

Talon's breath caught as he saw Sirona leaving the dressing room at the tailor's shop in town. It was two hours after dark and he'd paid a fortune for the tailor to accommodate his odd schedule. But it was worth every penny, he decided, as he saw the happiness on Sirona's face.

Her wedding gown was a pale blue that made her sky-colored eyes sparkle. Her blond hair was pulled up in a matching ribbon.

He'd smiled at her. "Thomas is a lucky man who had best take care of you."

She laughed and pressed her lips to his cheek, then rushed back inside to try on the rest of her wedding trousseau.

A few minutes later, the seamstress's assistant had run out to him. "She's fainted!"

Terrified, Talon had rushed to her and carried her home. He'd sent for a doctor only to be told no one knew what ailed her, but that she wouldn't live out the night.

He'd spent hours by her side, holding her in his arms, listening to her struggling to breathe.

Her young body had been racked with pain and she was covered in sweat.

"I will never marry Thomas now," she whispered. "I shall never be a mother." She looked up at him as tears seeped from the corners of her eyes. "There will be no one left to care for you, Uncle."

And she had died there in his arms, her hand on his cheek.

Talon had been inconsolable. He'd foolishly believed that the curse had been lifted and that she'd been a blessing. In the end, he'd learned that Camulus was once more toying with him.

He would never be able to love without loss.

The night Sirona was entombed, Talon had burned his plantation to the ground and headed into the swamp where he vowed to let no other human being near him again.

Deleted Scene from Seize the Night

The events that occurred during Seize the Night *took the Dark-Hunter world by storm. Much-beloved characters died, and suddenly nothing was sacred. What with Desiderius's massacre and everything that happened to Nick Gautier, the novel rattled off to its end at an insanely intense pace. Because of that, this soft, quiet, and beautiful scene featuring Acheron at Cherise Gautier's grave just didn't quite fit.*

Ash listened quietly as the priest spoke words of comfort outside the tomb in the St. Louis cemetery where Cherise Gautier had been laid to rest. Julian, Grace, Kyrian, Amanda, Tabitha, and

Valerius stood to his right while Talon, Sunshine, and the Peltiers were lined up on his left to pay respect to one of the finest women Ash had ever been privileged to know.

He was dressed in the same clothes he'd had on the day he'd first met the woman. A pair of slouchy black pants, an oversized black sweater, and a long leather coat. Cherise had taken one look at him and clucked her tongue.

"When was the last time you ate?" she'd asked him.

"An hour ago."

His words hadn't fooled her at all. Convinced he was lying to save his pride, she'd promptly sat him down in a chair and proceeded to make him a plate of Cajun hash browns while Nick had tried not to laugh at them.

In the last eleven thousand years, she had been one of the rare humans who had treated Ash like a human being. She hadn't seen him as anything more than a young man who needed a mother's love and a friend.

And he missed her more than anything.

As he stood with the cold wind cutting through him, he could hear his own soul screaming out in rage that he had caused this. How could one sentence uttered in anger cause so much damage? But then they could. Cuts and bruises always healed, but words spoken in anger were most often permanent. They didn't damage the body, they destroyed the spirit.

"I first met Cherise the day her mother birthed her," the old priest said to them. "And I was there the evening she brought her own child into this world. Nick was her pride and all of you who knew her know that if you'd ever asked her what her most prized possession was, she would have answered with Nick's name."

Kyrian slid a sideways look to Ash, who heard the former Greek general's thoughts. Since Nick's body hadn't been found after the vicious murder of Cherise, the consensus among the New Orleans Dark-Hunters and Squires, both former and current, was that Nick had become a Dark-Hunter himself.

They all knew better than to ask Ash for the truth.

The humans who didn't know of their world all assumed that Nick had been another casualty to whatever fate had befallen his mother, while the authorities believed Nick had killed her.

The latter was why Ash knew he couldn't bring Nick back to New Orleans. Not for a long time at least. The police were looking for him and they would convict him in a heartbeat.

Not to mention he didn't really want anyone to know about Nick. At least not until Nick was ready to deal with the world.

After the priest finished, Amanda and Tabitha placed the roses they held in their hands at the door of Cherise's tomb while the priest and Peltiers left.

Amanda paused beside Ash. "We're having a memorial service later for Nick at our house. Just the Dark-Hunters and Squires."

Ash nodded, but refused to meet her eyes. If he did, he was sure she'd know the truth.

He didn't move until he was alone. Sighing, he glanced around at the stone monuments that made up the cemetery. There were so many here whom he had personally known. So many he had seen live and die.

He could hear the sound of their voices on the wind, remember their faces, their lives.

"I'm sorry, Cherise," he whispered.

Stepping forward, he created a *mavyllo*, a sacred black rose that had been created by his mother, and laid it beside the red ones. Unlike the red ones, it would take root here and grow in memory of her.

It was the highest honor his kind could bestow on anyone.

"Don't worry, Cherise. I won't let anything else bad happen to your son . . . I promise."

Reading Order of the Dark-Hunter Stories and Novels

*Child, how naive of you. I want the soul of the woman who
has compelled you to make a deal with the devil.*
—Hades

If you're a stickler for making sure you've read everything in the
Dark-Hunter universe in the order in which it was released,
here's a checklist for you. It includes the novels as well as all the
Dark-Hunter-related stories, and where those stories were originally found.

Fantasy Lover

"The Beginning"

"Dragonswan" (from *Tapestry*)

Night Pleasures

Night Embrace

"Phantom Lover" (from *Midnight Pleasures*)

Dance with the Devil

"A Dark-Hunter Christmas"

Kiss of the Night

Night Play

"Winter Born" (from *Stroke of Midnight*)

Seize the Night

Sins of the Night

"Second Chances" (from the *Dark-Hunter Collectible Booklet*)

Unleash the Night

Dark Side of the Moon

"A Hard Day's Night-Searcher" (from *My Big Fat Supernatural Wedding*)

"Until Death We Do Part" (from *Love at First Bite*)

"Fear the Darkness" (2007 online e-mail exclusive)

The Dream-Hunter

Devil May Cry

Upon the Midnight Clear

Official Series Web Sites

Ahhh, the beauty of annihilation. There's nothing like it.
—Apollymi

Dark-Hunter Web site, www.Dark-Hunter.com

Dream-Hunter Web site, www.Dream-Hunter.com

Were-Hunter Web site, www.Were-Hunter.com

Daimon-Apollite Web site, www.Katoteros.com

Sherrilyn Kenyon Fan Club, www.vampirechick.com

Sherrilyn Kenyon MySpace Page, www.myspace.com/
officialdarkhunter

Exceptionally Brief Afterword

Baby, the world you know just got ugly.
—Ravyn Kontis

As Promised

Now that you're finished, go back to the beginning and start again. Read often. The information in this book tends to change as often as Ash's hair color. A smart Dark-Hunter is a breathing Dark-Hunter. Protect this book with your life.

Now, go on, go play. Save the human race from extinction. I've got work to do.

And so do you.

Acknowledgments

The ability of the human heart to sacrifice for the one it
loves . . . there is nothing on Olympus than can even begin to
compete with that.
—M'Adoc

Like me, this compendium would not be the amazing thing it is without a lot of help and inspiration from my friends and family.

First and foremost, I must thank the Dark-Hunter posse and my own personal muses—Dee Clingman; Lillie Rainey; Janet Lee; Tracy Willoughby; Kitti McConnell; Kristi Gillis; Mary Robinette Kowal; Nicole Hamilton; and Shannan Starnes—for keeping me in line, tossing ideas around, and helping at the drop of a hat. I must also thank the lovely and effervescent Jenny Rappaport and Lori Perkins. Jenny Hime, you're the best friend a fairy-godmother-in-training could hope to have.

Humongous hugs go to Eddie Coulter—whom most of you know from the Dark-Hunter message boards as EvylEd—for coming back from K-Con loaded down with maps, brochures, and pamphlets; for driving to my house at least once a month and forcing me to remember what the outdoors looks like; for giving me an ear to vent into and a shoulder to cry on; and for keeping me in *Stargate* episodes and temporary sanity.

For everything New Orleans, I must thank my Louisiana families: Robin and Beau Erwin; Aunt Nina, Uncle Robbie, and the rest of my Stringer clan; and the Ordoynes—Dale, Ora, Devin, and Megan. Who knew that Greeks and Cajuns could have so much in common? Big, big love to all y'all.

And for all those reminders on what it is to be Greek, I must thank Gloria and Angelo Metropolis, as well as my immediate family: my very cool, very patient, very giving (and very forgiving) parents George and Marcy Kontis; my talented sister Soteria, whose stories always make me laugh when I need it most; and my beautiful, immortal grandmother, Helen. That lady from Troy had nothing on you, Nana.

I would be remiss (and he would never forgive me) if I didn't mention Steve, my knight in shining armor, who has the amazing ability to love me and support me and kick me in the butt from halfway around the world. Thanks, babe.

Last but not least I, of course, have to thank the infamous Sherrilyn Kenyon—friend, mentor, and goddess with a generous heart. You're fabulous, sweetie. To infinity, and beyond.